Sisterhood, Science and Surveillance
in *Orphan Black*

ALSO OF INTEREST

EDITED BY JANET BRENNAN CROFT

Lois McMaster Bujold: Essays on a Modern Master of Science Fiction and Fantasy (2013)

Tolkien and Shakespeare: Essays on Shared Themes and Language (2007)

EDITED BY JOHN WM. HOUGHTON,
JANET BRENNAN CROFT, NANCY MARTSCH,
JOHN D. RATELIFF, ROBIN ANNE REID

*Tolkien in the New Century:
Essays in Honor of Tom Shippey* (2014)

Sisterhood, Science and Surveillance in *Orphan Black*

Critical Essays

Edited by JANET BRENNAN CROFT *and* ALYSON R. BUCKMAN

McFarland & Company, Inc., Publishers
Jefferson, North Carolina

ISBN (print) 978-1-4766-6854-3
ISBN (ebook) 978-1-4766-3783-9

LIBRARY OF CONGRESS AND BRITISH LIBRARY
CATALOGUING DATA ARE AVAILABLE

© 2019 Janet Brennan Croft and Alyson R. Buckman. All rights reserved

No part of this book may be reproduced or transmitted in any form or by any means, electronic or mechanical, including photocopying or recording, or by any information storage and retrieval system, without permission in writing from the publisher.

Front cover images © 2019 Shutterstock

Printed in the United States of America

McFarland & Company, Inc., Publishers
 Box 611, Jefferson, North Carolina 28640
 www.mcfarlandpub.com

Table of Contents

Introduction: *A Galaxy of Women*
    ALYSON R. BUCKMAN *and* JANET BRENNAN CROFT   1

"I am not your property": The Progressive Feminism
of *Orphan Black*
    GRAEME J. WILSON   5

Women's Rebellion or Radical Containment? Understanding
Orphan Black's Feminist Message
    DANI HOWELL   22

"To Hound Nature in Her Wanderings": Soccer Moms,
Punks and Postfeminist Mothers on *Orphan Black*
    ERIN BELL   41

Making Clones, Making Mothers: Motherhood in *Orphan Black*
    JENNY BONNEVIER   58

Motherless Bad Girl/Bad Girl Mother: Naturalizing
and Essentializing Motherhood in *Orphan Black*
    LAINE ZISMAN NEWMAN   77

Hell and Back: Helena as Kore and Shaman in *Orphan Black*
    JANET BRENNAN CROFT   95

Living in the Panopticon: Resistance to Surveillance
in *Orphan Black*
    BRANDI BRADLEY   113

"My story is an embroidery": Representing Trauma
Within the World of *Orphan Black*
    ALYSON R. BUCKMAN   128

Performing Bodies: Multiplying Cyborg-Clones, CGI
  and the Invisible Special Effect
    BRONWEN CALVERT   151
Sheeply Empowerment: An Analysis of M.K.'s Reappropriation
  in *Orphan Black*
    JENNIFER DEROSS   166
cDNA/©DNA in *Orphan Black:* Eugenics, Surplus Life
  and the Castor Virus
    JESSICA LEE MATHIASON   180

About the Contributors   205
Index   207

Introduction

A Galaxy of Women

ALYSON R. BUCKMAN *and*
JANET BRENNAN CROFT

Orphan Black (2013–2017) is a ground-breaking BBC-America television series set primarily in Toronto (where so much of today's contemporary film and television is filmed, though it usually stands in for other locations). The central plot concerns a group of young women discovering they are clones and the gradual stripping away of the mystery surrounding Sarah Manning, our primary viewpoint character, as well as Beth, Cosima, Alison, Helena, Rachel, M.K./Veera, Katja, Krystal, Tony, Jennifer, Charlotte, and 263 others. The series begins with Sarah meeting copies of herself when she attempts to run a scam which will allow her to run off with her daughter and foster brother. Soon she finds herself trying to evade a clone who is attempting to kill her sisters at the behest of religious extremists. That clone, Helena, will be brought into the fold, even as the sisters must contend with another "evil twin": Rachel, brought up within the organization that began the cloning program, is concerned only with besting her fellow clones, selling them out on the corporate level for her own illusory freedom and sense of self-worth. Not content with critiquing global capitalism and religion, *Orphan Black* engages with military and scientific realms as well, concluding with an intersectional feminist evisceration of patriarchy.

Part of the appeal of the serial is just how aptly it reflects contemporary concerns about the corporatization of science and ethics, the role of the military, sexual and gender equality, and toxic masculinity. While the birth of the first mammal cloned from an adult somatic cell (Dolly the sheep) occurred in 1996, He Jiankui very recently figured in the news when he claimed to have performed the first embryonic gene editing in twin girls, provoking an intense debate about the ethics and protocols of genetic engineering. Corporate, capitalist, and military (mis)use of such technology is an omnipresent worry, especially after such nightmarish collaborations as that of the American military with the Blackwater corporation in Iraq, which lined the pockets of several politicians, including those of Dick Cheney, the vice president of the United States during the second Gulf War. The ability to sterilize whole populations as a means of warfare, as hypothesized in *Orphan Black* through the male Castor clones (as opposed to the female Leda clones), would add a terrifying element to the arsenal of torture in subduing populations. The use of a property tag in the DNA of the clones illustrates the potential for the rise of slavery based upon genetic origins and is based on the implications of the 2013 *Myriad* Supreme Court case, as discussed in Jessica Lee Mathiason's essay herein.

The mainstreaming of toxic masculinity, the dehumanization of women and LGBTQIA+ people, and the exclusion of non-dominant groups are also central themes in *Orphan Black*, mirroring real-world news events contemporaneous with the production of the show: Donald Trump's rise to power even after famously boasting about "grab[bing] 'em [women] by the pussy" and making racist comments about immigrants and other countries, Mike Pence's support of gay conversion therapy, and the appointment of Brett Kavanaugh to the Supreme Court in the face of accusations of attempted rape and clear lack of respect for female senators during his confirmation hearing. The fifth season pulls back the curtain concealing the mastermind behind the scientific, military, and corporate misuses of science within the serial to reveal a narcissistic son of privilege determined to use the Leda clones for the extension of his own twisted life; he is aided and abetted by two women more interested in progressing their careers than in ethical action.

In tandem with the #metoo movement, the series illustrates the need for women's voices and control over our own bodies. Certainly, in a televisual environment with a dearth of female leads and strong female representation, *Orphan Black* is outstanding in providing a focus on not only the five main clones, as portrayed by Tatiana Maslany, but multiple other strong supporting female roles as well: Kira Manning, Siobhan Sadler, Virginia Coady, Susan Duncan, Delphine Cormier, Gracie Johanssen.

The socio-political commentary provided by the serial could have doomed it to a short shelf life or to narrative heavy-handedness, but this is not the case. It is not simply a political screed but an examination of what it would mean to be a clone, who might profit from that, and how such cloning would affect humanity and identity. While *Orphan Black* uses many of the staples of melodramatic television serials, it does so with cunning twists, layers of meaning, and excellence in acting and continuity. In short, it is an example of quality television, which begs multiple viewings and interpretations as a result of its complexity, depth, and astute contemporary commentary. The series also has taken advantage of multimedia platforms, engaging with its audience not only through the show but also through comics which extend the televisual world into a separate medium and further explore it. Other materials include *Orphan Black: Classified Clone Reports*, which purports to be files on the clones collated by Dr. Delphine Cormier, which further augment characterization through a pseudo-scientific lens.

One sign of the quality of the series is the number of critical studies already published and forthcoming. In addition to the usual mass market "behind-the-scenes" books, there are books on aspects of the science, bioethics, philosophy, and feminism of the series; our text furthers the discussion through consideration of mythological resonances, representation of trauma, posthumanism, motherhood, familial structures, sexuality, panopticism, special effects, performance art, and radical containment in the series.[1] Although we began this project in 2015, once we learned there would be a fifth and final season in 2017, we chose to delay it so that we could discuss the series *in totum* and come to more definitive conclusions.

Another marker of the series' quality is the multiple conclusions that can be drawn from it. For example, even within our own collection, there are essays which are more fully supportive of the series' feminism than others. Graeme J. Wilson argues the show supports progressive intersectional feminism in its exploration of motherhood in all its variety, its ongoing critique of toxic masculinity, its endorsement of alternate gender identities, and its subversion of television's standard female stereotypes. Dani Howell agrees it subverts stereotypes of femininity and queerness; however, she argues as well that the series privileges the standard Western ideal of female beauty, and that "only bodies that support dominant ideology are freed"; in this way, radical ideas are domesticated and made non-threatening.

Like Howell, Erin Bell and Jenny Bonnevier each assert that *Orphan Black* challenges conventional stereotypes of womanhood, specifically through the construction of diverse, fluid representations of motherhood. Laine Zisman Newman, conversely, explores the series' reiteration of the common trope of the "bad girl" and her salvation through redemptive motherhood.

Tropes of female and maternal representation are considered in Janet Brennan Croft's discussion of Helena as Kore/Persephone as well; Helena, she argues, repeatedly descends into hell and gains wisdom and maturity as well as the ability to become an angel of death and shaman. Her consumption of her own self-doubt in the shape of the scorpion Pupok illustrates the strength of this character, and this strength is derived, in part, from sisterhood, another element of the feminism of the series. Brandi Bradley argues that this sisterhood is what enables the resistance of the characters of the series to the panopticon in which they find themselves. While Foucault, as she argues, theorized a system of surveillance and group bonding which would ensure passivity in the service of the institution, the series illustrates connection as resistance. Connection also becomes a means to healing, as Alyson R. Buckman argues in her essay on the representation of trauma in the series: storytelling through shared community is one means through which the clones survive their various traumas and strengthen their ties to each other.

This introduction so far has not mentioned one of the essential elements that made *Orphan Black* such an excellent series: Tatiana Maslany and the special effects that made her performance of multiple roles possible. Bronwen Calvert analyzes the interaction of technology, embodied performance, and duplication with key themes of the series, discussing as well the woman who remains integral and yet invisible: Kathryn Alexandre, Maslany's body double. Issues of authenticity, invisibility, and the digital/human hybrid are central to Calvert's discussion.

Jennifer DeRoss concentrates on one of the less-central clones, M.K., as a trickster figure who reappropriates sheep imagery; regularly used within our cultural imaginary as a shorthand for a lack of agency, the sheep figure becomes one which represents all the clones and yet works against the notion that these clones are easily replaceable or lack individuality or humanity. Her use of a portion of her objectifying patent number to assert her own subjectivity functions similarly, as does her story's fragmentation across multiple platforms. Jessica Lee Mathiason draws our attention to the science behind the cloning and examines how neoliberalism, capitalism, and advanced scientific technologies converge with eugenics within the series, providing an exploration of corporate pressures on the modern legal system.

One of the last episodes of the series, "Guillotines Decide," 5.8, depicts Felix's art show; embraced as a brother-*sestra*, Felix has painted portraits of the clones which are then celebrated as different icons of womanhood. Sarah is Athena, goddess of war; Cosima is represented as Metis, goddess of wisdom and deep thought; Alison is Hestia, goddess of hearth and home. Other paintings depict Helena, MK, Rachel, and Krystal, as well as Mrs. S and Kira. "To my galaxy of women," Felix toasts, "thanks for the nurture." Felix here stands in for the creators of the series, Graeme Manson and John Fawcett, who have created a galaxy of women to whom we lift a glass as well even as we scribble down our ideas of what it all means.

NOTE

1. Examples include Andrea Goulet and Robert A. Rushing's collection Orphan Black: *Performance, Gender, Biopolitics* (Intellect, 2018), released just as we were completing editing; Gregory M. Pence's *What We Talk About When We Talk About Clone Club: Bioethics and Philosophy in* Orphan Black (Benbella, 2016); Orphan Black *and Philosophy: Grand Theft DNA*, edited by Richard Greene and Rachel Robinson-Greene (Open Court, 2016); and two books by Valerie Estelle Frankel, *The Women of* Orphan Black: *Faces of the Feminist Spectrum* (McFarland, 2018) and Orphan Black *and the Heroine's Journey: Symbols, Depth Psychology, and the Feminist Epic* (CreateSpace, 2017).

"I am not your property"
The Progressive Feminism of Orphan Black

Graeme J. Wilson

The current television landscape is populated by a wealth of acclaimed and innovative dramas that demonstrate cinema-level visuals and complex, serialized narratives. Popularly referred to as the Golden Age of Television by media scholars, this period ostensibly began with the debut of *The Sopranos* on premium channel HBO in 1999 (Damico and Quay viii; Sepinwall 41). *The Sopranos*, *Breaking Bad*, *Mad Men*, and other eminent series that have come to define this new Golden Age, often ruminate on the construction of masculinity in modern society (Damico and Quay 71). However, discourse on femininity has been largely marginalized within the current Golden Age.[1] For example, although *The Sopranos* and *Breaking Bad* feature multidimensional female characters, e.g., Carmela Soprano (Edie Falco) and Skyler White (Anna Gunn), they largely exist to expand the domestic backgrounds of the series' primary protagonists, i.e., their respective husbands, Tony Soprano (James Gandolfini) and Walter White (Bryan Cranston). This trend remains common amongst contemporary Golden Age dramas and does not deviate from traditional television roles written for women, which are largely defined by their relationships to the programs' male protagonists (Bacue and Signorielli 542). It remains relatively rare for a dramatic series to be headlined by a woman, and even more so for a dramatic series to feature a multitude of complex female characters in its ensemble. Resultantly, it is difficult to overstate just how innovate and groundbreaking the Canadian science fiction television series *Orphan Black* truly is.

Orphan Black, created by John Fawcett and Graeme Manson, premiered on cable channel BBC America on March 30, 2013. The series ultimately aired for five seasons, totaling 50 separate hour-long episodes before concluding on August 12, 2017. The main protagonist of *Orphan Black* is Sarah Manning

(Tatiana Maslany), a working-class grifter who discovers that she is one of several hundred genetically identical clones, all born through surrogacy. Other clones (all played by Maslany) include Alison Hendrix, a soccer mom, and Cosima Niehaus, a doctoral microbiology student. Sarah, Alison and Cosima decide to work together to locate other clones and investigate their mysterious origins, dubbing themselves "Clone Club." Over the course of the series, Sarah, Alison and Cosima come into violent conflict with the Dyad Institute, the scientific organization responsible for the illegal cloning program dubbed Project Leda. One clone, the power-hungry Rachel Duncan, is employed by Dyad and serves as Sarah's archrival. Clone Club eventually discovers that Dyad is merely a public front for Neolution, a controversial underground movement that aims to direct the course of human evolution through fringe science. Together, Clone Club must fight for their freedom and individual rights, asserting that they are more than Dyad and Neolution's property. Clone Club must simultaneously defend themselves from the Proletheans, an extremist religious cult, most sects of which view the clones as abominations. Dedicated to eradicating Clone Club, the Proletheans employ a brainwashed clone, Helena, to hunt down Sarah and the rest of her genetic siblings. However, Helena later betrays the Proletheans and is welcomed into Clone Club.

Throughout each of its five seasons, *Orphan Black* continually accrued both popular interest and critical acclaim. Much of *Orphan Black*'s success is generally attributed to its lead actress, Tatiana Maslany, who portrays Sarah, Alison, Cosima and numerous other Leda clones in the series; Maslany won an Emmy for her various performances in 2016. At a time when equal representation has become such a fundamental topic in media and entertainment, *Orphan Black* has received praise for its emphasis on strong female roles. Maslany herself acknowledged this in her acceptance speech for her Emmy, stating "I feel so lucky to be on a show that puts women at the center" (Highfill). However, *Orphan Black* also deserves notice for its socially conscious feminist themes.

It is common for science fiction texts to demonstrate "morally informed storylines" (Hockley 63), as the unique settings of the science fiction genre allow writers to comment on contemporary social issues through metaphorical narratives (Bressler and Lengel 23). When developing *Orphan Black*, Fawcett and Manson were originally interested in the notion of personal identity and viewed human cloning as a lens through which to explore that theme. Although science fiction commonly features male protagonists (Kray 39), Fawcett and Manson elected to write the lead clones as women (although a group of male clones is also featured in the series). Cosima Herter, a scientific consultant for the series and the model for Cosima Niehaus, pointed out to Fawcett and Manson that, by doing so, *Orphan Black* was in a unique position to address a variety of uniquely feminist themes. Fawcett and Manson agreed and subsequently expanded on this element of the text. The series has since "been hailed as a feminist masterpiece," with its overarching narrative functioning as an allegory for women's rights (Duca).[2] The feminism of *Orphan Black* is best encapsulated through three key elements: its exploration of motherhood, critique of toxic masculinity, and subversion of gender stereotypes. By deconstructing *Orphan Black*'s feminist ambitions, this essay aims to further promote and normalize the portrayal of feminist ideology in popular media.

Methodology

To deconstruct the portrayal of feminism in *Orphan Black*, this essay channels feminist film theory and queer theory for its theoretical framework. Feminist film theory is employed by media scholars to examine how the portrayal of women in mass media texts challenge or reinforce gender stereotypes in society (Erens xvi). Queer theory, which "discusses how power operates with sexuality in contemporary society to define social and cultural norms" (Avila-Saavedra 6), is used to critique and challenge societal heteronormativity, an ideology that posits heterosexuality is the only socially acceptable sexual orientation (Jenkins and Lovaas 8). For its methodology, this essay employs textual analysis, which is used to separate "the primary, linguistic meaning of a text's component parts [from its] secondary, or textual meaning" (Altman 15). Textual analysis includes several different systematic approaches, including feminist rhetorical criticism, which is specifically used to "understand [female] oppression as well as the communication used by and about women to overcome that oppression" (Griffin 395). Feminist rhetorical criticism was the most suitable method through which to deconstruct the thematic content of *Orphan Black* for this essay, due to Fawcett and Manson's own acknowledged promotion of feminist ideology throughout the series (Duca).

Analysis

Motherhood

Motherhood is one of the primary themes of *Orphan Black*, one that the series examines at both a personal and sociocultural level. All patriarchal societies, to different degrees, glorify motherhood as the ultimate marker of feminine validation (Tsuge 848). In the United States, this conception has historically been reflected in portrayals of motherhood in popular media

(Stavrianos 10). However, feminism has worked to deconstruct the allegedly and implicitly biological imperative connecting womanhood to motherhood entrenched in the cultural imagination. In recent decades feminist movements have broken several entrenched taboos relating to mothering, in particular deromanticizing the experience by discussing the difficulties and isolation it can inflict on women (Snitow 33). However, patriarchal expectations regarding motherhood are critical to the policing of femininity. Thus, being a "bad mother" represents a serious societal transgression (Lotz 127). The figure of the bad mother is a social construction, a maternal failure that is incompetent or outright disinterested in raising her offspring.

At the beginning of the series, Sarah flirts with the bad mother archetype. She is a grifter with no steady employment, instead earning a living solely through petty theft and scams. A year prior, Sarah had absconded with her boyfriend, Victor Schmidt (Michael Mando), a known drug dealer, abandoning her young daughter, Kira (Skyler Wexler), to be raised in the interim by Siobhan Sadler (Maria Doyle Kennedy), Sarah's adoptive mother. However, Sarah herself is not a bad mother—merely a flawed one. Sarah truly loves her daughter, and upon her return in the series pilot, admits to Sadler, whom Sarah calls Mrs. S, that she was not mature enough to be a mother yet ("Natural Selection," 1.1). Sarah declares that she is ready to leave Victor and commit to raising Kira, but Mrs. S refuses, stating that Sarah needs to prove herself to her first, a condition which Sarah reluctantly accepts. It is not uncommon for male protagonists in contemporary dramatic television, such as Tony Soprano and Walter White, to demonstrate numerous shortcomings in their roles as fathers, but they are judged far less harshly. *Orphan Black* directly addresses this double standard, asserting that motherhood is a complex role and should not simply be taken for granted.

In *Orphan Black*, each Leda clone displays various degrees of maternal instinct. Sarah is fiercely protective of Kira, and her daughter's safety serves as Sarah's driving motivation in the series. This is a prominent trope in popular fiction, in which female protagonists act "to protect [their] children, whether biological or adoptive" (Tasker 69). Alison, who had always wanted children, adopted a young boy and girl with her husband, Donnie (Kristian Bruun), after learning that she was infertile. Cosima is similarly infertile, although she is uninterested in having children of her own. Instead, Cosima, as well as Alison and Helena, project their maternal instincts onto Kira, who refers to them as her "aunties." Mrs. S is the undisputed matriarch of Clone Club, occupying both a grandmaternal role towards Kira and maternal role towards Sarah and the other clones. In this regard, Mrs. S is a classic "mother hen" archetype, a notion reinforced by her term of endearment towards Sarah and Kira, "chicken." Even Rachel, who is arguably the most cold and aloof character in the series, begins to bond with Kira during their interactions later in the series. Rachel desperately wants to be a mother and flies into an uncharacteristic rage after learning that not only is she infertile, but intentionally so. It is revealed that the Leda clones were purposefully engineered to be infertile when Rachel is informed she and her genetic siblings are "barren by design." However, Sarah and Helena are anomalies in that they are capable of breeding and thus dubbed "failure[s]" by Ethan Duncan ("Variable and Full of Perturbation," 2.8).

At the beginning of the series, Sarah is the only clone with any biological offspring. However, in the second season, Henrik Johanssen (Peter Outerbridge), the leader of the Proletheans, forcibly harvests Helena's eggs ("Governed as It Were by Chance," 2.4) and manipulates her into having the fertilized embryos implanted in her womb ("Things Which Have Never Yet Been Done," 2.9). This plot development is dark, tragic, and sadly almost inevitable, as Project Leda was originally named after the Greek myth of Leda and the Swan. In the myth, the god Zeus, who has taken the form of a swan, seduces and rapes the queen of Sparta, Leda (Barnwell 63).[3] Even the name of the cloning program alludes to male invasiveness of women, both physically and metaphorically. With the exception of Sarah and Helena, for whom fate intervened on their behalf, motherhood is a choice that has been intentionally and inhumanly denied to the various women of Clone Club. This particular plot thread illustrates issues related to women's reproductive rights, which have been historically influenced and decided by patriarchal corporate, governmental, and religious factions (Dixon-Mueller 14), circumstances *Orphan Black* replicates in its plot to assert its social relevance. In the series, Dyad and the Proletheans represent such factions, as both organizations attempt to exert their authority over the women of Clone Club, particularly regarding their reproductive rights.

In the penultimate episode of the second season, Helena kills Henrik before burning down the Prolethean compound, ending their threat forever (2.9). Helena subsequently joins Clone Club. Despite her offspring being conceived through what could be defined as a form of rape, Helena decides not to terminate her pregnancy, as the prospect of motherhood excites her. However, breaking from historical treatment of abortion in mainstream television, *Orphan Black* does not portray Helena's decision to carry the pregnancy to term as the only morally correct choice, but rather as just as legitimate as the choice *to* terminate the pregnancy.

Although abortion-related storylines have increased in popular television in recent decades, abortion is often characterized as, although legal, disreputable and dangerous. It is not uncommon for women in television narratives who decide to have an abortion to die from complications during the procedure, thus exaggerating the physical danger of abortion and contributing to its stigmatization (Kimport and Sisso 417). Even when television characters do have successful abortions, subsequent storylines generally emphasize their guilt and regret (Cole and Press 26). In contrast, the decision to have an abortion and its personal impact are portrayed with much more nuance in *Orphan Black*. A flashback in the series finale ("To Right the Wrongs of Many," 5.10) reveals that Sarah considered having an abortion after learning she was pregnant with Kira. Mrs. S says to Sarah that "Bringing a life into this world is a really big responsibility [...]. Only you can decide, chicken. [...] It's a woman's choice. It's the most personal one you can make." In the second season finale ("By Means Which Have Never Yet Been Tried," 2.10), it is revealed that Sarah *did* previously have an abortion, although no details are given whether Sarah was pregnant before or after Kira, or regarding Sarah's specific motivations behind the abortion. Echoing Mrs. S's earlier words, Sarah should not have to justify her decision to anyone but herself. Although television has historically presented abortion "as a questionable and selfish solution" to an unplanned or unwanted pregnancy (Cole and Press 27), *Orphan Black* correctly asserts that abortion is a much more complex and personal decision than typically represented in popular media.

Ultimately, *Orphan Black* recognizes motherhood as an amazing privilege, but not one that should represent the ultimate validation of womanhood in society. Instead, *Orphan Black* contends that motherhood is a choice, and one that rightfully belongs in the hands of women, regardless of their desire to have children or not. While the theme of motherhood receives intense focus across each of *Orphan Black*'s five seasons, it receives slightly less emphasis in the third season in favor of a new but equally relevant theme: toxic masculinity.

Toxic Masculinity

Toxic masculinity refers to the perspective that idealized masculinity is embodied by norms such as "domination, the devaluation of women, [and] wanton violence" (Kupers 714). In *Orphan Black*, toxic masculinity is personified in the Castor clones (all portrayed by Ari Millen), who serve as the main antagonists for the third season. Although Dyad managed Project Leda independently, they also collaborated with the military on Project Castor, which in turn produced a number of male clones. The Castor clones, named after one of Leda's sons (Yeats 210), are the genetic brothers of the Leda clones, being collectively raised within a military setting. Unlike the Leda clones, the Castor clones are generally more aggressive and vicious, even more so than Helena, who was raised as an assassin. Also unlike the Leda clones, the Castor clones possess a genetic defect that sterilizes their sexual partners, rendering them infertile, as well as suffering from a neurological defect that eventually kills them. It is eventually revealed that the military intends to harvest and weaponize this gene from the Castor clones, further alluding to the control patriarchies attempt to exert over women's reproductive rights.

Notably, instead of the stereotypical male military general or sergeant, Project Castor is rather managed by a woman: Dr. Virginia Coady (Kyra Harper), a high-ranking Neolution figure.[4] Coady acknowledges and even endorses the military's plans for the Castor clones, satisfied that her own career will be advanced in the process. Despite her sex, Coady is entirely dismissive of the women whom the Castor clones infect, content at having data procured for her research, and is also largely ambivalent towards the Castor clones themselves. Although the Castor clones view Coady as a mother figure, she views her adoptive sons largely as pawns, willing to experiment on and even terminate them if it benefits her research. Resultantly, Coady neatly fits the parameters of the bad mother archetype, manipulating her children through faux maternal affection (Lotz 128). This subtext is made explicit in *Orphan Black*'s penultimate episode, when Coady complies with orders to euthanize the last remaining Castor clone, prompting Helena to declare to Coady that, "You are shit mother" ("One Fettered Slave," 5.9). Ultimately, by encouraging her sons' sexual deviancy instead of tempering it, Coady's actions affirm that both men *and* women effectuate the continued conservation of rape culture[5] (May and Strikwerda 183).

Through *Orphan Black*'s third season, the Castor clones are utilized as a prism through which to explore not only toxic masculinity, but also the phenomenon of rape culture. In the second episode of the season ("Transitory Sacrifices of Crisis," 3.2), two of the Castor clones, Rudy and Seth, sexually assault a young woman named Patty (Natalie Krill) in a hotel room. While Patty had originally consented to sex with Rudy, Seth appears unexpectedly and begins to initiate a threesome. An unnerved Patty protests, arguing, "This is not what I signed up for." In response, Rudy simply replies that, "But we're brothers. We were taught to share," words that dehumanize Patty and reduce her to mere property. When Patty recounts her story to Sarah, Patty suggests that Rudy felt she "had insulted them by rejecting [Seth]." This scene establishes that Rudy, Seth and the other Castor clones share a "bro" mentality, a male subculture that prioritizes male bonding over romantic relationships with women. Encompassing this particular ideology is the popular phrase "bros before hos" (Radner 55). Bro subculture is strongly equated with American collegiate fraternities, which gender theorists have varyingly characterized as hypermasculine, misogynistic, and heteronormative (Hummer and Martin 460), all recognized traits of toxic masculinity (Kupers 714). For many collegiate fraternity members, engaging in heterosexual sex both affirms their own personal masculinity and validates male superiority over women (Hummer and Martin 467). Because it actively promotes the sexual objectification of women, the bro subculture popular amongst collegiate fraternities is also linked to rape culture (Boswell and Spade 134; Hummer and Martin 470; Sanday 4). Similar social structures and misogynistic practices have also been observed within militarized masculinities (O'Toole 219, 221; Projansky 9).

In *Orphan Black*, Castor functions as a makeshift fraternity, with its members loyal only to each other and regarding women as dehumanized, sexual objects to which they are entitled. However, Rudy ultimately faces judgment for his actions in the third season finale, during which he is fatally stabbed after a struggle with Helena. As Rudy bleeds out, he appeals to Helena's violent nature, stating, "We're just like you, Helena." Helena simply replies, "You poisoned women. […] You are rapist," asserting that Rudy's sexual crimes will not be forgiven or overlooked ("History Yet to Be Written," 3.10). *Orphan Black* strongly denounces the toxic masculine characteristics of Rudy and the other Castor clones, instead advocating for other masculine models that display more progressive qualities. One such model is embodied by Felix Dawkins (Jordan Gavaris), Sarah's younger foster brother and closest friend. Felix is openly gay, which compliments *Orphan Black*'s condemnation of toxic and hegemonic masculinity.

Hegemonic masculinity is a distinct concept from toxic masculinity, although it is not uncommon for the two to overlap. Hegemonic masculinity describes both patriarchal society's subordination of women and its hierarchal arrangement of masculinities (Connell and Messerschmidt 831–832; Demetriou 340, 343; Donaldson 645). While hegemonic masculinity encompasses masculine traits that "embod[y] the currently most honored way of being a man" in society (Connell and Messerschmidt 832), toxic masculinity specifically refers to the traits "that are socially destructive, such as misogyny [and] homophobia" (Kupers 716). While aggressive and physical homophobia is recognized as a prominent feature of toxic masculinity, hegemonic masculinity nevertheless prioritizes heterosexual masculinity in society, with gay men experiencing subordination "not only in terms of social status and prestige but also by a series of material practices, which include political, cultural, economic, and legal discrimination" (Demetriou 341). The reason gay masculinities "are subordinated to the hegemonic model [is] because their object of sexual desire undermines the institution of heterosexuality, which is of primary importance for the reproduction of patriarchy" (Demetriou 344) and the continued dominance of men over women.

In *Orphan Black*, Felix is often abused and harassed by the Castor clones, Victor, and other heterosexual men who display machismo attitude. Resultantly, Felix begins to develop a strong kinship with the women of Clone Club, based on their mutual marginalization. The relationship that the women of Clone Club develop with Felix complements the intersectional philosophies of modern feminist activism, which emphasize solidarity with other communities marginalized within heteronormative and patriarchal society, including the LGBT community (Miller 441). When inducting Helena into Clone Club, Sarah demands that Helena treat Felix with respect, explaining, "That's my brother. Which means he's one of our sisters. Family" ("*Ipsa Scientia Potestas Est*," 2.5). Felix similarly verbalizes the strong familial bond he shares with the women of Clone Club in the fifth season episode "Guillotines Decide" (5.8). When hosting his art show dedicated to his "galaxy of women," Felix delivers a heartfelt monologue about the nurturing influence Mrs. S provided him and Sarah, and how Mrs. S is directly responsible for their moral values and commitment to their family, which now include Sarah's genetic sisters (5.8).

Besides Felix, the LGBT community is also represented through Cosima, who identifies as lesbian. However, *Orphan Black* treats their sexuality as secondary to their actual personalities. Cosima herself asserts to Rachel during their initial meeting that "my sexuality is not the most interesting thing about me" ("Governed by Sound Reason and True Religion," 2.2), further rejecting historical television stereotypes where LGBT characters are defined almost entirely by their sexual identity. This is especially true for homosexual men, whose storylines often revolve around their attempts to reconcile their sexual orientation with popular societal expectations of masculinity (Gross 31). Instead, Felix has already attained self-actualization (Maslow 382) prior to the beginning of the series. Felix never feels compelled to validate his masculinity to himself, unlike the Castor clones, who continually pursue this self-validation through displays of sex and violence. Felix rejects these macho and toxic masculine practices, which are often celebrated in popular media (Scharrer 615) and instead embodies a more progressive masculine identity in which his queer sexuality and platonic association with women do not detract from his masculinity. *Orphan Black*'s condemnation of hegemonic masculinity specifically is further represented through its subversion of gender stereotypes.

Gender Stereotypes

Gender refers to the social and cultural expectations related to each biological sex. Specifically, "*gender role*[s] and *gender display*[s] focus on behavioral aspects of being a woman or a man (as opposed, for example, to biological differences between the two)" (West and Zimmerman 126–127). The term "cisgender" then refers to individuals whose gender conforms to their birth-assigned sex (Aultman 61; Curling et al. 125). A traditional feminine gender role is "working full-time within the home rather than taking employment outside of [it]," while a traditional masculine gender role is "providing financially for the family and making important family decisions" (Blackstone 337). Prominent gender roles such as these, which popular television has helped to normalize in society (Bacue and Signorielli 543), are largely rooted in persisting gender stereotypes. Such stereotypes include women being more inherently emotional, passive, and yielding, and men being more inherently ambitious, dominant, and assertive (Carranza and Prentice 269–270). Consequently, "the feminist movement [works] to deconstruct gender stereotypes and offer alternative visions of gender roles that emphasize equality between women and men" (Blackstone 337), a cause to which *Orphan Black* contributes. Even though the primary Leda clones derive from specific archetypes, such as the housewife (Alison) or "dumb blonde" (Krystal), they operate outside traditional gender norms and subvert popular gender stereotypes, particularly regarding the notion of women being inherently weaker and submissive.

A prescriptive gender stereotype is that assertiveness, independence, self-reliance, and leadership are more masculine traits (Carranza and Prentice 270). However, the primary Leda clones all display these qualities without compromising their femininity. Alison is neither meek nor submissive, both stereotypical characteristics especially associated with the housewife archetype, as represented in popular fiction such as *Desperate Housewives* (Merskin 161). In contrast, Alison is easily the stronger personality in her marriage with Donnie. Notably, Donnie, né Chubbs, took Alison's surname upon their marriage, breaking typical marital convention. Alison is also unafraid of confrontation and is physically capable of defending herself. Although these traits are coded as masculine (Connell 28), Alison, Sarah, Helena, and Mrs. S all demonstrate a capability for self-defense over the course of the series, demonstrating that aggressive physicality is easily compatible with femininity. While Cosima does not share her siblings' physical attributes, she occupies another role as Clone Club's self-designated "geek monkey" ("To Hound Nature in Her Wanderings," 2.6).

Commonly, intelligent "genius" characters on mainstream television are not only portrayed as awkward and socially repressed (Carlson 1), but also explicitly identify as male (5). Cosima demonstrates both strong social skills and extensive scientific understanding, subverting expectations of the "genius" archetype not only through personality, but also just by being a woman. Genius women are unfortunately rare in mainstream television, especially in contrast to the vast prominence of the "dumb blonde" stereotype, which describes a physically attractive woman with shallow interests and limited intelligence (Inness 2). *Orphan Black* also subverts this stereotype through the character of Krystal Goderitch, a Leda clone introduced in the third season. Krystal is blonde, frivolous, and wears provocative clothing that prominently displays her breasts; all recognized elements of the "dumb blonde" stereotype (Greenwood and Isbell 342). Both the Castor and Leda clones quickly assume from her fatuous personality that Krystal is unintelligent. However, Krystal surprises Clone Club by breaking ground in the Dyad conspiracy through her own investigations. Although Krystal amusingly draws the wrong conclusions from the evidence, believing Dyad are knowingly selling poisonous cosmetics instead of participating in illegal human cloning, Sarah, Alison, and Cosima are forced to admit that their efforts to expose Dyad and Neolution would have failed without Krystal. *Orphan Black* asserts that intelligence and physicality should not be exclusively coded as masculine and can naturally coexist alongside femininity, as demonstrated by the women of Clone Club. Even Rachel, one of the primary antagonists of the series, defies typical gender conventions.

In earlier seasons of the series, Rachel is distinguished for her cold and emotionless demeanor. However, because women working in male-dominated fields often suffer "the perception that they are overly emotional (and thereby cannot control the influence of their emotions on their thoughts and behaviors)" (Brescoll 423), these women are forced to restrict displays of emotion so as to not undermine their peers' perception of their competence. This in turn is responsible for generating stereotypical terms "such as *bitch, ice queen, iron maiden,* and *dragon lady* [...] to describe women who have successfully climbed the organizational ladder" (Heilman et al. 426). Although Rachel would appear to conform to the stereotype of the "ice queen" because she "display[s] very little (feminine) emotion at work" (Brescoll 423), this is in fact a role forced onto her by dominant gender stereotypes, particularly those of women being inherently weaker and more passive than men, whose supposed stronger personalities make them more effective leaders (Carranza and Prentice 269–270). In contrast, Rachel actively combats these stereotypes in order to succeed at Dyad, although she ultimately earns a reputation as an "ice queen" in the process. However, Rachel's desire for children and eventual friendship with Kira also challenge this reputation, thus presenting a more complex and three-dimensional depiction of successful corporate women (Rachel's infertility is the primary source of her jealousy of Sarah, who conceived Kira naturally).

Even more so than Rachel, Sarah resists conforming to cultural expectations of feminine behavior. In *Orphan Black*, Sarah's femininity is firmly established through her strong maternal relationship with Kira. Despite this, Sarah, besides displaying physical toughness throughout the series, also wears leather jackets and boots, abuses alcohol, enjoys casual sex, and reflexively resists authority. Sarah thus portrays a more complex depiction of gender, as these attributes are popularly coded as either working class masculine traits (Pyke 538) or butch lesbian traits (Bimbi et al. 91). However, rather than as lesbian, Sarah identifies as either bisexual or pansexual, as confirmed by Maslany during a panel for *Orphan Black* at the 2016 San Diego Comic-Con ("Orphan Black"). Pansexuality refers to romantic and sexual attraction

16 Sisterhood, Science and Surveillance in *Orphan Black*

towards "individuals of any sex or gender identity. Often people choose this identity label to reflect inclusion of trans people in their sexual attractions" (Curling et al. 125). The trans community is represented in *Orphan Black* through the character of Tony Sawicki, a transgender male clone introduced in the second season of the series.

A key argument of queer theorists is that "sexuality is not restricted to heterosexuality or homosexuality, [which is] a binary system reinforced by hegemonic patriarchal societies" (Avila-Saavedra 6–7). Instead, sexual and gender identities are much more varied and diverse, with the transgender identity being one such category. Because their "gender is on the other side (trans-) of their birth-assigned sex" (Aultman 61), transgender individuals embody a conscious rejection of conventional cisgender normativity. Trans representation is a fairly recent phenomenon in popular television (Kidd 102), especially compared to other LGBT identities that began to experience more widespread and progressive representation in the 1990s. Some notable examples include the sitcoms *Will & Grace* and *Spin City*, both of which aired on broadcast networks and featured normalized gay protagonists (Mitchell 87). During the 1990s, transgender activists and their allies described such practices as homonormative, privileging gay and lesbian norms over those of the more marginalized transgender identity (Bryant 456). However, because cisnormativity is hegemonic in American culture, "conventional sex-gender alignment" has traditionally dominated television in order to maximize commercial appeal and attract the widest possible audience (Booth 115). Therefore, *Orphan Black*'s inclusion of a transgender character in its ensemble is particularly noteworthy.

In his debut episode, Tony—originally named Antoinette Sawicki—explains to Felix and Sarah that, like many members the trans community, he was uncomfortable with his assigned sex at birth. Tony has since begun the transitioning process and is explicitly seen injecting testosterone throughout the episode (2.8). While being interviewed for feminist culture blog Pajiba during the 2014 ATX Television Festival, Fawcett and Manson explained they had sought input and advice from GLAAD in developing Tony's character (Chaudhury). During a panel at the festival, Fawcett and Manson further explained that they wanted to avoid perpetuating stereotypes regarding the trans community and for Tony's portrayal to feel authentic, affirming that *Orphan Black* is, at its core, "a show about identity and we celebrate diversity" (Bricker).

Ultimately, television and other mass entertainment mediums have participated in "oppressive work […] by addressing the dominant audience [exclusively]" (Condit 112). Besides its narrow depiction of gender roles, mainstream television often ignores marginalized communities that deviate wholly from cisgender norms. However, *Orphan Black* celebrates such diversity. *Orphan Black* challenges the narrow and hegemonic portrayal of gender in popular television, portraying a wider range of gender options through its depiction of alternate gender identities and subversion of feminine stereotypes. Not only does the latter contribute to *Orphan Black*'s rumination on the nature versus nurture debate, but it also functions as a feminist assertion of female complexity, an appreciable progression from what is often represented on television.

Conclusion

Although women account for more than half of the population, they have historically been underrepresented on television (Bacue and Signorielli 529; Kidd 102). Additionally, their roles are more often those of plot devices rather than fully formed characters. Traditional television roles written for women are more sexualized and skew younger (Bacue and Signorielli 531), with their overall value in the programs primarily dependent upon their relationships with male characters (542). However, *Orphan Black* deviates from such regressive portrayal of women, instead championing their autonomy. This is reflected by the tagline for the show's third season, "I am not your property," which on promotional billboards was superimposed over Sarah's defiant face. Similar posters were produced for Alison, Cosima, and Helena. This tagline directly alludes to a scene from the first season finale, in which Cosima and Delphine (Évelyne Brochu) discover a sequence within the Leda clones' genome that states, "This organism and derivative genetic material is restricted intellectual property," revealing that Dyad—and, by proxy, Neolution—has patented the women of Clone Club, as well as any potential offspring they produce, and thus "own" them ("Endless Forms Most Beautiful," 1.10). Although P.T. Westmorland (Stephen McHattie), the founder of Neolution, claims the organization's goals are entirely prosocial, it is eventually divulged that Westmorland is dying and simply seeking to extend his own life, as he suffers from a pathological fear of death. The Leda and Castor clones comprise an extensive genetic breeding program, with the singular goal of isolating and reproducing a genetic "fountain of youth" to restore Westmorland ("Ease for Idle Millionaires," 5.5). Resultantly, the entire conspiracy is revealed to be exploiting women simply and entirely to benefit the vanity of an old, white, upper class man—a scenario sadly not without historical precedent. Even before this revelation, Clone Club rejects both Dyad and Neolution, fighting for their freedom and individual rights. Throughout *Orphan Black*, the women of Clone Club assert that they are more than Dyad's property and that Dyad does not own their bodies or lives—a message that remains as relevant today as ever before.

In conclusion, the feminism of *Orphan Black* can be compartmentalized into three separate factors: its exploration of motherhood, critique of toxic masculinity, and subversion of gender stereotypes. This progressiveness has resulted in a strong, dedicated fandom for the series, itself collectively referred to as Clone Club after the community in the series (Derschowitz). *Orphan Black*'s portrayal of normalized LGBT sexuality, represented through both Felix and Cosima, has also resulted in a strong LGBT fandom for the series, whose members often refer to themselves as "Clonesbians" on social media (Ross). Today, with the rise of white nationalism during the present U.S. political context, masculine power norms have evinced resurgence, with feminism experiencing newfound hostility and prejudice within patriarchal societies. However, the popular and critical success of *Orphan Black* identifies the series as representing a new milestone in normalizing the portrayal of feminisms in popular media.

Notes

1. Although the current television landscape is predominantly male, several contemporary Golden Age dramas have been recognized for their emphasis on femininity, including *Homeland*, *Orange Is the New Black*, *Nurse Jackie*, and *Weeds*.
2. See Erin Bell, Jenny Bonnevier, and Dani Howell in this volume for other perspectives on the representation of women within the series.
3. For more on the mythological elements of the series, see Janet Brennan Croft in this volume.
4. Subsequent essays in this volume consider Coady in greater detail.
5. Rape culture describes the normalization of sexual objectification and assault in a society (Boswell and Spade 133) and is largely perpetuated through "fundamental attitudes and values [that] are supportive of gender stereotypes and violence against women" (McMahon 357).

Works Cited

Altman, Rick. "A Semantic/Syntactic Approach to Film Genre." *Cinema Journal*, vol. 23, no. 3, 1984, pp. 6–18.
Aultman, B. Lee. "Cisgender." *TSQ: Transgender Studies Quarterly*, vol. 1, nos. 1–2, 2014, pp. 61–62.
Avila-Saavedra, Guillermo. "Nothing Queer About Queer Television: Televised Construction of Gay Masculinities." *Media, Culture & Society*, vol. 31, no. 1, 2009, pp. 5–21.
Bacue, Aaron, and Nancy Signorielli. "Recognition and Respect: A Content Analysis of Prime-Time Television Characters Across Three Decades." *Sex Roles*, vol. 40, no. 7, 1999, pp. 527–544.
Barnwell, W.C. "The Rapist in 'Leda and the Swan.'" *South Atlantic Bulletin*, vol. 42, no. 1, 1977, pp. 62–68.
Bimbi, David S., et al. "Butch Bottom–Femme Top? an Exploration of Lesbian Stereotypes." *Journal of Lesbian Studies*, vol. 16, no. 1, 2012, pp. 90–107.
Blackstone, Amy M. "Gender Roles and Society." *Encyclopedia of Human Ecology*, edited by Julia R. Miller et al., ABC-CLIO, 2003, pp. 335–338.
Booth, E. Tristan. "The Provisional Acknowledgement of Identity Claims in Televised Documentary." *Transgender Communication Studies: Histories, Trends, and Trajectories*, edited by Jamie C. Capuzza and Leland G. Spender, Lexington Books, 2015, pp. 111–126.
Boswell, A. Ayres, and Joan Z. Spade. "Fraternities and Collegiate Rape Culture: Why Are

Some Fraternities More Dangerous Places for Women?" *Gender & Society*, vol. 10, no. 2, 1996, pp. 133–147.
Brescoll, Victoria L. "Leading with Their Hearts? How Gender Stereotypes of Emotion Lead to Biased Evaluations of Female Leaders." *The Leadership Quarterly*, vol. 27, no. 3, 2016, pp. 415–428.
Bressler, Nancy, and Lara Lengel. "Mothering in Dystopia: Lone Parenting in a Post Apocalyptic World." *Motherhood and Lone/Single Parenting: A 21st Century Perspective*, edited by Mari Motapanyane, Demeter Press, 2016, pp. 19–52.
Bricker, Tierney. "You'll Never Guess Who Came Up with the Idea for Orphan Black's Transgender Clone." *E! News*, 2014, www.eonline.com/news/549539/you-ll-never-guess-who-came-up-with-the-idea-for-orphan-black-s-transgender-clone.
Bryant, Karl. "In Defense of Gay Children? 'Progay' Homophobia and the Production of Homonormativity." *Sexualities*, vol. 11, no. 4, 2008, pp. 455–475.
"By Means Which Have Never Yet Been Tried." Writ. Graeme Manson. Dir. John Fawcett. *Orphan Black*. Season 2, episode 10. First aired 21 June 2014.
Carlson, Ashley Lynn. "Introduction." *Genius on Television: Essays on Small Screen Depictions of Big Minds*, edited by Ashley Lynn Carlson, McFarland, 2015, pp. 1–10.
Carranza, Erica, and Deborah A. Prentice. "What Women and Men Should Be, Shouldn't Be, Are Allowed to Be, and Don't Have to Be: The Contents of Prescriptive Gender Stereotypes." *Psychology of Women Quarterly*, no. 26, 2002, pp. 269–281.
Chaudhury, Nadia. "A Chat with 'Orphan Black' Creators Graeme Manson & John Fawcett About Saturday's Game-Changing Episode." *Pajiba*, 2014, www.pajiba.com/movie_and_tv_facts/a-chat-with-orphan-black-creators-graeme-manson-john-fawcett-about-saturdays-gamechanging-episode.php.
Cole, Elizabeth R., and Andrea L. Press. *Speaking of Abortion: Television and Authority in the Lives of Women*. U Chicago P, 1999.
Condit, Celeste Michelle. "The Rhetorical Limits of Polysemy." *Critical Studies in Mass Communication*, vol. 6, no. 2, 1989, pp. 103–122.
Connell, R.W. *Which Way Is Up? Essays on Sex, Class, and Culture*. Allen & Unwin, 1983.
Connell, R.W., and James Messerschmidt. "Hegemonic Masculinity: Rethinking the Concept." *Gender & Society*, vol. 19, no. 6, 2005, pp. 829–859.
Curling, Deone, et al. "LGBT Identity, Untreated Depression, and Unmet Need for Mental Health Services by Sexual Minority Women and Trans-Identified People." *Journal of Women's Health*, vol. 26, no. 2, 2017, pp. 116–127.
Damico, Amy M., and Sara E. Quay. *21st-Century TV Dramas: Exploring the New Golden Age*. Praeger, 2016.
Demetriou, Demetrakis Z. "Connell's Concept of Hegemonic Masculinity: A Critique." *Theory and Society*, vol. 30, no. 3, 2001, pp. 337–361.
Derschowitz, Jessica. "Orphan Black Star Tatiana Maslany on the Clone Club: It's the Reason You Do Your Job.'" *Entertainment Weekly*, 2017, ew.com/tv/2017/08/04/orphan-black-tatiana-maslany-clone-club/.
Dixon-Mueller, Ruth. *Population Policy and Women's Rights: Transforming Reproductive Choice*. Greenwood Publishing Group, 1993.
Donaldson, Mike. "What Is Hegemonic Masculinity?" *Theory and Society*, vol. 22, no. 5, 1993, pp. 643–657.
Duca, Lauren. "The Real-Life Cosima Had to Tell the 'Orphan Black' Creators the Show Was a 'Feminist Bomb.'" *The Huffington Post*, 2015, www.huffingtonpost.com/2015/06/13/orphan-black-feminist_n_7528978.html.
"Ease for Idle Millionaires." Writ. Jenn Engles. Dir. Helen Shaver. *Orphan Black*. Season 5, episode 5. First aired 8 July 2017.
"Endless Forms Most Beautiful." Writ. Graeme Manson. Dir. John Fawcett. *Orphan Black*. Season 1, episode 10. First aired 1 June 2013.
Erens, Patricia. "Introduction." *Issues in Feminist Film Criticism*, edited by Patricia Erens, Indiana UP, 1990. pp. xv–xxv.
"Governed as It Were by Chance." Writ. Russ Cochrane. Dir. David Frazee. *Orphan Black*. Season 2, episode 4. First aired 10 May 2014.

"Governed by Sound Reason and True Religion." Writ. Karen Walton and Graeme Manson. Dir. John Fawcett. *Orphan Black*. Season 2, episode 2. First aired 26 April 2014.

Greenwood, Sarah, and Linda M. Isbell. "Ambivalent Sexism and the Dumb Blonde: Men's and Women's Reactions to Sexist Jokes." *Psychology of Women Quarterly*, vol. 26, no. 4, 2002, pp. 341–350.

Griffin, Cindy L. "Feminist Rhetorical Criticism." *Encyclopedia of Communication Theory, Volume 1*, edited by Karen A. Fodd and Stephen W. Littlejohn, SAGE Publications, 2009, pp. 395–396.

Gross, Larry. "Out of the Mainstream: Sexual Minorities and the Mass Media." *Gay People, Sex, and the Media*, edited by Alfred Kielwasser and Michelle Wolf, the Haworth Press, 2013, pp. 19–46.

"Guillotines Decide." Writ. Aisha Porter-Christie and Graeme Manson. Dir. Aaron Morton. *Orphan Black*. Season 5, episode 8. First aired 29 Jul 2017.

Heilman, Madeline E, et al. "Penalties for Success: Reactions to Women Who Succeed at Male Gender-Typed Tasks." *Journal of Applied Psychology*, vol. 89, no. 3, 2004, pp. 416–427.

Highfill, Samantha. "Emmys 2016: Tatiana Maslany Win Best Actress in a Drama." *Entertainment Weekly*, 2016, www.ew.com/article/2016/09/18/emmys-2016-tatiana-maslany-drama-actress/.

"History Yet to Be Written." Writ. Graeme Manson. Dir. John Fawcett. *Orphan Black*. Season 3, episode 10. First aired 20 June 2015.

Hockley, Luke. "Science Fiction." *The Television Genre Book*, edited by Glen Creeber, 3rd ed., Palgrave, 2015, pp. 62–64.

Hummer, Robert A., and Patricia Yancey Martin. "Fraternities and Rape on Campus." *Gender & Society*, vol. 3, no. 4, 1989, pp. 457–473.

Inness, Sherrie A. "Introduction: Who Remembers Sabrina? Intelligence, Gender, and the Media." *Geek Chic: Smart Women in Popular Culture*, edited by Sherrie A. Inness, Palgrave Macmillan, 2016, pp. 1–10.

"*Ipsa Scientia Potestas Est.*" Writ. Tony Elliott. Dir. Helen Shaver. *Orphan Black*. Season 2, episode 5. First aired 17 May 2014.

Jenkins, Mercilee M., and Karen E. Lovaas. "Introduction: Setting the Stage." *Sexualities and Communication in Everyday Life: A Reader*, edited by Mercilee M. Jenkins and Karen E. Lovaas, SAGE Publications, 2007, pp. 1–19.

Kidd, Dustin. *Pop Culture Freaks: Identity, Mass Media and Society*. Westview Press, 2014.

Kimport, Katrina, and Gretchen Sissin. "Telling Stories About Abortion: Abortion-related Plots in American Film and Television, 1916–2013." *Contraception*, vol. 89, no. 5, 2014, pp. 413–418.

Kray, Susan. "Things Women Don't Say." *Science Fiction, Canonization, Marginalization, and the Academy*, edited by George Slusser and Gary Westfahl, Greenwood Press, 2002, pp. 37–50.

Kupers, Terry A. "Toxic Masculinity as a Barrier to Mental Health Treatment in Prison." *Journal of Clinical Psychology*, vol. 61, no. 6, 2005, pp. 713–724.

Lotz, Amanda D. "Really Bad Mothers: Manipulative Matriarchs in *Sons of Anarchy* and *Justified*." *Television Antiheroines: Women Behaving Badly in Crime and Prison Drama*, edited by Milly Buonanno, Intellect, 2017, pp. 125–139.

Maslow, Abraham H. "A Theory of Human Motivation." *Psychological Review*, vol. 50, no. 4, 1943, pp. 370–396.

May, Larry, and Robert Strikwerda. "Men in Groups: Collective Responsibility for Rape." *Bringing Peace Home: Feminism, Violence, and Nature*, edited by Karen J. Warren and Duane L. Cady, Indiana UP, 1996, pp. 175–191.

McMahon, Sarah. "Understanding Community-Specific Rape Myths: Exploring Student Athlete Culture." *Affilia: Journal of Women and Social Work*, vol. 22, no. 4, 2007, pp. 357–370.

Merskin, Debra L. *Media, Minorities, and Meaning: A Critical Introduction*. Peter Lang Publishing, 2011.

Miller, Shae. "Sexuality, Gender Identity, Fluidity, and Embodiment." *The Oxford Handbook*

of U.S. Women's Social Movement Activism, edited by Rachel L. Einwohner, et al., Oxford UP, 2017, pp. 440–461.
Mitchell, Danielle. "Straight and Crazy? Bisexual and Easy? or Drunken Floozy? The Queer Politics of Karen Walker." *The New Queer Aesthetic on Television: Essays on Recent Programming*, edited by James R. Keller and Leslie Stratyner, McFarland, 2006, pp. 85–98.
"Natural Selection." Writ. Graeme Manson. Dir. John Fawcett. *Orphan Black*. Season 1, episode 1. First aired 30 March 2013.
"One Fettered Slave." Writ. Alex Levine. Dir. David Frazee. *Orphan Black*. Season 5, episode 9. First aired 5 Aug 2017.
"Orphan Black FULL PANEL—San Diego Comic-Con 2016." *YouTube*, uploaded by BBC America, 23 July 2016, www.youtube.com/watch?v=kvO8a48t4js.
O'Toole, Laura. "Subcultural Theory of Rape Revisited." *Gender Violence: Interdisciplinary Perspectives*, edited by L. Kiter Edwards, et al., 2nd ed., New York UP, 2007, pp. 214–221.
Projansky, Sarah. *Watching Rape: Film and Television in Postfeminist Culture*. New York UP, 2001.
Pyke, Karen D. "Class-Based Masculinities: The Interdependence of Gender, Class, and Interpersonal Power." *Gender & Society*, vol. 10, no. 5, 1996, pp. 527–549.
Radner, Hilary. "Grumpy Old Men: Bros Before Hos.'" *Reading the Bromance: Homosocial Relationships in Film and Television*, edited by Michael DeAngelis, Wayne State UP, 2014, pp. 52–78.
Ross, Dalton. "'Orphan Black': Tatiana Maslany on Cosima's Sexuality." *Entertainment Weekly*, 2014, www.ew.com/article/2014/03/14/orphan-black-tatiana-maslany-cosima-gay/.
Sanday, Peggy Reeves. *Fraternity Gang Rape: Sex, Brotherhood and Privilege on Campus*. 2nd ed., New York UP, 2007.
Scharrer, Erica. "Tough Guys: The Portrayal of Hypermasculinity and Aggression in Televised Police Dramas." *Journal of Broadcasting & Electronic Media*, vol. 45, no. 4, 2001, pp. 615–634.
Sepinwall, Alan. *The Revolution Was Televised: The Cops, Crooks, Slingers, and Slayers Who Change*. Touchstone, 2015.
Snitow, Ann. "Feminism and Motherhood: An American Reading." *Feminism Review*, no. 40, 1992, pp. 32–51.
Stavrianos, Cynthia. *The Political Uses of Motherhood in America*. Routledge, 2015.
Tasker, Yvonne. *Working Girls: Gender and Sexuality in Popular Cinema*. Routledge, 1998.
"Things Which Have Never Yet Been Done." Writ. Alex Levine. Dir. T.J. Scott. *Orphan Black*. Season 2, episode 9. First aired 14 June 2014.
"To Hound Nature in Her Wanderings." Writ. Chris Roberts. Dir. Brett Sullivan. *Orphan Black*. Season 2, episode 6. First aired 24 May 2014.
"To Right the Wrongs of Many." Writ. Renée St. Cyr and Graeme Manson. Dir. John Fawcett. *Orphan Black*. Season 5, episode 10. First aired 12 Aug 2017.
"Transitory Sacrifices of Crisis." Writ. Aubrey Nealon. Dir. John Fawcett. *Orphan Black*. Season 3, episode 2. First aired 25 April 2015.
Tsuge, Azumi. "Fertility and Fertility Treatment." *Routledge International Encyclopedia of Women: Global Women's Issues and Knowledge*, edited by Kramarae, Cheris, and Dale Spender, Routledge, 2000, pp. 848–850.
"Variable and Full of Perturbation." Writ. Karen Walton. Dir. John Fawcett. *Orphan Black*. Season 2, episode 8. First aired 7 June 2014.
West, Candace, and Don H. Zimmerman. "Doing Gender." *Gender & Society*, vol. 1, no. 2, 1987, pp. 125–151.
Yeats, William Butler. "Leda and the Swan." *The Classic Hundred Poems: All-time Favorites*, edited by William Harmon, Columbia UP, 1998, pp. 210–211.

Women's Rebellion or Radical Containment?
Understanding Orphan Black's *Feminist Message*

Dani Howell

The *Orphan Black* narrative begins when the protagonist, Sarah Manning (Tatiana Maslany), sees a woman who looks just like her commit suicide. Sarah steals the dead woman's identity, and this impersonation is the series' catalyst. Sarah eventually discovers she and the woman, Beth Childs, are clones. The story focuses on a group of these cloned women—Sarah, Alison Hendrix, and Cosima Niehaus—who are referred to as the Project Leda clones (and all played by Maslany)—the name of the experiment that led to their creation.

In an advertisement for this series, the dialogue "I am not your toy. I am not your experiment. […] I am not your property" plays over a video crosscutting between these cloned women ("Catch Up on ORPHAN BLACK"). As the ad suggests, a central theme throughout the series is women's desire for and attempt at autonomy. These cloned women face a constant threat: those in power trying to take control over their lives and their bodies. Viewers see this attempted oppression from corporations, the government, and religious institutions. In focusing on these women, this female-driven narrative defies television's tendency to privilege stories that place men in the active role and use women as passive objects. Since traditional television series tend to reinforce male value, critics often comment that *Orphan Black*'s focus on women's attempts to possess autonomy seems like a feminist oasis in a culture that perpetuates restrictive views of women.[1] All that said, while the series dramatizes a journey for women's autonomy, I am hesitant to label this artifact a paragon of feminist media. The series offers a potentially radical message;

however, upon closer analysis, *Orphan Black* tempers this idea. This imagined freedom is available only to a small group of women, suggesting *Orphan Black* cannot fully break away from the influence of the patriarchal culture that produced it.

Because *Orphan Black*'s feminist message is often attributed to its imagined spaces and scenarios that allow women to subvert male power, my analysis examines the narrative's portrayal of women, the freedoms it imagines for these women, and the women permitted to have these freedoms. As I will explain, there are inconsistencies in the ways *Orphan Black* wrestles with gender, heteronormativity, and sexuality, domesticating its radical ideas about gender and sexuality. The series conceives of scenarios and spaces in which female bodies wrest freedom from normative gender roles and narrow views of sexuality. However, the narrative does not imagine these freedoms for all; only bodies that support dominant ideology are freed, a vision of freedom that is limited at best. Women are only granted freedom if they fulfill a patriarchal desire for an ideal and legible female body, making this potentially revolutionary message less threatening and echoing the workings of contemporary patriarchal power. This power grants women enough freedom to create an illusion of autonomy, but it only provides limited forms of freedom to a specific set of privileged bodies: the thin, white bodies that align with cultural norms.

Theoretical Framework

I use Antonio Gramsci's conceptions of hegemony and ideology to analyze *Orphan Black*'s portrayal of feminist rebellion. According to Gramsci, ideology refers to a specific system of ideas; contradicting ideologies—dominant culture and oppositional views—interact until one proliferates throughout society, creating and altering the "hegemony of a fundamental social group over" subordinate groups (211). The conflicting ideologies in *Orphan Black* that I am analyzing are feminist and patriarchal, revealing the ways the series both subverts and reinforces the dominant power structures that subjugate women.

Popular culture plays an important role in circulating ideologies because, as Tony Bennett posits, it exists in constant tension between the governing group's attempt "to win hegemony" and "the forms of opposition to this endeavor" (xv). The result is a cultural hegemony that mixes dominant and oppositional ideology (xv–xvi). Our contemporary dominant ideology is that of the Western white male subject position, which views other races, genders, and groups as inferior and subservient (Kellner 61). This patriarchal ideology creates social hierarchies that further benefit those already in power. We see ideological negotiation play out when *Orphan Black* presents and then domesticates views of gender and sexuality that are still uncommon in television. This negotiation conveys, at times, a radical feminist message while ultimately supporting a cultural logic that privileges hegemonic ideas of gender (Bennett xv–xvi).

My analysis focuses on the oppositional ideologies of feminist and queer values, such as equality, community, cooperation, and antinormativity (Johnson 7; Tong 7).[2] These oppositions counter a dominant ideology that glorifies patriarchy and disparages typically feminine qualities (Hartmann 21). As Heidi Hartmann argues, dominant ideology is "a set of social relations between men" that creates both "solidarity among men that enable them to dominate women" and hierarchies—both between men and women and groups within each (11). Furthermore, she contends that these hierarchies work because "those at the higher levels can 'buy off' those at the lower levels by offering them power over those still lower" (11). In this sense, we can see what Elisabeth Schüssler Fiorenza termed "kyriarchy"—a system of oppression not limited to "the sex/gender system but conceptualize[d] in terms of interlocking structures of domination"—at play (8). A woman may be oppressed because of her gender but still have privilege because of her race, sexuality, or any number of other factors, and using a multifaceted approach allows these various intersections to be recognized.

To examine the ways these ideologies interact, I draw on Todd Gitlin's Gramscian cultural Marxist approach to television media. He argues that television relays, reproduces, and packages ideology that develops "both from social elites and from active social groups" and shapes views on everything from race to sexuality (253). According to Gitlin, "social conflicts are transported *into* the cultural system," and in this hegemonic process, conflicts are framed to align with culture's dominant system of meaning (264). These potentially subversive ideas still exist but are less threatening to the governing. For example, dominant culture domesticates a message of gender equality if this equality results in the further Othering of a different subjugated group, say, women of color, as is the case in *Orphan Black*. The series articulates oppositional ideology when it subverts contemporary depictions of gender roles and offers well-developed, non-normative views of sexuality. However, the series circulates dominant ideology to contain this opposition: it reinforces stigma around queer sex, and it values a female body that is legibly heterosexual and fulfills patriarchal desire through visual stimulation.

Thin White Female—The Acceptable Body

While television critics often hail *Orphan Black* as a prime example of feminist media, viewers should remain aware of Bennett's idea: popular culture is a negotiation between oppositional and dominant ideology (xv). If we analyze how the series negotiates contradicting ideologies, we can better understand the ways *Orphan Black* both reflects women's changing role in society but also attenuates ideas about women's freedoms or, more specifically, about the women permitted to have these freedoms. The series shows women no longer confined to traditional gender roles. Yet, to gain this liberation, women must be thin, white, and attractive.

Most media put male characters in an active narrative role, relegating women to passive positions that progress men's stories; however, *Orphan Black* complicates these traditional male/female roles. *Slate*'s Jessica Roake argues that straight men in the first season of "*Orphan Black* are stupid, weak, simple, [and] unethical [...]. Like most women in the history of entertainment," the men are "reactive. [...] [T]hey don't show any agency [or] display any power of individual thought." In short, heterosexual men serve little independent plot function. They take on roles typically reserved for women: their narratives advance women's plots, and they are not developed outside of their relationships with female characters.

Furthermore, *Orphan Black* subverts traditional gender roles beyond which gender takes an active narrative position; the series complicates normative roles of men and women in public and private spheres. Alison and Donnie Hendrix (Kristian Bruun), a suburban married couple, best exemplify the series' re-envisioning of gender norms. They start a business selling (illegal) prescription drugs to suburban housewives. Their business dynamics become clear when Donnie is in charge of menial tasks, like transporting the product, while Alison is responsible for more complicated jobs, like managing the cover operation. Alison is better at physically strenuous tasks, easily lifting heavy storage containers Donnie cannot. Moreover, when Alison and Donnie want to buy Alison's mother's soap company (Bubbles) to launder money, Alison's mother—Connie (Sheila McCarthy)—hesitates. She thinks Donnie is incompetent. Connie worries Donnie cannot successfully co-run a business, so she sells them her company only after confirming that Alison will "wear the pants at the new Bubbles" ("Community of Dreadful Fear and Hate," 3.7). Alison also takes on challenging tasks; Donnie's only responsibility is following orders, which he is still unable to do well. Alison is free to adopt an active, typically masculine relationship role instead of occupying a passive position. The couple's switch in gender roles reverses what is expected in a male-dominated society.

Here, the gender roles subvert patriarchal ideology. When Alison and Donnie occupy these unconventional positions, they demonstrate men and women functionally taking on nontraditional social roles. It is not just that Alison has better business sense than Donnie. She is physically stronger and can lift more than her husband, threatening to make the male's position obsolete. However, Connie repeatedly references Donnie's failure at traditional masculinity, hinting at a dominant ideology that requires men to perform a specific display of masculinity. Traditional masculinity puts men in socially controlling positions, so it is crucial for maintaining current power relations. That said, Connie is characterized as narcissistic and judgmental, so it is unlikely viewers are meant to agree with her assessment of Donnie. Nevertheless, her view holds weight since Donnie is consistently portrayed as incompetent, and he is often used as comic relief. In contrast, Alison is not depicted as less of a woman for taking on typically masculine positions, allowing the series to suggest it is a natural role for women. At times, though, Alison's type–A personality does face some scrutiny, especially from Donnie early in the series. This becomes clear when Donnie tells Neolution leader Dr. Aldous Leekie (Matt Frewer) that living with Alison is not easy, and, given Donnie and Alison's interactions up until this point, viewers know he is talking about her personality and her desire to take charge in their relationship ("Endless Forms Most Beautiful," 1.10). However, during this conversation, viewers also learn that Donnie has been spying on his wife for years, aligning him with the antagonists. This moment of betrayal, while suggesting Alison's personality can make her difficult to live with, in the end, encourages viewers to feel empathy toward her since Donnie has been deceiving her for years.

Orphan Black has a feminist moment with its depiction of Alison and Donnie's relationship but, in doing so, reinforces a specific masculine gender code. The series also ends with Donnie taking on a career that adheres more to traditional masculinity. In the finale, he is dressed in a suit and tie, heading to his job as a regional manager for a concrete flooring business, which is also a callback to when he shot Dr. Leekie and buried him in his garage ("To Right the Wrongs of Many," 5.10). Instead of taking orders from his wife, Donnie's career now involves managing other employees, reclaiming a more masculine, assertive role. Through these characters, one can see that it is more appropriate for women to take on traits typically coded as masculine than it is for straight men to take on characteristics more often coded as feminine. Thus, while Alison's gender role reversal is an instance of feminist empowerment, Donnie's lack of masculinity is a punchline that is eventually corrected, leaving viewers with the understanding that it is acceptable to adopt traits typically coded masculine but humiliating to give up masculinity.

Even though *Orphan Black* depicts women who are liberated from stereotypical gender roles, it does so at the expense of those who do not align with traditional views of Western beauty. Therefore, the series effectively upholds hegemonic standards of female beauty and domesticates the narrative's radical message about gender. This negotiation is particularly apparent in the physical bodies displayed on the screen. The well-developed adult women embody stereotypical Western beauty as they are thin, white, and attractive.[3] There are women who do not fit this ideal, but they function differently than the women who do fulfill it. For example, Sarah Stubbs (Terra Hazleton), a member of Alison's theatre group, is the only overweight female character. She is naïve and often used as comic relief. Additionally, characters use Sarah S. and her naiveté for their own benefit, giving her a passive narrative role. The presentation of the thin female body juxtaposed against a less traditional one creates a hierarchy between bodies that positions the former as superior.

Orphan Black also presents a hierarchy between the white protagonists and people of color, the latter of which—besides Detective Art Bell (Kevin Hanchard)—are positioned almost exclusively as supporting characters or antagonists. Early in the series, viewers are introduced to Alison's adopted children, however, the narrative never directly addresses that they are of a different race. This transracial adoption seems to act as a shorthand acknowledgment to let the audience know that Alison cannot have children without the series having to mention that the children are not biologically related to her and Donnie. There is also never any in-depth reference to the Hendrixes trying to get their children to maintain a connection to their culture, effectively whitewashing their race. The children are then subsumed into white suburbia with seemingly all connection to their background erased.

This hierarchy becomes most apparent when looking at the adult women in the series.[4] The early seasons are especially devoid of named recurring characters who are clearly legible as women of color. In Season 1, only two women of color appear for three or more episodes. Meera Kumar (Priya Rho), Alison's neighbor, has few lines and only functions as a background character who judges Alison's parenting skills. The other is Janis Beckwith (Jean Yoon), a member of the forensics team at the police station, who appears three times in Season 1 and once in Season 4. She is developed only insofar as viewers know she is dedicated to her career and has a morbid sense of humor—once referring to the machinery that mutilated Katja Obinger's body as an "industrial sausage maker" ("Variation Under Nature," 1.3). In the second season, Yvonne (Raven Duada) is a black woman who works as a rehab orderly. She appears briefly in three episodes. The series starts to open more salient roles to women of color in Season 3. However, these women are rarely, if ever, ones with whom viewers are intended to align. Marci Coates (Amanda Brugel) is a black woman who is the incumbent of the school board position Alison is vying for. While Marci plays a comparably substantial role in her season, she is uppity, conceited, and self-serving, suggesting the audience is not supposed to identify with her. She tries to rezone the school, which will require Alison's adopted children to switch to a worse district: an idea that horrifies Alison.

It is important to note that, historically speaking, the idea of a worse district stands as code for a more economically, ethnically, and racially diverse school. This possibility seems even more likely given that viewers are asked to worry about the possibility of Alison's children switching schools. Marci poses a threat to Alison's wealthy, white suburban lifestyle and her children. *Orphan Black*, as a result, asks us to side with Alison and her white privilege over the season's one recurring woman of color.

Season 4 has two recurring women of color: Roxie (Miranda Edwards) and Evie Cho (Jessalyn Wanlim). Roxie has little, if any, agency as she spends most of her on-screen time following the orders of her superiors. Her actions almost exclusively put her at odds with *Orphan Black*'s protagonists. First, she helps her partner assail Sarah in an empty laundromat ("Transgressive Border Crossing," 4.2). The next time Roxie appears, she attempts to apprehend Cosima at Brightborn Industries and instead aggressively captures Krystal (another Project Leda clone) and locks her in a room ("Human Raw Material," 4.5). Due to the consistency of these attacks, her presence begins to suggest that some type of trauma is about to occur to the protagonists. And, in the end, she is literally contained when Detective Art Bell handcuffs her. Roxie's final conversation ends with Art informing her that he is taking her to the police precinct, quite clearly taking away her freedom ("The Mitigation of Competition," 4.9).

Evie Cho, director of Brightborn Industries, is the most prominent woman of color throughout the series, appearing in eight of Season 4's ten episodes. Like Marci and Roxie, Evie opposes the female collective the audience roots for. She poses a threat to the well-being of the Project Leda clones, encouraging Beth Childs to kill herself and giving Detective Martin Duko (Gord Rand) the order to kill the clone's original, Kendall Malone (Alison Steadman) ("The Scandal of Altruism," 4.6). With Evie serving as the season's main antagonist, *Orphan Black* pits white and non-white women against each other, further enforcing a hierarchy between them. Furthermore, while the series often has non-traditional portrayals of women, Evie's eventual death illustrates the plot's reliance on at least one common trope: killing characters of color.[5] Moreover, Evie is not the only woman of color to die in the *Orphan Black* universe; Amelia (Melanie Nicholls-King)—Sarah's surrogate mother—and Maggie Chen (Uni Park)—a member of the religious Prolethean cult—are both murdered after little on-screen time. While the series has a high death count, it is notable how many non-white women die, considering how few there are. When a white woman dies, there are still other well-developed ones represented on screen. Therefore, the impact of these deaths sends a different message. It is clear to viewers that white women are not invincible, but, given the series' focus on white bodies, their deaths raise the stakes for our protagonists rather than erasing the presence of a marginalized group.

Viewers are left with a message that suggests non-white bodies are disposable. And, with Evie in particular, the series hints that when a non-white body wrests power and independence, as she does from the scientific cult Neolution, it is punished. Ultimately, her death brings with it the possibility that the Project Leda clones will gain their own independence.

Thus, while these Othered bodies are present, these women of color are not developed in the same radical manner as white women. Instead, viewers are invited to ignore, denounce, or discard women of color for the sake of furthering white women's narratives. We are left with the message that these women exist to bolster and progress white women's stories. To this end, the series' use of non-white bodies suggests women in *Orphan Black* can only claim freedom if they fulfill some patriarchal desire, in this case, reifying white safety and privilege. This hierarchy among women, while granting freedom to those on the higher end, further subjugates bodies that lie outside of traditional Western beauty standards.

Orphan Black further enforces a physical female ideal by having the same actor, Tatiana Maslany, play over half of the main female characters.[6] Maslany is white, approximately 5'4", and has an athletic build, so she does not completely align with our culture's ideal body, which is 5'7" and 114 pounds according to the national model staffing company TSM Agency.[7] Thus, it seems the series is beginning to challenge hegemonic beauty standards with these slight variations, visually demonstrating Bennett's point that popular culture negotiates between dominant and oppositional ideology (xv). Maslany is shorter and more athletic than the "ideal" body, but she is still thin, white, and attractive, making the variations in these other areas more acceptable. And while each female clone Maslany plays differs in appearance, most come close to a pre-determined beauty standard. However, Mika (also referred to as M.K.), the Project Leda clone from Helsinki, does stray from this ideal body. While Maslany still plays her, the character wears jackets and cardigans that hide her shape, often puts on a large sheep mask, and has burns covering part of her face. She comes across as small and childlike when compared to the other clones, and, through her, the series does begin to depart from this norm. Unfortunately, she's also the only Project Leda clone to appear in multiple seasons and then be killed. In fact, her death in "Clutch of Greed" (5.2) is one of the most violently graphic deaths in the series. As a result, *Orphan Black* then contains this deviation, removing the female clone who does not fit dominant ideology's desired body.

When viewers examine the male characters, the series' female ideal becomes even more apparent. The leading male cast varies in race and weight, whereas the women mainly vary in height and fitness level. Having more variance in male characters does not negate the need for a more inclusive depiction of women, especially women of color. Black feminist critic Kimberlé

Crenshaw calls for an intersectional approach and refers to this tendency to address race and gender as separate categories of experience as a "single-axis framework," which is common in both feminist and antiracist theory and undermines the efforts of both (139). With the white female leads and a black male lead (Art), viewers can see Crenshaw's argument embodied on screen. The result leaves no available imaginative space for women of color, revealing a tendency for even modern-day feminist works to perpetuate this race/gender division. Viewers are never able to see developed, positive experiences of independence for women of color, subtly revealing that they may not be privy to the freedom allotted to white bodies (Crenshaw 139–140). Looking at the series' women, one can see *Orphan Black* follows the norm in privileging a white female body. By doing so, the series makes its feminist notions more palatable to dominant culture.

Taking these cultural influences on media into account, feminist scholar Christine Gledhill explains that feminist criticism of popular culture must "perform a dual operation": examine a text's negotiation on an "'imaginary' level, internal to fictional production, and on a 'realist' level, referring to the sociohistorical world outside the text" (245, 246). This approach can help people better understand the ways *Orphan Black* circulates conflicting messages about women's freedom. Following Gledhill's suggestion to use this dual operation, we see how, on the imaginary level, the series suggests women can be freed from gender roles that place them as subservient to men. In this fictional world, women take active, assertive roles in their lives. On the realist level, however, the series limits the bodies capable of escaping these traditional roles. Viewers are given a narrative that imagines potentially liberating ideas about women while simultaneously, at the sociohistorical level, suggesting these bodies can only be granted independence at the expense of the Othered female body.

At the same time that *Orphan Black* reifies traditionally beautiful bodies, it implicates patriarchal institutions in the duplication of this ideal. The series places the responsibility of creating these clones on the government and a scientific corporation (Dyad Institute). These institutions replicate a body that closely follows hegemonic beauty standards. That said, one cannot completely discount the series' role in advancing a limited body type, undermining its message that governing groups illegitimately shape the bodies that our culture values. Women outside of the Project Leda clones, such as Delphine (Évelyne Brochu), still meet this narrow definition of the acceptable body. If one reads the series' negotiation this way, even a seemingly radical subversion of gender roles is only possible at the expense of already marginalized groups, specifically plus-sized women and women of color. Based on the portrayal of women, as the social hierarchy between men and women breaks down, the hierarchy between different groups of women is further enforced. In this way, *Orphan Black* embodies Hartmann's assertion that subjugated groups can be bought off with the idea of power over those who are more marginalized, demonstrating just how pervasive these interlocking oppressions are in our kyriarchal culture. While there are steps towards progress, the radical message is not as far reaching or all-encompassing as the current conversation around the series may suggest. Unfortunately, the most underprivileged are not privy to this progress. Within the narrative, equality for all women is an illusion. The freedom must, in some way, be domesticated. *Orphan Black* suggests society makes allowances for women only if their bodies align with cultural beauty standards, further reifying dominant beliefs.

Sexuality—How Much Is Too Much?

While *Orphan Black* presents oppositional gender ideals, it still upholds dominant culture's views about what type of woman is privy to this freedom. When we look at the way sexuality is represented in the narrative, a similar pattern emerges. The series imagines a world where women depart from traditional views and tropes of sexuality and gender identity; however, these women must somehow be contained. Television shows often rely on tropes when they incorporate a queer character. These tropes offer a limited representation of LGBTQIA+ individuals.[8] Narratives repeatedly display gay/straight binaries that ultimately privilege heterosexuality. In contrast, an oppositional take offers queer characters who are not confined to limited plot devices. When viewers consider the ways dominant and oppositional ideologies interact within *Orphan Black*, contradictory messages arise in the treatment of queer bodies. In the inconsistencies of the series' portrayal of gender and sexuality, we see the mobilization of Gitlin's theory that social conflicts are framed into dominant systems of meaning (264). The series humanizes queer characters and avoids tropes often integral to mass media depictions of LGBTQIA+ characters. However, while the queer women are well developed and have narrative freedom, these representations are restricted in visual presentation: the series will not explicitly illustrate queer sex, and it reifies a gender binary.

The series presents queer characters' sexualities as an important aspect of their character but not as the defining characteristic. In doing so, the narrative deviates from stereotypical portrayals of LGBTQIA+ people. While my analysis focuses on the show's queer women, Roake's description of Felix (Jordan Gavaris), a gay man, illuminates the series' ability to achieve this delicate balance. She explains that Felix's portrayal celebrates his queerness rather than forcing him to conform to heteronormativity. She writes: *"Orphan*

Black's one fantastically vital, multidimensional male character is Felix, Sarah's foster brother and moral compass. Felix is an artist/rent boy given to swanning about his loft in open shorty kimonos." Felix's sexuality is not hidden. He takes an active role in narrative arcs, and these arcs exist independently of his queerness, so he does not function as the sassy gay friend. Furthermore, as Roake notes, Felix embraces his sexuality and femininity, as evidenced by his "open shorty kimonos." He is the most developed male character and is therefore not pigeonholed as a stereotypical, effeminate gay man. Furthermore, when compared to the heterosexual male characters, like Donnie and Paul (Dylan Bruce), Felix is given more freedom to openly explore gender roles. He is allowed to be independent, feminine, and strong, and he is not confined to the rigid masculinity codes the other men adhere to. In this way, the series validates his queer gender and sexuality.

Like Felix, the queer female characters in *Orphan Black* are developed beyond their sexual orientation. One of Cosima's main arcs focuses on her scientific research to cure the clones' genetic illness, and Delphine's narrative often revolves around her career at Dyad. Both arcs suggest the characters' orientation is not their defining quality. In these characters, we locate the series' recognition that LGBTQIA+ individuals are as complex as heterosexual ones when not reduced to queer tropes.

The queer romantic relationships are both essential to the plot and depicted as natural: a rare feat in network and basic cable television. Cosima and Delphine's storylines incorporate their same-sex relationship, which is important for characterizing them in the same manner as their straight counterparts. Furthermore, the narrative focuses on romantic connections rather than gender. In "Variable and Full of Perturbation" (2.8) after Delphine approaches Cosima about Cosima's worsening illness, the two women decide to consume marijuana and get "completely baked" together. While high, Delphine looks at Cosima, saying: "There's something important I want to tell you: Je t'aime." The two then discuss how Delphine's feelings led her to lie to Cosima in an ill-conceived attempt to discover a cure for Cosima's sickness. Cosima tells Delphine that to love her, she must love the other Project Leda clones as well. When Delphine agrees, Cosima states: "And I love you, too." While the two women had recently broken up, this conversation marks the rekindling of their monogamous relationship. Cosima and Delphine are not eroticized for the male gaze, nor is this scene intended to titillate viewers. Camera shots do not linger on either woman's physique, and neither woman is overly sexualized or naked. The relationship is not depicted as aberrant. In fact, Cosima and Delphine's romance is a fundamental storyline. Most of the clones' romantic/sexual partners rarely interact with the clones with whom they are not in a relationship. Cosima and Delphine's romance is so salient to the plot, however, that Delphine often interacts with other central characters, especially Sarah. Delphine repeatedly demonstrates her dedication to Cosima as she puts Cosima's personal well-being before their relationship, drawing viewers to value and care about these women's connection. Through these characters, the series invites us to see queer relationships as equal to their straight counterparts. In doing so, the narrative expands cultural norms surrounding sexuality as it reflects developed and lived experiences of a group rarely seen on television.

This queer relationship is depicted similarly to heterosexual ones but maintains non-normative qualities, keeping a heteronormative cultural logic from subsuming it. The women's relationship differs as it values the female clone collective in a way the straight relationships do not. Cosima requires Delphine to love all her sisters, but her sisters are also her genetic identicals. When analyzing this scene, one must keep in mind that "queer" can refer to more than sexuality. To borrow the words of Eve Kosofsky Sedgwick, queer is "the open mesh of possibilities, gaps, overlaps, dissonances and resonances"; the term "can't be subsumed under gender and sexuality" (8–9). In this scene, more is queer than the women's sexuality. In Cosima and Delphine's relationship, the recognizable is mixed with the unfamiliar. To begin with the familiar, this scene elucidates the cultural value of monogamy. Heteronormativity emphasizes fidelity, so it makes sense that this expectation extends to queer partnerships. For viewers to care about this queer couple, the characters must partake in committed relationships in imitation of their heterosexual equivalents. By having this relationship fulfill some normative characteristics, *Orphan Black* legitimizes it. Overall, the series upholds monogamy, but this scene creates an interesting and queer emphasis on family and community. Unlike typical relationships, Delphine must love all the clones for her romance with Cosima to work, so their relationship places an unconventional value on the larger community, thus creating a non-normative family dynamic. While a romantic partner usually must love the other's family, this dynamic is queered as the family is comprised of clones, not the family in which Cosima was reared. Incorporating both traditional and unfamiliar elements complicates conventional conceptions of family. In this overlap, the series presents a queer relationship that benefits a larger community: the clone collective. This community focus does not extend to straight relationships. Cosima and Delphine subvert normative notions of family when they value an ethics of care and shift the focus from masculine to feminist values. *Orphan Black* instills the feminist shift that Rosemarie Tong discusses as the series suggests "women's capacities for care as a human strength rather than a human weakness" (163). The series values a feminist ethics of care, supporting the idea women are not confined to one path or quality.

Orphan Black also presents a nuanced view of sexual identity. The series depicts sexuality as a fluid spectrum, which challenges common notions that sexuality is a rigid either/or quality and that queer individuals just need to find the right partner of the opposite sex. The characters display a range of sexualities that the series reveals at various points throughout the narrative. Viewers learn Cosima is queer halfway through Season 1 when she flirts with and kisses Delphine; however, she does not self-identify as a lesbian (or with any label) until Season 3. By not immediately defining her sexuality, the series develops her character and attraction to women without relying on labels. While Cosima's sexuality is stable, Delphine's is fluid, allowing the series to deviate from a stable sexual binary. In "Entangled Bank," Delphine arrives at Cosima's apartment (1.8). Cosima apologizes for trying to kiss Delphine during their previous encounter because, as Cosima says to Delphine, "I know, you're not gay." Moments later, however, Delphine confesses to Cosima that she enjoys being around someone who "gets" her and "can't stop thinking about that kiss." Delphine explains her thought process about her sexuality: "I've never thought about bisexuality. I mean, for myself. But as a scientist, I know that sexuality is a, is a, is a spectrum. But, you know, social biases, they codify attraction. It's contrary to the biological facts, you know?" When Delphine caresses Cosima's cheek and kisses her, she moves past the social biases that previously organized her understanding of her sexuality.

Delphine calls attention to a dominant ideology that codifies attraction in opposition to human's natural biology. In this moment, the series illuminates the restrictiveness of social beliefs that paint sexuality as a permanent, stable binary, and it presents the possibility of fluid, non-binary sexualities. By having Delphine consciously process her sexual fluidity and the cultural logic surrounding sexuality, the series presents a prevalent belief—sexuality as pre-determined and stable—and then deconstructs it. In doing so, the series articulates sexuality as fluid. Acknowledging a sexual spectrum and incorporating characters with fluid sexualities disrupts the hierarchy between homo- and heterosexuality. Without a binary, the series begins to dismantle the idea that one sexuality is superior and all else is deviant. Furthermore, presenting this spectrum reflects an increasing acceptance for those who do not identify with a stable label, especially since characters never disparage Delphine for her evolving understanding of her sexuality. One should note Cosima identifies as a lesbian, so the series recognizes both stable and fluid possibilities. This is important because labels can allow marginalized groups to form a community around the quality that makes them outcasts.

Orphan Black presents sexuality as fluid and usually portrays queer and straight relationships in a similar manner; however, this equality is not extended to the representation of straight and queer sex. This discrepancy suggests there is still stigma around queerness—even this progressive series domesticates non-normative sexuality. The main heterosexual Project Leda clones are depicted having sex: Sarah and Paul are shown several times, Rachel and Paul have a sadomasochistic sex scene, and Alison is shown having sex (separately) with Donnie and Chad (Eric Johnson) (her neighbor's husband). The actors clearly simulate sex in these scenes. For queer characters, however, sex is heavily implied but never shown. While Cosima and Delphine date throughout the show, the two are only seen kissing or lying in bed together. Cosima's relationship with Shay (Ksenia Solo) follows the same pattern. Comparing these depictions of straight and queer sex reveals a hierarchy between them. Queer relationships are not permitted the same on-screen freedom as heterosexual ones. This reluctance to show gay sex suggests and perpetuates stigma.

It seems simulating queer intercourse is still taboo on basic cable when a series with otherwise radical depictions of sexuality refrains from showing queer sex. If it were only queer female characters not shown having sex, one could argue the series is taking extra care to avoid fetishizing queer women. However, this pattern is consistent for gay male characters: Felix is never depicted having sex. Not fetishizing women may be a factor, but the aversion to visualizing any type of LGBTQIA+ sex suggests a link between queer intercourse and cultural anxieties around non-normative sexualities. Since straight sex is repeatedly depicted, one can see a hierarchy that places heterosexual sadomasochistic relationships and extramarital affairs as more television appropriate than same-sex intercourse. It appears the series can portray LGBTQIA+ relationships in a more liberal way only because the relationships are less sexual. *Orphan Black* does not go as far as desexualizing the queer characters (a common trope in television); however, their sexuality is domesticated. On screen we see a less threatening portrayal of non-normative sexuality, suggesting stigmas of disgust still surround queer sex. Now that stigma just takes the form of avoidance rather than outright shaming.[9]

Furthermore, queer female characters only have sexual freedom if they clearly identify on the male/female gender binary. There are few realistic non-binary characters on television. In this lack, it is apparent that gender must be intelligible as one of these two options. *Orphan Black*'s dependence on legibly gendered female bodies exemplifies the way this binary circulates in mass media. Judith Butler's theory of gender performativity allows us to understand how avoiding liminal bodies in narratives reifies traditional perceptions of gender. As Butler explains, gender is a construction that "conceals its genesis; the tacit collective agreement to perform, produce, and sustain discrete and polar genders as cultural fictions," with punishments for those who do not agree to believe in the binary, which "'compels' our belief" that this construction is necessary (*Gender Trouble* 140). Since *Orphan Black* includes only legibly gendered women, the series feeds into this tacit agreement to perform polar genders as natural.

Even as the series includes well-developed queer women, the narrative suggests these women must adhere to heterosexual gender norms. Women can have queer sexuality but not queer gender. Butler explains that cultural norms govern gender intelligibility. Gender norms allow "for certain kinds of practices and action to become recognizable as such, [...] defining the parameters of what will and will not appear within the domain of the social" (*Undoing Gender* 42). *Orphan Black* maintains fairly restrictive parameters for gender performativity, suggesting just how ingrained "normal" gender performance is. These norms are most apparent in the female characters. The women do display different levels and varieties of femininity, with Alison adhering most to a traditional version of it. She often wears feminine puffy vests and pink clothes, like her bright-pink school-board-campaign shirt and hat. Sarah's gender performance is the furthest from traditional femininity as she typically wears unadorned dark colors, leather, and jackets. Her outfits, while approaching androgyny and playing with gender expectations, are often form fitting, which keeps a sense of femininity to her style, so it is never fully masculine. Cosima, Delphine, and Shay—the series' three queer women—are also usually presented as femme. All three wear attire typically coded as feminine: dresses, floral patterns, heels, and jewelry. However, there is one episode in the final season that subverts gender. When Cosima and Delphine are on the island, they have dinner with the clones' creators, P.T. Westmorland (Stephen McHattie) and Susan Duncan (Rosemary Dunsmore). When they arrive at the house, one of Westmorland's employees tells the women they must dress up for the meal. Instead of wearing one of the available dresses, though, Cosima confidently and defiantly puts on one of the available suits ("Ease for Idle Millionaires," 5.5). While the suit fits well, it is not form fitting or feminine. In fact, Cosima's posture becomes more masculine: her hands slightly in her pockets and elbows sticking out as she physically takes up more space than she typically does. In this moment, with her hair pulled up, in non-normative attire, and a masculine stance, she challenges gender conventions. However, this scene is notable because it differs from the series' standard. Since gender is created through sustained social performance, having women consistently perform feminine iterations of gender enforces dominant views and shows a limited depiction of women, even with this momentary glimpse of antinormativity (Butler, *Gender Trouble* 141).

Felix is the only character consistently freed from gender legibility norms. While he identifies as male, his gender performance is feminine and fluid. He wears decorative scarves, kimonos, and makeup and, at times, wears more masculine sweaters and button-up shirts. He is never mocked for his appearance or dehumanized for performing femininity. It is notable that, while there are more queer women with prominent roles, it is the one gay male lead who repeatedly challenges gender norms. So, while the series imagines a space where women can be freed from traditional gender roles, this freedom does not often extend to their gender.

To understand how *Orphan Black* addresses gender performativity, one must also look at Tony, the Project Leda transgender clone. Through Tony, the series begins to complicate the pervasive idea that gender is a stable, natural binary. He calls viewers' attention to the idea of gender as a social construction; therefore, we cannot pigeonhole *Orphan Black*'s gender performance parameters as solely normative. While Tony is genetically identical to the female clones, he presents as male: he identifies with male pronouns, has facial hair, takes testosterone, and has a deeper voice than the female clones ("Variable and Full of Perturbation," 2.8). By including Tony, *Orphan Black* suggests biology does not pre-determine gender since his gender performance differs from the clones with whom he shares identical genetics. If gender were natural and pre-determined, all the clones would perform gender in the same way. However, the clones are not restricted to the gender they were assigned at birth, hinting at expanded possibilities. Furthermore, the series never depicts Tony as ill or aberrant for his gender identity. There is one moment when Art refers to Tony as "her," but Felix quickly corrects him, telling Art to use male pronouns.

Since Tony demonstrates gender as a social performance rather than a biological fact, the series expands gender possibilities. These possibilities are essential because, to borrow the words of Judith Butler, "Possibility is not a luxury; it is as crucial as bread. [...] [W]e should not underestimate what the thought of the possible does for those for whom the very issue of survival is most urgent" (*Undoing Gender* 29). Besides Art's misgendering of Tony, the characters accept him with open arms, with Sarah referring to him as "one of our own" the first time they meet (2.8). Since the characters we have aligned with for eighteen episodes never question or doubt the validity of Tony's gender identity, viewers are encouraged to root for a trans character. In this instance, the series expands the acceptable non-normative ways of life it presents and begins to deconstruct a stable view of gender. Since a strict, pre-determined gender binary reinforces gender as biological fact, it is easier to hierarchize gender when it is viewed as a clear divide. This hierarchy tends to place women as subordinate to men. Therefore, characters like Tony call attention to gender's construction and contest a stable hierarchy, working to reveal its illegitimacy. Unfortunately, Tony's destabilizing presence only lasts for this episode. The characters reference him again occasionally, such as the series finale when Cosima mentions to Delphine that they cured Tony of the deadly illness that afflicts the clones, but he never appears again on-screen (5.10). While viewers know Tony survived—which is more than many trans characters on television—the series never fully engages in a sustained dialogue that elevates Tony's status to that of the cisgender characters. He is not introduced until the end of the second season and appears in only one episode; his presence expands traditional understandings of gender but only for a fleeting moment. And so with Tony, *Orphan Black* imagines some gender possibilities, but the narrative is incapable of further explicating and sustaining gender's complexities beyond the framework of a single 43-minute episode.

Conclusion

The current conversation around *Orphan Black* focuses on the series' offering of a feminist narrative through characters and plotlines, and to an extent, I agree with this view. However, this conversation overlooks the ways the show limits the women who can imagine this freedom. The narrative has feminist ideas at the forefront, yet they are accompanied by a more obfuscated, deep-rooted message that attenuates these radical ideas. Disseminated in this feminist message is the suggestion that women must a look certain way, domesticating the potentially liberating and revolutionary themes. It is important to understand how *Orphan Black* tempers its radical notions because of the potential risks in reading the series as a paragon of feminist values. If we take its lauded feminist message at face value, we overlook the need for intersectionality and risk assuming we are in a post-feminist society and that no more work needs to be done to challenge current gender power relations.

Orphan Black meditates on the theme of women's autonomy from patriarchal expectations. However, while the clones may insist, "I am not your property," the series itself, to some degree, can never truly be free from the quagmire that is our cultural system. Like the female bodies that must be legible for their queerness to be acceptable, the series itself inherits a cultural vocabulary it must use to be intelligible to its audience. As a result, any potentially radical message is articulated through restraints. One cannot completely ignore the feminist messages being conveyed; yet, to fully understand what the series suggests about femininity, identity, and gender, one must investigate the surface meaning and subtexts. The idea of not being one's property is hypothetically empowering, but in a capitalistic patriarchal society, it seems near impossible to fully function outside of a power system when that system determines the vocabulary we have to examine these types of social and cultural issues.

Notes

1. Since *Orphan Black*'s inception, popular culture critics have hailed it as a rare progressive depiction of gender and sexuality on basic cable television. It does not relegate women and queer characters to secondary roles. Lili Loofbourow of the *New York Times*

describes it as "TV's strangest—and most sophisticated—meditation on femininity," and *The New Yorker*'s Jill Lepore states, "it could be said that 'Orphan Black' is a feminist 'Frankenstein,' if it weren't true that 'Frankenstein' was a feminist 'Frankenstein.'"

2. While my analysis uses these feminist/queer values, it is important to note there is no monolithic or unitary set of feminist/queer values; these stated traits, however, are most relevant to this analysis (Tong 1).

3. For the purposes of this analysis, when I refer to adult women, I specifically mean adult women in the age range of approximately 20–60. I am not including youths or seniors in this specific examination of the female body.

4. The male cast is more diverse. There are non-white recurring characters like Art, who is one of the leading characters from episode one onward and is crucial to the narrative, and Vic, who appears in more than ten episodes. While there is room for further analysis on these characters, the male cast is outside the scope of this paper.

5. Killing characters of color is so pervasive in popular culture that *Variety* published an article in 2016 discussing how characters in this group are killed off at shockingly high numbers. Maureen Ryan writes: "the sheer volume of these deaths—a number of which were shocking for the wrong reasons—has been notable. When considered as a whole, it is difficult for the suspicion that these characters are expendable not to harden into belief."

6. Media psychologist Kristen Harrison argues that an analysis of television reveals that "thinness has become the norm, and the most desirable or successful female characters and media personalities are typically thin" (256).

7. The TSM Agency's statistics come from a review of their database of more than 30,000 models.

8. When *Orphan Black* started in 2013, most non-premium cable shows with queer characters focused narratives on coming out or coming to terms with one's sexuality (ex. *Glee*) or desexualized and sanitized the queer characters, who were usually male (ex. *Modern Family*).

9. Martha Nussbaum explains, "For a long time, our society, like many others, has confronted same-sex orientations and acts with a politics of disgust, as many people react to the uncomfortable presence of gays and lesbians with a deep aversion akin to that inspired by bodily wastes, slimy insects, and spoiled food" (xiii). She goes on to argue that this view is still present today, writing "the politics of disgust is alive and well in America today, as many groups aggressively depict same-sex practices in such a way as to arouse disgust" (xiv).

WORKS CITED

Bennett, Tony. "Introduction: Popular Culture and 'The Turn to Gramsci.'" *Popular Culture and Social Relations*, edited by Tony Bennett, Colin Mercer, and Janet Woollacott, Open UP, 1986, pp. xi–xix.
Butler, Judith. *Gender Trouble: Feminism and the Subversion of Identity*. Routledge, 1990.
_____. *Undoing Gender*. Routledge, 2004.
"Catch Up on ORPHAN BLACK." YouTube, uploaded by BBC America, 24 Feb. 2015, www.youtube.com/watch?v=a0BsVQJoWi4.
"Clutch of Greed." Writ. Jeremy Boxson. Dir. John Fawcett. *Orphan Black*. Season 5, episode 2. First aired 17 June 2017.
"Community of Dreadful Fear and Hate." Writ. Sherry White. Dir. Ken Girotti. *Orphan Black*. Season 3, episode 7. First aired 30 May 2015.
Crenshaw, Kimberlé. "Demarginalizing the Intersection of Race and Sex: A Black Feminist Critique of Antidiscrimination Doctrine, Feminist Theory and Antiracist Politics." *University of Chicago Legal Forum*, 1989, pp. 139–167.
"Ease for Idle Millionaires." Writ. Jenn Engles. Dir. Helen Shaver. *Orphan Black*. Season 5, episode 5. First aired 8 July 2017.
"Endless Forms Most Beautiful." Writ. Graeme Manson. Dir. John Fawcett. *Orphan Black*. Season 1, episode 10. First aired 1 June 2013.
"Entangled Bank." Writ. Karen Walton. Dir. Ken Girotti. *Orphan Black*. Season 1, episode 8. First aired 18 May 2013.

Gitlin, Todd. "Prime Time Ideology: The Hegemonic Process in Television Entertainment." *Social Problems* vol. 26, no. 3, 1979, pp. 251–66.
Gledhill, Christine. "Pleasurable Negotiations." *Cultural Theory and Popular Culture: A Reader*, edited by John Storey. 2nd ed., University of Georgia Press, 1998, pp. 236–224.
Gramsci, Antonio. "Hegemony, Intellectuals and the State." *Cultural Theory and Popular Culture: A Reader*, edited by John Storey. 2nd ed., University of Georgia Press, 1998, pp. 210–216.
Harrison, Kristen. "Television Viewers' Ideal Body Proportions: The Case of the Curvaceously Thin Woman." *Sex Roles*, vol. 48, no. 5/6, 2003, pp. 255–64.
Hartmann, Heidi. "The Unhappy Marriage of Marxism and Feminism: Towards a More Progressive Union." *Capital & Class*, vol. 3, no. 2, 1979, pp. 1–33.
"Human Raw Material." Writ. Kate Melville. Dir. David Wellington. *Orphan Black*. Season 4, episode 5. First aired 12 May 2016.
Johnson, Allan. *The Gender Knot: Unraveling Our Patriarchal Legacy*. Temple UP, 1997.
Kellner, Douglas. *Media Culture: Cultural Studies, Identity, and Politics Between the Modern and the Postmodern*. Routledge, 1995.
Lepore, Jill. "The History Lurking Behind *Orphan Black*." *The New Yorker*, 16 April 2015, www.newyorker.com/culture/cultural-comment/the-history-lurking-behind-orphan-black. Accessed 4 January 2018.
Loofbourow, Lili. "The Many Faces of Tatiana Maslany." *The New York Times*, 2 April 2015, www.nytimes.com/2015/04/05/magazine/the-many-faces-of-tatiana-maslany.html. Accessed 4 January 2018.
"The Mitigation of Competition." Writ. Alex Levine. Dir. David Frazee. *Orphan Black*. Season 4, episode 9. First aired 9 June 2016.
Nussbaum, Martha. *From Disgust to Humanity: Sexual Orientation and Constitutional Law*. Oxford UP, 2010.
Roake, Jessica. "Empty Suits: The Brilliant Misandry of *Orphan Black*." *Slate*, 18 April 2014, www.slate.com/articles/arts/culturebox/2014/04/male_characters_on_orphan_black_are_undeveloped_making_the_show_s_feminist.html. Accessed 4 January 2018.
Ryan, Maureen. "'Anyone Can Die?' TV's Recent Death Toll Says Otherwise." *Variety*, 13 April 2016, variety.com/2016/tv/opinion/tv-deaths-walking-dead-the-100-arrow-1201751968/. Accessed 4 January 2018.
"The Scandal of Altruism." Writ. Chris Roberts. Dir. Grant Harvey. *Orphan Black*. Season 4, episode 6. First aired 19 May 2016.
Schüssler Fiorenza, Elisabeth. *But She Said: Feminist Practices of Biblical Interpretation*. Beacon Press, 1993.
Sedgwick, Eve Kosofsky. *Tendencies*. Duke UP, 1993.
"To Right the Wrongs of Many." Writ. Renée St. Cyr and Graeme Manson. Dir. John Fawcett. *Orphan Black*. Season 5, episode 10. First aired 12 Aug 2017.
Tong, Rosemarie. *Feminist Thought: A More Comprehensive Introduction*. 3rd ed., Westview Press, 2009.
"Transgressive Border Crossing." Writ. Russ Cochrane. Dir. John Fawcett. *Orphan Black*. Season 4, episode 2. First aired 21 April 2016.
"Variable and Full of Perturbation." Writ. Karen Walton. Dir. John Fawestt. *Orphan Black*. Season 2, episode 8. First aired 7 June 2014.
"Variation Under Nature." Writ. Graeme Manson. Dir. David Frazee. *Orphan Black*. Season 1, episode 3. First aired 13 April 2013.
"What Is the Average Model Height and Weight?" *TSM Agency*, 2017, http://www.blog.tsmagency.com/average-model-height-and-weight-requirements/.

"To Hound Nature in Her Wanderings"

Soccer Moms, Punks and Postfeminist Mothers on Orphan Black

Erin Bell

Described as sci-fi, bio-punk, thriller, mystery, and dystopic drama, BBC America's genre-blending *Orphan Black* reached cult status, in part, due to Tatiana Maslany's award-winning depiction of some dozen clone characters, ranging from British punk-rock hustler Sarah Manning to the uptight and well-coiffed soccer mom Alison Hendrix. Focusing on a group of women who discover they were clandestinely created as part of an experiment, *Orphan Black* follows several central characters (all played by Maslany) as they become self-aware and attempt to uncover who created them and for what purpose. Though many of the episodes of *Orphan Black* focus on the consequences of creating life in the laboratory and the impact of biotechnology on humanity, the program also probes how families function in any number of unique combinations. The subjects of science and family are not mutually exclusive, but, in fact, are closely related to one another as the processes of cloning, in vitro fertilization (I.V.F.), genetic modification and manipulation point toward contemporary concerns about maternity and reproduction. For all of its speculation about "weird science," *Orphan Black* is just as much about parenting as it is about scientific and epistemological concerns.

To that end, the series is populated by a number of parental figures, including adoptive parents, co-operative parents at a commune, foster parents, married heterosexual parents, single parents, and surrogate mothers, among others. Fathers like Donnie Hendrix (Kristian Bruun), Ethan Duncan (Andrew Gillies), and Cal Morrison (Michiel Huisman) play significant roles on the program as do father figures, including Detective Art Bell (Kevin Hanchard), Dr. Aldous Leekie (Matt Frewer), and P.T. Westmorland (Stephen McHattie) to name just a few. Maternal figures on *Orphan Black*, however, are more numerous and drive the action of the program forward. Of the clones who frequently appear in episodes, twin clones Sarah and Helena are mothers to biological offspring. Alison is the mother of two adopted children, and, though Rachel is not a mother, her desire to become a parent motivates her actions in several episodes of the program. The clones are complemented and contrasted by many other maternal characters, from Sarah's foster mother, Siobhan Sadler, affectionately called Mrs. S (Maria Doyle Kennedy) to Rachel's adoptive mother, Susan Duncan (Rosemary Dunsmore). Virginia Coady (Kyra Harper) is a mother figure to the male line of clones (called Castors, played by Ari Millen). Additional mother figures play cursory roles in the show, including Amelia (Melanie Nicholls-King), the surrogate who carried Sarah and her twin sister, Helena ("Nature Under Constraint and Vexed," 2.1) and Siobhan's mother, Kendall Malone (Alison Steadman). Malone makes several appearances in the series and is eventually revealed as the genetic "parent" of the female Leda and their male counterparts ("Insolvent Phantom of Tomorrow," 3.9). Malone's unique status as a human chimera allows for the artificial reproduction of her two separate cell lines to create the female and male clones.

What is noteworthy about the mother figures listed above is not just their number, but how each challenges commonly circulated representations of maternity and what is supposedly "natural" behavior in social and family structures.[1] Mothers on *Orphan Black*, whether biological, foster, surrogate, or adoptive, embody maternity and caregiving in vastly different modes, suggesting the breadth of the maternal experience today.[2] Unlike mothers depicted in the sitcoms and primetime dramas common to the 20th century, *Orphan Black* demonstrates that motherhood can be expressed in a number of methods and that *becoming* a mother occurs via multiple routes—not just through heterosexual intercourse resulting in a pregnancy. With its interest in biotechnology and cloning, *Orphan Black* suggests multiple ways of being human, indicating the contemporary turn toward posthumanity, or ways of being which move beyond past permutations of human embodiment and subjectivity. At the same time, *Orphan Black* explores cultural shifts in how women and mothers are defined and depicted, suggesting what feminist theorist Rosalind Gill determines a "postfeminist sensibility," that which demonstrates the ambivalent and often contradictory attitudes about women in today's society. In its depiction of cloned women as mothers, the program presents and problematizes numerous intersections between biology, sociology, and technology, calling attention to many critical issues facing female parents in contemporary society.

Though emergent forms of biotechnology such as cloning and genetic engineering offer new possibilities for parenting, today's cultural climate also perpetuates old-fashioned values regarding mothers. With conservative pundits and critics calling for a return to the way things used to be, many mothers feel pressured to replicate an old image of domesticity whilst concurrently fulfilling work and other obligations outside of the home. The tension between old and new ideals for women is indicative of what feminist cultural theorist and media commentator Rosalind Gill describes as the postfeminist turn. In her essay "Postfeminist Media Culture: Elements of Sensibility" (2007), Gill explains that postfeminist media culture reflects the dialectical tension between feminist and anti-feminist values all at once.[3] For Gill:

> [P]ostfeminism is understood best neither as an epistemological perspective nor as an historical shift, nor (simply) as a backlash in which its meanings are pre-specified. Rather, postfeminism should be conceived of as a sensibility. From this perspective postfeminist media culture should be our critical object—a phenomenon into which scholars of culture should inquire—rather than an analytic perspective [148].

Gill's claim has important implications for understanding how mothers are portrayed on *Orphan Black*. Though mother characters like Sarah and Alison are often assertive and empowered in their lives, they are also frequently scrutinized, objectified, and surveyed. Running parallel to this plot point, *Orphan Black* also demonstrates the contradictions in moving toward posthumanity. Though bio-technology seems to carry the promise of a more egalitarian society, especially for women and mothers, the posthuman still inhabits a very human world. Biotechnology may offer exoneration from past social mores based on gender and biology, but on the program, the clones' status as beyond human often restricts their lives and objectifies them, rather than the opposite.

Interestingly enough, feminist theorists have recently begun to develop theories which connect posthumanism to postfeminism. In their *Postfeminism: Cultural Texts and Theories* (2009), Stéphanie Genz and Benjamin A. Brabon, for example, focus on "the relationship between cyborg and feminism," noting "the category of the postfeminist cyborg as a figure that moves along the border between conformity and transgression" (145). Alison, Sarah, and all the other clones on *Orphan Black* have a "beyond human" status as their genesis occurred via the artificially replicated genes of a human chimera; they also move between conforming to social rules and transgressing them. In many senses, the clones *are* illustrative of Donna Haraway's cyborg (1991), an entity that is both "animal and machine" (149). The cyborg's technological origins often allow it to move beyond the limitations of humanity's rules and ideologies as well as to evade limitations and stereotypes about gender and maternity. On *Orphan Black*, the clones were not created via organic reproduction, although they each had to be carried in a human surrogate mother's womb. Such developments suggest that the ability to create a child is no longer limited to heterosexuals or to women as, hypothetically, cloned embryos can also be implanted into an artificial womb. As such, Genz and Brabon note that "cyborg technologies are being used by women (and men) in a postfeminist era to rescript heteronormative categories" (145). Such procedures seem to offer the promise of freedom from traditional conceptions of women and mothering. At the same time, however, there is also renewed anxiety about women's roles as mothers and a desire to control women's bodies and their reproductive rights. Genz and Brabon note that the postfeminist woman "is involved in working with and against the power structures inherent within subjectivity as she becomes object (of the heterosexual male gaze) and subject (to a 'new' self)" (151). Because such ambivalent attitudes about mothers play out in *Orphan Black*, it is helpful to build an understand of the program through a postfeminist and posthumanist framework.

On the program, the posthuman clones are surveyed, watched, manipulated and objectified. In fact, their genetic coding has not only been augmented but patented.[4] Late in Season 1, Leda clone and Ph.D. student Cosima Neihaus discovers coding on the clones' strands of DNA which declares they are the property of the Dyad Institute. Cosima and her girlfriend, Delphine, (Évelyne Brochu) painstakingly unravel the code only to discover a message which states, "This Organism and Derivative Genetic Material is Restricted Intellectual Property" ("Endless Forms Most Beautiful," 1.10). This moment of discovery is both significant and troubling for the clones on the program, suggesting that they are an amalgamation of technology and biology—not quite human, or, perhaps, beyond human, as well as objects owned by a biotech company. Both the female Leda and male Castor clones have been genetically altered in other ways, beginning with the genetic manipulations that created them. Ethan Duncan, one of the scientists responsible for creating the clones, reveals that the Ledas were "design[ed]" to be infertile ("Variable and Full of Perturbation," 2.8.). As Duncan explains to his adopted daughter, the self-aware clone Rachel Duncan, Sarah and Helena's ability to have children is an anomaly (not an attribute) because infertility was purposefully grafted into the clones' genome. Later in the series, it is revealed that the clones' DNA was augmented with a gene that promotes accelerated healing, but that its properties remain inexplicably dormant in the first-generation clones. Such genetic alterations are indicative of the passage toward posthumanity.

Thus, the program highlights how technology can be used by men to control women's bodies; some of the very technologies that may seem liberating are the very same ones that objectify them. *Orphan Black* encapsulates such tensions throughout its five seasons, and they are particularly present in the lives of characters who are mothers. Both Alison and Sarah are depicted as progressive in some areas of life, and yet they are both subject to the scrutiny of their friends, family, and others to determine if they are fit to be mothers. As such, each of the characters embody the tensions and conflicts facing mothers in a postfeminist world.

Sarah Manning: Punk Rock Feminist

In online synopses and reviews of *Orphan Black*, protagonist Sarah Manning is usually described using a number of similar signifiers. Articles on the BBC America site designate Sarah as a "grifter" and a "born outsider." Writing for *InStyle*, Marianne Mychaskiw describes Sarah as "rebellious," "edgy" and "punk rock," while Alicia Lutes at *The Nerdist* writes that Sarah is simply "badass." This "streetwise hustler," as Sarah is billed on the Internet Movie Database (IMDB), is also a loving mother, sister, and daughter. Because of such variances in her character as well as her ambivalence about being a mother, Sarah both subverts and falls into line with idealized representations of mothers and motherhood. Sarah can be just as selfish as she can be *selfless*; her character is complicated and complex, and, in these contradictions, Sarah's character embodies the postfeminist sensibility. Sarah is the edgy, rebellious, cocaine-snorting punk in the black hoodie and leather jacket on a bender ("The Antisocialism of Sex," 4.7). And yet Sarah is also an attentive mother, agonizing over whether her daughter will recover from being hit by a car ("Unconscious Selection," 1.9), as well as the engaged parent, painting a mural on her daughter's wall ("Human Raw Material," 4.5). Sarah is a renegade, but, as her brother, Felix (Jordan Gavaris), reminds her, she is also "a good mum" (3.2). From the middle of Season 1 until the end of the Season 5, Sarah's actions are often motivated by her love for daughter. Although Sarah's role as a mother is a very important part of her identity, it is not the *only* aspect of her life that defines her. She is also a sister, daughter, investigator, and sexual being—in short, anything but the one-dimensional image offered by the prime-time mothers of the programs past.

One way Sarah differs from previous televised representations of mothers is in how her physicality—her body—is used for her own pleasure as well as other purposes. Sarah's corporeality is the focus of many images in the program, and it is depicted as both a source of power and of pain. Throughout the series, a great deal of attention is paid to Sarah's body, and this focus is indicative of the postfeminist aesthetic, as her sexuality suggests both empowerment and objectification. The pilot episode "Natural Selection" (1.1), for example, dedicates a good deal of screen time to surveying Sarah's body. As the episode opens, the camera focuses in on her diminutive frame as she sleeps through a train ride home. Her body is shown through a window-like opening between two seats, giving the impression that Sarah is being watched (1.1, 00:16). Sarah's wild hair is unkempt, her sooty eye make-up smudged, and with her earphones on and eyes shut, she nearly misses her stop, causing her to blurt out an expletive. A woman across the aisle catches Sarah's eye. This woman is well-dressed, holding a young girl close, and appears to be rather perturbed at Sarah's choice of language in front of the child. A flicker of emotion sweeps across Sarah's face, and she mutters a quiet "sorry" before hurrying off the train.

Within less than one minute into the first episode of the program, Sarah's punk aesthetic is posed against that of a woman who seemingly adheres to conventional ideals about propriety and caregiving. Such images remind viewers of how women like Sarah, particularly mothers, are surveyed and critiqued. Gill writes that the "surveillance of women's bodies constitutes perhaps the largest type of media content across all genres and media forms. Women's bodies are evaluated, scrutinized and dissected by women as well as by men, and are always at risk of 'failing'" (149). In this scene, the woman on the train scrutinizes Sarah, demonstrating how women are surveyed and judged, often by other women. Later, surveillance becomes a key theme in the program when Sarah and her sister clones discover they are all watched by assigned "monitors" who report to the Dyad Institute—the nebulous biotech company with connections to the futurist group/cult, the Neolutionists, both of which have ties to the cloning program that brought the women into existence.

While the early close-up shots focus on Sarah on the train, the episode quickly moves into the action sequence whereby Sarah catches her first sight of a doppelgänger, police officer Beth Childs, and witnesses her suicide. In the moments before Sarah spots Beth, Sarah exits the train, finds a payphone, and makes a call, emphatically telling the person on the other end of the line: "I wanna see Kira, okay?" (1.1). Context clues suggest that Kira is Sarah's child, but the full scope of Sarah's parental situation is revealed over the next few episodes of Season 1. As Sarah ends the call, Beth momentarily comes into view before she jumps in front of an incoming train, setting the events in motion that ultimately lead Sarah to uncover the truth about her beginnings. In addition to providing the impetus for the series' primary plot, these early scenes are significant to Sarah's character arc in another meaningful way. Though Sarah has been estranged from her daughter for months, it is clear she wishes to re-establish a connection with her child, although both Felix and Mrs. S question Sarah's intentions and whether or not such behavior is fair to Kira, who has lived with Mrs. S intermittently for most of her life.

While Sarah's relationship with her daughter may subvert expectations about mothering, her interest in sexuality challenges old ideals of maternity as well. In the program, Sarah is both sexual subject and object, reflecting a postfeminist sensibility. In scenes that highlight Sarah's sexuality, empowerment is posed against objectification. Throughout the five seasons of *Orphan Black,* many of the clones, including Sarah, participate in a fair amount of sexual activity. Such interludes frequently highlight the power dynamics between female and male partners which often put women in positions of control. Rachel Duncan engages in some light B.D.S.M. with both Ferdinand Chevalier (James Frain), a "cleaner" for the Dyad Institute, as well as with Paul Dierden (Dylan Bruce), Beth's former monitor and romantic partner. Rachel is typically the dominant in these encounters while the men are forced into or accept a submissive role. Alison has a quick rendezvous with neighborhood dad Chad (Eric Johnson) in an SUV, which serves as a way for both to act against their spouses. Sarah's sex scenes are worth noting for several reasons. Sarah has sex for pleasure, but she also uses her sexuality to dominate and control people and situations, such as in "Natural Selection" (1.1). By this episode, Sarah has commandeered Beth's flat, clothing, identity, and even Beth's sexual partner to keep up her charade. Sarah's impetus for stealing Beth's money and identity is to reclaim Kira, move away, and resettle as mother and daughter. When the ruse starts to goes sideways, Sarah turns to sex as means of distracting Paul from discovering her true identity.

In this sequence, a note on the refrigerator indicates that Paul will not be home for a couple of days, so Sarah is startled when he arrives earlier than expected. Hair wet, fresh from the shower, and wearing nothing more than black lace underpants and a sleeveless Clash T-shirt, Sarah is forced to keep up her charade as Beth, a woman she has never met. Switching from her British accent to a modest attempt at an American one, Sarah tries her best to answer Paul's litany of questions. Finally unable to stop Paul from presenting queries she cannot answer, Sarah pushes him into a passionate embrace, using her sexuality as defense. Before long, Sarah unbuckles Paul's belt, pulls down his pants, and they have sex on the kitchen table, Sarah situated on top. Though she initiates the act and seems to be actively enjoying it, as the scene fades out and the camera focuses in on Sarah's face, her eyes are vacant and expressionless (1.1, 32:15). It is difficult to tell whether Sarah is, in fact, engaged in the act, or simply using her body as a means of controlling the situation. Her body is a source of power, but it is also an object to be used, and Sarah's only means of escaping an impossible situation. The scene may echo countless other images of sex in which female characters in heterosexual relationships are depicted as faking it in order to please their partner or for various other reasons. Here, Sarah may be pretending, but she initiates the act, and she is in the dominant position. Having sex on an antiseptically clean, modern, kitchen table seems to both mock old adages about mother's work in the kitchen and deconstruct them.

Sarah occasionally engages in sexual activities throughout the remainder of *Orphan Black*, but another series of events which also highlight the postfeminist sensibility occur in the bathroom of a sleazy club in "The Antisocialism of Sex" (4.7). By this point in the season, Sarah has a "bot" implanted in her check against her will, consequently had the implant removed with the risk of death looming in the background, lost hope for finding a cure for an illness killing the clones, and acted in ways which indirectly led to the murder of Kendall Malone. Scenes at the Bovine Sex Bar are ironically juxtaposed with scenes from Alison Hendrix at her home, blowing up balloons for her daughter's birthday party.

Sarah begins her night at the bar with a few shots of bourbon before she runs into Dizzy (Joel Thomas), an underground conspiracy theorist who attempted to help her research and remove the implant in her check. As Dizzy and Sarah engage in titillating conversation, a young woman sidles up to the bar and offers Sarah a slippery nipple shot, flirtatiously emphasizing the implied sexual innuendo in the drink's name. There are more shots, more drinks, and, soon, Sarah is sandwiched between the woman, named Elle (Brook Palsson), and her tattooed partner, Tito (James Cade). Grinding against one another, electronic artist Peaches's post-punk vocals reverberate and resonate with Sarah's behavior. In the next vignette, Sarah, Elle, and Tito have made their way to the bar bathroom, and, after snorting lines of cocaine, they engage in an energetic *ménage à trois*. Out near the entrance of the club, Sarah's brother, Felix, enters and starts asking people if they have seen Sarah. Felix's comments to Dizzy quickly reveal the gravity of the situation, bringing viewers back to Sarah's role as mother. "Try not to piss about," Felix tells Dizzy. "It concerns her daughter." Surprised, Dizzy asks, "She has a daughter?" Felix replies, "Yeah, sometimes." Felix's deadpan reply reveals the complexity of Sarah's maternal role.

In the club, Sarah's behavior represents more than sexual desire—it also denotes her desire for control. She has been powerless in many of the recent events in her life and engaging in these behaviors suggests her need for agency, but it is difficult to say if such images are truly empowering. The sex scenes in "The Antisocialism of Sex" are illustrative of another of Gill's claims about postfeminism. She explains that, "Where once sexualized representations of women in the media presented them as passive, mute objects of an assumed male gaze, today sexualization works somewhat differently in many domains. Women are not straight-forwardly objectified but are portrayed as active, desiring sexual subjects" (151). Sarah is anything but passive in the scenes, but it is difficult to discern whether she is sexual subject or object.

In these encounters, as well as during those where Sarah is drinking and doing drugs, she can also be understood as a "phallic girl," a term coined by cultural theorist Angela McRobbie. The "phallic girl," according to McRobbie, "gives the impression of having won equality with men by becoming like her male counterparts. [...] This is a young woman for whom the freedoms associated with masculine sexual pleasures are not just made available but encouraged and also celebrated" (83). The "phallic girl" is indicative of Sarah on a bender, since, according to McRobbie, such a character's exploits include "heavy drinking, swearing, smoking, getting into fights, having casual sex," and so on (83). McRobbie suggests that such behavior is "a tightrope" and a "masquerade" for women, because taking on this role is never truly empowering. According to McRobbie and a host of other feminist scholars, no woman can have true power with a patriarchal and hegemonic society, regardless of how much they may act in a way that is characterized as masculine (84). In the episode, Sarah's façade of exuberance fades as soon she leaves the club. Alone, drunk, and hallucinating, she considers jumping in front of the train, just as Beth did. Genz and Brabon write that "both posthuman and postfeminism are impure discourses that blend and bind the forms that they 'post'—reifying and rewriting the categories of human, feminism, woman" (153). Here, Sarah's postfeminist, phallic behavior has bound and objectified her. The pleasure and/or sense of control the sex act supposedly creates quickly dissipates, and Sarah is left feeling miserable and alone.

One last way that Sarah's character as mother reflects a postfeminist sensibility is in her adherence to the politics of choice in her own life as well as in her daughter's. As Gill explains, "Notions of choice, of 'being oneself,' and 'pleasing oneself,' are central to the postfeminist sensibility" (153). Sarah's notion of choice extends beyond herself and to her daughter, Kira, who is finally given the autonomy to make her own decisions. Throughout the first four seasons of *Orphan Black.*, Rachel Duncan and others at the Dyad Institute repeatedly try to gain access to Kira's genetic material. As the only offspring of a clone (until Helena gives birth to her twin boys), Kira is important to their research. It is finally revealed that Kira has a mutation in gene LIN28A, which leads to accelerated healing powers ("Ease for Idle Millionaires," 5.5). Both the Dyad Institute and the Neolutionists want access to Kira's "unique physiology" ("Clutch of Greed," 5.2). After years of running from Rachel, however, Kira decides to work with her rather than hide from her because Kira wants to know more about her identity. Though Sarah is adamantly opposed to allowing Kira to work with Rachel, she eventually allows her daughter to make her own choice—even though the choice may also represent Kira's tie to Dyad (5.2).

Just as Sarah must fight to exert control in her existence, she realizes she must grant her daughter the same control over *her* own life and body. Ultimately, the choice to cooperate with Rachel and the Neolutionists becomes Kira's rather than Sarah's, which is an important gesture towards autonomy for all women. However, Kira's arrangement with Rachel and Dyad demonstrates how in many cases, the use of the term "choice" is a ruse and emblematic of no real choice at all. Ideologies about the politics of choice come full circle in the season finale, which includes a number of flashbacks depicting Sarah's choice to have Kira ("To Right the Wrongs of Many," 5.10). Scenes from the past are spliced into the episode. Close-up shots focus in on Sarah and Mrs. S parked outside a women's clinic discussing whether or not Sarah should have an abortion. Just as Sarah grants Kira the opportunity to make her own decision earlier the season, Mrs. S allows Sarah to come to her own conclusion about the unplanned pregnancy. Based on her knowledge of Sarah's birth, it is feasible that Mrs. S might realize the significance of Sarah's pregnancy (in regard to her status as a clone), but she does not indicate as such. Mrs. S offers Sarah perspectives supporting either having an abortion or keeping the baby but does not push Sarah in either direction. Ultimately, notes Joelle Renstrom, "Reckless, rough Sarah surprises herself (and Mrs. S, her foster mother) by deciding to keep the baby. Years before she learns how many decisions others have made about her body, she makes a decision for herself." This decision is Sarah's alone, illustrating a central tenet of the politics of choice. While themes regarding autonomy are understandable to most, the freedom to choose is of the utmost importance to women and mothers fighting to assert control over their bodies in the 21st century.

Soccer Moms, Self-Surveillance and "Having It All"

Control, or the lack thereof, is a theme that also resonates with the character Alison Hendrix. At first glance, Alison seems to be everything that Sarah is not. While Sarah's fashion aesthetic veers from grunge to punk, Alison's eye-makeup is often color coordinated to her hair scrunchie, and her sleek ponytail is pulled so tight it looks like it hurts. *Orphan Black* costume department set supervisor Peter Webster, quoted in Trudeau, notes that Alison is "little miss prep," and "that kind of housewife/mom, where everything's steamed and pressed." Alison is "always done up, she's always just perfect." Alison's "perfect" looks are one component of her seemingly picturesque life in a well-appointed, two-story suburban colonial where she resides with her husband, Donnie, and their two children, Gemma (Millie Davis) and Oscar (Drew Davis). A queen bee in her Bailey Downs subdivision, Alison appears to be the quintessential soccer mom.

Though, at the outset of the series, it looks like Alison and Sarah could not lead more different lives, it is soon revealed that, beneath the surface,

Alison's world is just as chaotic as Sarah's. Alison is depicted as an overachieving, scrap-booking, helicopter parent—a parody of the most extreme mother—but she is also a closeted alcoholic and prescription pill addict. Though Alison attempts to present the image of the perfect mother, eventually, her world of images falls apart. Alison's character parodies stereotypical representations of a flawless mother persona, showing how such images are false. Alison's interest in image is also representative of a postfeminist sensibility.

Like Sarah, Alison's character is far more complex than a cursory reading of her reveals. Her pressed clothes and perfectly maintained home evoke the ideals of the television mothers of the past, highlighting how contemporary ideologies about mothers are still invested in impossible images as well. Like an updated version of Donna Reed (*The Donna Reed Show*), June Cleaver (*Leave It to Beaver*), or Carol Brady (*The Brady Bunch*), Alison is devoted to her domestic duties. The earlier maternal characters represent the "happy housewife heroine" that pioneering feminist Betty Friedan critiqued in her seminal text *The Feminine Mystique* (1963). Friedan notes that the image of a woman/mother which surfaces in such media artifacts is one that is "young and frivolous, almost childlike; fluffy and feminine; passive; gaily content in a world of bedroom and kitchen, sex, babies, and home" (83). Alison, however, moves beyond the role of housewife heroine, which aligns with shifts in ideologies about mothers in current culture. As noted earlier, such ideologies suggest it is simply not enough to have a well-maintained home and carefully cared-for children.

According to feminist scholar Judith Lakämper, "The myth of the 'woman who has it all' has replaced the myth of the 'happy housewife,' which was at the heart of second-wave feminist critiques" such as Friedan's work (120). In her essay, "Affective Dissonance, Neoliberal Postfeminism and the Foreclosure of Solidarity," Lakämper maps out the concept of affective dissonance in relationship to current ideologies regarding motherhood, noting that the very things that are meant to make women feel good about their role as mothers often have quite the opposite effect. Drawing on the work of affect theorist Sara Ahmed, Lakämper reports "how particular objects can be identified with a likelihood to make us feel a certain way, i.e. to raise a particular set of affective expectations," particularly for mothers, but "we may become alienated from our affective community if we fail to experience the objects in the expected ways" (125). This description helps forge an understanding of Alison's character, who does not necessarily experience said objects/experiences in the expected ways, leading to her disillusionment. These points can be further supported by theories detailing the postfeminist cyborg. Genz and Brabon argue that "what looks like individual empowerment, agency and self-determination can also signal conformity and docility," suggesting just one of the inconsistencies postfeminist women often face in their lives. (151). While Alison engages in behaviors that she assumes are empowering, such behaviors likewise signal her conformity to repressive ideals.

At the beginning of the series, Alison seemingly embodies and embraces the "have-it-all" attitude. While Sarah is frequently shown in scenes with Kira, Alison's children are present in episodes less frequently. While some may suggest this is simply because Kira is a main character and Gemma and Oscar are not, there is a deeper meaning to their lack of screen time. In her attempt to do it all, Alison ends up spending her time in other areas besides the home. Alison coaches a soccer team, performs in the community theatre, works at her mother's soap emporium, exercises, and even launches a successful campaign for School Trustee. The more that Alison endures throughout the first seasons of the show, the more her pretense of perfection begins to crack. Alison's character highlights the problematic dimensions of trying to live by such myths about "leaning in," and taking on so much in one's life. Part of Alison's value system is invested in appearances—of her family, of her home, her marriage, and of herself—making her character indicative of an important claim Gill suggests about the surveillance of women by themselves and by others. Gill writes:

> Arguably, monitoring and surveying the self have long been requirements of the performance of successful femininity—with instruction in grooming, attire, posture, elocution and "manners" being "offered" to women [...]. However, what marks out the present moment as distinctive are three features. First, the dramatically increased intensity of self-surveillance, indicating the intensity of the regulation of women (alongside the disavowal of such regulation). Second, the extensiveness of surveillance over entirely new spheres of life and intimate conduct. Third, the focus upon the psychological—upon the requirement to transform oneself and remodel one's interior life [155].

Alison personifies and parodies these three features in a number of areas of her life, from her religious adherence to practicing the *Hip Hop Abs* video to the fact that she (rather hilariously) does not use swear words. Likewise, just as Alison is watched and surveyed by mothers in her community, she perpetuates the same behaviors, frequently critiquing the parenting abilities of those around her.

It is ironic that while Alison has been so invested in her image and how people in her community see her and her family, she actually has been covertly surveyed by outside forces for years. In Season 1, Alison slowly pieces together that she has been the object of observation by the Dyad Institute. In one of the most darkly humorous scenes of the series, Alison turns her tidy craft room into a torture cell in order to find out if Donnie, her husband, is her monitor ("Variations Under Domestication," 1.6). After knocking Donnie unconscious with a golf club, Alison ties him to a chair with a crocheted scarf, ribbons, and craft tape, using the very trappings of her soccer mom persona to imprison her husband. Dressed in pink and white gingham pajamas, Alison interrogates Donnie about his hidden "special box," which turns out to house several pornographic DVDs rather than the secret files Alison is looking for.

As Alison presses Donnie for information, she menacingly twirls a caddy of scissors around, rendering her tools of domesticity into instruments of terror. While the scissors imply violence, they also offer a parodic moment regarding Alison's world, leading viewers to ask why one person would need more than a dozen pairs of craft scissors. Alison continues to interrogate Donnie, dripping hot glue onto his chest (1.6). After calling Donnie a spy, Alison laments that he has turned her "whole life into a big, embarrassing lie." It is upsetting to think that her husband may by her "monitor," but Alison is also troubled by the fact her sphere is false. It is worth noting that, after Alison undergoes an interior self-transformation which includes getting a tattoo and a new, purple bob hairstyle in Season 5, she ultimately vows to do away with the craft room altogether and refashion it into a space for freeform activities like music and art.

Alison's image is also deconstructed during an intervention for her in her home (1.9). By this point in the series, viewers have seen Alison sneaking shots from bottles of liquor, taking handfuls of pills on the sly, and even smoking pot with her friend Aynsley's husband, Chad, and subsequently having sex with him. Though these behaviors are presented to viewers, the rest of the characters are not privy to them. Such methods of secret self-medication indicate the stress that accompanies trying to be the perfect wife and mother. In the intervention episode, Alison enters her living room and finds it filled with people, including her pastor, mother-in-law, and Aynsley (Natalie Lisinska). Alison immediately calls "bullshit," recognizing the attempt at an intervention. Donnie demands that "the pills and the drinking" have to stop while Aynsley claims that Alison may have ruined her marriage and demands Alison recognize the damage she has done. Such behaviors also fit within Gill's framework about being made-over. The idea here is that Alison can be "fixed," that she can be remade and refashioned to align with the values of the neighborhood community.

Though the intervention scene also has moments of dark comic relief, themes of surveillance resonate here as well. After Aynsley and Donnie speak, Alison directs the conversation back toward Aynsley, reminding the group of her dalliance with a roofer and noting that Aynsley's flaws make her just as imperfect as Alison. Alison condemns Aynsley, "For scrutinizing every detail of my life since the day I moved into this fishbowl. You have pried, and snooped, and gossiped about me. Like I was your own personal laboratory subject." "No more words!" she yells at the pastor. Though Alison does eventually enter a treatment center, her words reflect the affective dissonance that many mothers experience. The social networks of mothers that they belong to should bring feelings of solidarity and support, but, instead, may function as a source of stress and comparison to others, resulting in feelings of inadequacy.

Though Alison rails against being scrutinized and watched in this intervention-inspired tirade, ironically, Alison is just as guilty of analyzing Aynsely and other women in her community. It is clear that Alison has performed the same type of surveillance on her friends, as she notes the liaison with the roofer as well as Aynsley's other flaws. As much as Alison progresses in her attempts to loosen up over the next few seasons, she eventually evokes judgment and surveillance on Helena after she becomes a mother. In the series finale, Alison suggests that it is "ridiculous" that Helena has nicknamed her twin boys "Orange" and "Purple" rather than giving them appropriate names. Later, Alison reveals to Sarah, Cosima, and Delphine that Helena "needs a little guidance" and criticizes Helena for giving the twins rocks to play with instead of more appropriate baby toys ("To Right the Wrongs of Many," 5.10). Ironically, while Alison feels trapped and watched, she perpetuates the same behavior upon other women in her life, highlighting a common tension among mothers. In their attempts to be the best, many mothers feel scorned and belittled by their peers rather than supported by them.

It is Alison's tortured relationship with Aynsely, however, which takes this theme of competition and surveillance between mothers to its horrific and darkly comic conclusion (1.10). After the intervention, Alison is convinced Aynsely is her monitor and confronts her. In an exchange of insults, Aynsely strikes a particularly low blow, exclaiming to Alison, "You're barren, and you can't have your own children!" This particular comment is more than Alison can bear. In the midst of the disagreement, Aynsley's scarf gets caught up the garbage disposal. Though Aynsley begs Alison to help her escape, Alison watches by as her former best friend is strangled to death. It is a disturbing scene; even though Alison does not murder Aynsley *per se*, she certainly could have saved her. This example is just one of many moments in Alison's character arc that challenges the notion of being a "perfect" mother. Further into the series Alison moves from soccer mom to full-fledged gangster, concealing a dead body beneath the floor of her garage and later becoming a drug dealer.

By Season 3, both Hendrixes are immersed in a prescription pill selling operation, using the Bubbles soap store as front for the business. Celebrating the successes of their recent career change, one of the most iconic scenes occurs in "Certain Agony of the Battlefield," 3.6. "Dolce & Gabbana" by RiFF RAFF plays in background, and Donnie and Alison celebrate in frenetic booty dance, throwing fat stacks of cash and rolling around in Alison's craft glitter—until they are interrupted by Gemma, dressed for karate, who reports her brother has "put ear wax in her gi." The scene shows the depth of Alison's character and how multi-faceted she has become.

As a less conventional mother character, Alison, like Sarah, taps into a greater trend in contemporary television. Feminist scholar Panizza Allmark notes a cultural shift in the depiction of mothers on television programs, indicating "a turn in the media towards a postfeminist subject who is relatable through her flaws and vulnerability, and yet defiantly transgresses traditional conventions of motherhood" (3). Both Sarah and Alison are such postfeminist protagonists. Each transgress idealized versions of motherhood, challenging and revising past ideologies about what it means to be a mother. However, while Sarah and Alison (and Helena) are beyond human, they also must face many of the challenges that contemporary mothers confront. Though the series finale of *Orphan Black* ends on an empowering note as the four *sestras* come together in celebration after reclaiming their freedom, the final scenes also circle back to the ongoing discussion of mothering and maternity. Sarah, still grieving the loss of her own mother, prepares to take the G.E.D. exam. In the quick vignette leading to the scenes before the celebration, Sarah calls herself an "idiot," for forgetting to do the shopping again. A quick scan of the refrigerator reveals several bottles of beer and a couple of carry-out boxes, hardly the stuff of a well-stocked kitchen. Apologizing to Kira, Sarah tells her she'll have to buy lunch again. Kira, on the other hand, seems content with her mother's parenting skills and when she tells Sarah to "do her best" in reference to the G.E.D. exam, the comment seems to double as advice for her parenting style.

Kira leaves for school, and in a poignant reference to the lasting influence of mothers, the camera pans to Felix's portrait of Mrs. S, with a teacup in one hand and a shotgun close to the other. The painting's position on the mantle as well as its cloudy background suggest Mrs. S as a religious icon, looking down in protection over her family. Juxtaposed, however, with the earlier scene highlighting Sarah's small mistake, it almost appears as though Mrs. S is not looking down in protection but simply "looking down" on Sarah. As the finale plays out, Sarah goes to the G.E.D. testing site, but leaves without even attempting to begin her exam.

Reconvening with her sisters at the party, Sarah is almost as sullen and moody as she was in Season 1. As her well-meaning friends and family pester her about the G.E.D. test, she finally releases a torrent of emotion, focusing on the fact that even though she has conquered many of her demons, she is still coping with being a parent. "There's no one left to fight," cries Sarah, "and I'm still a shit mum." Agonized, Sarah notes how she is lying to her own child about taking the exam and "making things up for appearances," coming back once again to the discussion of expectations about what it means to mother as well as how women are surveyed and critiqued. Even though Sarah has managed to defeat a multi-million-dollar biotech company and reclaim her freedom, she still feels inadequate as a mother. "I don't know what I am doing," reveals Sarah. Rather than berating Sarah, the sisters come together in solidarity, explaining many of their own short-comings in relationship to gender and parenting. Each of the women express their own insecurities and failures, from Alison's confession that Gemma drove her so crazy she nearly stuck a dirty sock in her mouth to Cosima's admittance that she is terrified of babies.

In spite of the fact that the clones have created their own unique posthuman family, each still contends with commonly circulated ideologies regarding motherhood and maternity. Sarah, Alison, and Helena may be freed from an organic model of the family as suggested in Haraway's "Cyborg Manifesto," yet they are still overwhelmed by social expectations about parenting. In the end, *Orphan Black* not only blends elements from multiple genres, but it presents a distinct range of maternal characters which encompass the complexities of gender and sexuality, gesturing toward emergent ideologies about postfeminism and posthumanism as well as many contemporary anxieties and expectations about mothering.

NOTES

1. For more on the subject of maternity, see Dani Howell's "Women's Rebellion or Radical Containment? Understanding *Orphan Black*'s Feminist Message" in this volume.

2. One common abbreviation for the program *Orphan Black* is O.B., a clever reference to obstetrics, also abbreviated O.B., the science and study of the female reproductive system.

3. For additional interpretations of postfeminism see Susan Faludi's *Backlash: The Undeclared War Against Women* (Three Rivers Press, 1991), or Angela McRobbie, quoted later in this essay, in her *The Aftermath of Feminism: Gender, Culture and Social Change* (Sage, 2009), who reports that "postfeminism positively draws on and invokes feminism as that which can be taken into account, to suggest that equality is achieved, in order to install a whole repertoire of new meanings which emphasise that it is no longer needed, it is a spent force" (12).

4. For more on the representation of patenting people, see Jessica Lee Mathiason's "cDNA/©DNA in *Orphan Black*: Eugenics, Surplus Life and the Castor Virus" in this volume.

WORKS CITED

Allmark, Panizza. "Pushing the Boundaries: *Weeds*, Motherhood, Neoliberalism and Postfeminism" *Outskirts*, vol. 35, 2016, pp. 1–23.
"The Antisocialism of Sex." Writ. Nikolijne Troubetzkoy and Graeme Manson. Dir. David Frazee. *Orphan Black*. Season 4, episode 7. First aired 26 May 2016.
"Certain Agony of the Battlefield." Writ. Aubrey Nealon. Dir. Helen Shaver. *Orphan Black*. Season 3, episode 6. First aired 23 May 2015.
"Clutch of Greed." Writ. Jeremy Boxson. Dir. John Fawcett. *Orphan Black*. Season 5, episode 2. First aired 17 June 2017.
"Ease for Idle Millionaires." Writ. Jenn Engles. Dir. Helen Shaver. *Orphan Black*. Season 5, episode 5. First aired 8 July 2017.
"Endless Forms Most Beautiful." Writ. Graeme Manson. Dir. John Fawcett. *Orphan Black*. Season 1, episode 10. First aired 1 June 2013.
Faludi, Susan *Backlash: The Undeclared War Against Women*. Three Rivers Press, 1991.

Friedan, Betty. *The Feminine Mystique*. Norton, 2001.
Genz, Stéphanie, and Benjamin A. Brabon. *Postfeminism: Cultural Texts and Theories*. Edinburgh University Press, 2009.
Gill, Rosalind. "Postfeminist Media Culture: Elements of a Sensibility." *European Journal of Cultural Studies*, vol. 10, no. 2, 2007, pp. 147–166.
Graham, Elaine. *Representations of the Post/Human: Monsters, Aliens and Others in Popular Culture*. Manchester University Press, 2002.
Haraway, Donna J. "A Cyborg Manifesto: Science, Technology, and Socialist-Feminism in the Late Twentieth Century." *Simians, Cyborgs, and Women. the Reinvention of Nature*. Free Association Books, 1991, pp. 149–182.
"Human Raw Material." Writ. Kate Melville. Dir. David Wellington. *Orphan Black*. Season 4, episode 5. First aired 12 May 2016.
"Insolvent Phantom of Tomorrow." Writ. Russ Cochrane. Dir. Vincenzo Natali. *Orphan Black*. Season 3, episode 9. First aired 13 June 2015.
Lakämper, Judith. "Affective Dissonance, Neoliberal Postfeminism and the Foreclosure of Solidarity." *Feminist Theory*, vol. 18, no. 2, 2017, pp. 119–135.
Lutes, Alicia. "ORPHAN BLACK PLAYLISTS: BE BADASS LIKE SARAH MANNING." *The Nerdist*. 1 July 2014. nerdist.com/orphan-black-playlists-be-badass-like-sarah-manning/.
McRobbie, Angela. *The Aftermath of Feminism: Gender, Culture and Social Change*. Sage, 2009.
Mulvey, Laura. *Visual and Other Pleasures*. Palgrave, 2009.
Mychaskiw, Marianne. "Calling All Orphan Black Fanatics: Here's Exactly How to Recreate Sarah Manning's Trademark Hairstyle." *InStyle*. 7 June 2014. www.instyle.com/news/calling-all-orphan-black-fanatics-heres-how-recreate-sarah-mannings-signature-hairstyle.
"Natural Selection." Writ. Graeme Manson. Dir. John Fawcet. *Orphan Black*. Season 1, episode 1. First aired 30 March 2013.
"Nature Under Constraint and Vexed." Writ. Graeme Manson. Dir. John Fawcett. *Orphan Black*. Season 2, episode 1. First aired 19 April 2014.
"Orphan Black." BBC America. www.bbcamerica.com/shows/orphan-black/cast-crew/.
"Orphan Black." IMDB. www.imdb.com/title/tt2234222/.
Renstrom, Joelle. "*Orphan Black* Was Never About Cloning: The Show's Examination of Science Ethics Went Far Beyond a Single Technology." *Slate*. 13 August 2017, www.slate.com/articles/technology/future_tense/2017/08/orphan_black_was_never_about_cloning.html.
"Sarah Manning." BBC America. www.bbcamerica.com/shows/orphan-black/cast-crew/sarah.
"To Right the Wrongs of Many." Writ. Renée St. Cyr and Graeme Manson. Dir. John Fawcett. *Orphan Black*. Season 5, episode 10. First aired 12 Aug 2017.
Trudeau, Tessa. "On the *Orphan Black* Set: We've Got All the Costume Details!" *InStyle*. 10 May 2014. www.instyle.com/fashion/costume-department-insider-orphan-black.
"Unconscious Selection." Writ. Alex Levine. Dir. TJ Scott. *Orphan Black*. Season 1, episode 9. First aired 25 May 2013.
"Variable and Full of Perturbation." Writ. Karen Walton. Dir. John Fawcett. *Orphan Black*. Season 2, episode 8. First aired 7 June 2014.
"Variations Under Domestication." Writ. Will Pascoe. Dir. John Fawcett. *Orphan Black*. Season 1, episode 6. First aired 4 May 2013.

Making Clones, Making Mothers
Motherhood in Orphan Black

JENNY BONNEVIER

Orphan Black raises numerous questions concerning reproduction, centering as it does on a set of female clones (created through a project called Leda and all played by Tatiana Maslany) and their discovery of each other and of their origin. While the term *orphan* evokes the absence of parents, the term *clone* signifies their non-existence; in order for a clone to exist, there can be no genetic mother or father in the sense we commonly employ those terms. Clones have genetic originals; in traditional biological terms at least, they do not have parents. The signifying spaces occupied by mother and father in kinship discourses are thus in their default positions empty in a narrative that centers on clones. While *Orphan Black* certainly interrogates meanings of fatherhood, most notably perhaps through the character Ethan Duncan (Andrew Gillies), its engagement with motherhood is both more persistent and more central to the core concerns of the narrative. To some extent, the emphasis on motherhood can be read as an expression of a culture where mothers are primary care-givers and where female identity is mainly constructed in relation to motherhood, but the series also challenges these cultural assumptions. In the following discussion I have chosen to focus primarily on motherhood as it is constructed through female relationships, rather than in relation to fatherhood. This focus enables a better understanding of the potential of motherhood outside of the dominant framework of heterosexual nuclear families.

Orphan Black activates many tropes associated with reproductive technologies, and, as Robyn Wiegman points out, "new reproductive technologies bring with them a crisis of signification, pressuring the naturalized assumptions that have enabled the most common of kinship terms—family, mother, father, brother—to operate as if they require no critical attention to their social constitution" (862). That reproductive technologies such as in vitro fertilization (IVF) and surrogacy destabilize kinship terms and traditional conceptions of family has been recognized and explored in kinship studies by scholars such as Marilyn Strathern and Sarah Franklin. While assisted reproduction is not a new phenomenon, the IVF technologies developed over the last forty years force us to rethink biological motherhood in new ways. As Jenny Gunnarsson Payne notes, "[t]oday it is possible, for the first time in human history, to distinguish not only between social and biological motherhood but also between various modalities of biological motherhood, such as genetic motherhood, gestational motherhood, and even, some might argue, mitochondrial motherhood" (483).

To understand the different ways that kinship in general and motherhood in particular is being (re-)articulated, Gunnarsson Payne suggests three "grammars of kinship": those of blood, genetics and epigenetics (485). But while assisted reproductive technologies such as surrogacy and IVF disturb or displace meaning in kinship formations, cloning removes the mother completely, leaving an empty space that—at least in the narrative of *Orphan Black*—needs to be filled. In a sense, rather than presenting a competing grammar of kinship, an alternative way in which the various parts that constitute a family can be read as meaning-giving in relation to each other, I would argue that cloning results in an incomplete grammar. Cultural representations of cloning thus both highlight the importance of the missing mother and activate the competing discourses that constitute her. This text, then, will explore the ways in which *Orphan Black* fills the signifying space of mother, inscribing motherhood with complex and conflicting meanings through the mobilization of different cultural discourses on what mothers are and what they should or should not be.

The opening scene of the first episode of Season 1 ("Natural Selection," 1.1) can be read as staging a simultaneous insistent presence and haunting absence of motherhood. We see a young woman (Sarah Manning) asleep on a train approaching Toronto. When the loudspeakers announce "Huxley Station!," she wakes with a start, exclaiming, "Shit!" and drawing disapproving looks from her fellow passenger, a mother with her arm protectively around her daughter. Clearly, Sarah is not scripted as a (good) mother, but, just as clearly, the idea of good motherhood is activated. We start to understand that she might be a mother, albeit probably not a good one, when the first thing she does as she exits the train is to make a phone call, asking to see someone named Kira. While the dramatic and effective opening that introduces Sarah to her double just as that woman is committing suicide holds the viewer's attention, the character that is established is that of a stereotypically bad mother (young, single, unstable, a grifter). She is also a mother lacking something vital—a child. Sarah, one might say, is simultaneously defined by her being a mother and by her absence as a mother, her failure at mothering. The opening of *Orphan Black* performs an interesting narrative sleight of hand in focusing on mothers that are clearly present, for better (as with the woman on the train) or worse (as in Sarah without her daughter), while introducing a narrative whose basic premise is the non-existence of genetic motherhood.

Below I will trace some of the different ways in which the space of mother is filled, and emptied, through the extended narrative of the five seasons. The full complexity of the discourses mobilized, their implications, and their cultural and scientific references and resonances cannot be mapped in a text of this length; the main focus will be on the women who attempt to mother the clones in different ways, and on some of the important ways in which these clones themselves inhabit the space of mother.

Motherhood—A Matter of Life and Death

That motherhood is associated with the power to give life goes without saying. However, in many mythological and cultural contexts the mother figure has a double or a flip-side in the form of someone bringing destruction and death. One example of such a double figure is the Hindu goddess Kali, but 19th and 20th century psychoanalytical traditions also draw on this duality. As psychologist Erich Neumann puts it in his 1972 *The Great Mother: An Analysis of the Archetype*, "the Archetypal Feminine is not only a giver and protector of life but, as container, also holds fast and takes back; she is the goddess of life and death at once" (45). In *Orphan Black* the interconnections between life-giving and death-dealing in both reproductive situations and in the trope of the mother are many. At the core of the central plot of the extended series are the pairs of infertility/fertility and death/life. The clones are dying, and their disease is directly linked to their infertility. It is first assumed that both the infertility and the disease are mistakes. However, the infertility, it turns out, was genetically engineered, whereas the disease this genetic manipulation triggered was unintended. When the clones were made infertile, then, they were not only denied the right to procreate and the form of immortality that is often culturally connected with the idea of passing on your genes, but also their genes became carriers of their own deaths. Instead of the common story of assisted reproduction where science helps fix nature's mistake—bringing about natural outcomes through unnatural means—science here not only violates the personhood of the women it creates through the patents encoded in their genes, but it kills them through their engineered infertility as well.

If infertility literally means death for the Leda clones, fertility entails the absence of the associated fatal disease and is thus life-giving in a double sense. However, fertility in *Orphan Black* does not unequivocally align with life. Both Sarah and Helena, Sarah's twin clone, are kept alive as a result of their fertility and the possibility to use their biology, both in terms of the knowledge that can be gleaned from it and in very literal terms, as in the planned removal of one of Sarah's ovaries ("By Means Which Have Never Yet Been Tried," 2.10). It is thus specifically their genetic materials, the research resources they represent for the corporations and organizations involved, that are valued. Their fertility, and Kira (Skyler Wexler) as an expression of that fertility, is repeatedly the reason for imprisonment, coercion, and forced submission to invasive medical procedures. We see fertility as life-saving but simultaneously life-threatening and oppressive in the first episode of Season 3, in which Helena has been captured by the Castor project, which is developing a male clone line. She is tortured, but the torture is interrupted by the scientist in charge, Virginia Coady (Kyra Harper), when she discovers that Helena is pregnant. Helena, captured and tortured because of her fertility, escapes torture—but not captivity—because of that same fertility. The strong ambivalence which has characterized at least second and third wave feminist attitudes about motherhood is present in this narrative sequence; motherhood, or the female body as a potential vehicle for motherhood, is a source of power and life, but it is also the reason for controlling, constraining, and manipulating women. (See, for instance, the introduction to *Representations of Motherhood* for a discussion of this ambivalence.)

Destructive, even deadly, manipulation of women's (fertile) bodies is a central recurring theme in the series, and this manipulation is connected to both corporate and military interests. In addition to the corporate interests that control and fight over the female Leda clones, the Castor clones (all played by Ari Millen) are under the control of the military and intelligence complexes. Interestingly, while the Castors too suffer from a fatal disease connected to their engineered infertility, their disease can be sexually transmitted, making infected women infertile. Thus, this male infertility not only means death for individual male clones, it is a means of hurting women. It is exploited as such by Coady, who, while searching for a cure, is also using the Castor clones to conduct a large-scale experiment on uninformed women subjects with the aim of developing a large-scale weapon. Conducting warfare through women's bodies is of course a common and horrifically recognizable aspect of real-life warfare, and the appearance of this motif in the series emphasizes the potentially abusive, rape-like aspects of the scientific employment of reproductive technologies. Infertility not only brings death to the clones suffering from it, it can be wielded as a weapon. Both fertility and infertility are expressions and means of—sometimes deadly—control of women, control that the Leda clones are constantly negotiating or fighting. But motherhood is not only something imposed or withheld by others, it is something that women experience as part of their identities. Culturally, it is also something that we tend to read as origin, as source of identity in multiple ways.

Mothers and Daughters: Identity and Origin

Motherhood is an important component of female identity in our cultural narratives, but motherhood also serves as the privileged locus of a cultural fantasy of origins. As the embodiment of this fantasy, the figure of the mother is both powerfully alluring and threatening; she is the source of life and the threat of death. In *Orphan Black*, an important storyline of Seasons 3 and 4 centers on finding the originals from which the Castor and Leda clones were made. This search evokes themes common in current culture of finding your identity through discovering your roots, either in terms of lost relatives, unknown ancestors, or the information in your DNA.[1] A typical narrative of the search for origins ends with these origins found, along with a new sense of belonging, and of connections established. Finding your origins is supposed to bring about closure—identity is now certain.[2] The search in *Orphan Black* is believed to involve two separate originals: the Castor original that needs to be destroyed, in order to thereby destroy the threat that the Castor clones and the associated research pose, and the Leda original, who holds the cure to both infertility and disease. These two presumed originals, one male and one female, hold the final answers; one does so in the form of death, the other in the form of life. However, the narrative cleverly sidesteps this neat division and simultaneously explodes the idea of origins as identity. There is only one original, it turns out, and this original, Kendall Malone (Alison Steadman), is a chimera. Instead of an original, instead of identity, we find the mythological beast that signals hybridity, non-identity. Possessing both a male and a female cell-line, the two originals are in a sense one common original, but in a more profound sense, there is no original, and thus no origin as source of identity. The narrative refusal of establishing a secure source of origin both helps demystify motherhood, highlighting its contingent and continuously constructed character, and, as I will return to in the concluding section of this text, sets the stage in *Orphan Black* for a more communal understanding of what motherhood can be.

Once discovered, Kendall Malone, still valuable in terms of the life-saving information her genome can provide, is quickly "dethroned" from the ur-mother position she has inhabited in the narrative. Rather than almost-mythological original, she is presented as a rude, chain-smoking, cancer-ridden ex-convict and working-class woman, and as a real-life bad mother. For Kendall is the mother of Siobhan Sadler (Mrs. S, played by Maria Doyle Kennedy), Sarah's foster mother, and was sent to jail for killing her daughter's husband. Their relationship is so bad that, when Mrs. S first sees her mother, she attempts to kill her. Eventually, a reconciliation is reached. Mrs. S learns that her mother is dying, and gradually recognizes her mothers' attempts at protecting both her and Sarah—who was put in her foster care with Kendall's assistance. In the scene where they finally reach out to each other, Kendall tells her daughter, "I couldn't expect forgiveness. But I wanted you to have her [Sarah]. She's your blood, too. A little piece of me. All I had left of my foul life to give" ("History Yet to Be Written," 3.10). Mothers and daughters in emotionally wrought relationships abound in the series, as in so many narratives. Freeing yourself of your mother's destructive and controlling influence, as clone Alison tries to do in relation to her gestational mother (who believes she is also Alison's genetic mother), is more or less a staple in stories of female identity, and Sarah's angry rejection of Mrs. S in the early parts of the series makes clear that this kind of rebellion is not only reserved for biological mother/daughterhood. However, Sarah's growing recognition of what Mrs. S has done, and is doing, for her, Kira, and the rest of their extended family helps Sarah find her own feet as a mother. As Kira reports to Rachel, Sarah has told her "she's all grown up now" (2.10) and will no longer run away from Kira and her responsibilities. Her process of maturation is not about a rejection of her mother, but rather mirrors the deepening of their relationship and an increasing recognition of Mrs. S as an example to emulate (even if their relationship continues to have serious up and downs). The importance of Mrs. S to Sarah's ability to be a mother becomes clear in the final episodes of the last season, when Mrs. S's death leaves Sarah adrift as she reverts to her old pattern of running away, planning to take Kira and leave.

A mother-daughter relationship that remains destructive, murderous even, is that between Rachel and Susan Duncan (Rosemary Dunsmore). Rachel herself is not a mother by standard legal or biological definitions. Understood as someone who performs acts of mothering, however, she can be read as inhabiting the space of mother temporarily in relation to two girls during the series. Rather than expressing a genuine wish to mother, those instances exhibit her need to prove herself as daughter, while rejecting her mother's authority and any claims of gratitude or affection. Her character activates several discourses that construct women who are not mothers. On the one hand, her extreme fury at her infertility and envy of Sarah's fertility come across as mentally unbalanced. One of the "fathers" of IVF, Patrick Steptoe, expressed this cultural commonplace at a conference in the 80s: "[i]t is a fact that there is a biological drive to reproduce. Women who deny this drive, or in whom it is frustrated, show disturbances in other ways" (cited in Raymond 4). Rachel embodies both this disturbed, barren woman and the cold, successful career-woman that became such a staple of the 80s and 90s media landscape, associated with a rejection of everything caring and compassionate, of motherliness. One scene in particular stages this duality neatly. When Ethan Duncan, Rachel's adoptive parent and one of the scientists behind the Leda project, tells Rachel that her infertility was intentionally designed, we hear her rational, emotionless answers of agreement and acceptance of the scientific rationale of the decision, while simultaneously witnessing her rage when, alone, she trashes her office, screaming in abandoned rage ("Variable and Full of Perturbation," 2.8). Her first mothering practices simply reinforce the sense that she is driven by hurt and wish for revenge as a daughter rather than a desire to mother as Kira is held in a monitored cell dressed as a pink princess room, with Rachel commenting, "Dear child, I know how frightening this must be for you. But you'll get used to it. You may even grow to like it here, just as I did" (2.10). Rachel is staging this scene for the benefit of Sarah, who is watching powerlessly on the other side of a mirror window. Her desire for fertility and fury with Sarah for possessing it, should be read primarily as a wish for control. As the only clone to be raised self-aware, Rachel is obsessed with distinguishing herself from the other clones through her position of power and control in the corporate world in which the other clones are simply property, and her infertility exposes her position of control and power as a fantasy.

But if Rachel's performance of motherhood with Kira is parodic, her interactions with the young clone girl Charlotte (Cynthia Gallant) are more ambivalent. Her relationship with Charlotte is set up by Susan, while Rachel is held in Susan's house in a manner similar to how Rachel previously held Kira. Rachel is more or less asked to "play house," taking on the role of Charlotte's mother. She connects with the child, perhaps in order to use her to communicate with the outside world, perhaps also out of a sense of kinship or sympathy. At dinner one night, Susan casually tells Rachel that "Charlotte was cloned from you" ("The Stigmata of Progress," 4.3). Clearly taken aback, Rachel composes herself and responds drily, "Adam's rib." This brief response moves the relationships of the women involved out of a mother—daughter paradigm, activating a mythological context and casting Susan in the role of scientist-as-god, evoking the emblematic feminist sf text *Frankenstein*, an echo that becomes stronger as the created accuses its creator of failure: "You failed to find the original. You failed to cure us by other means. Just leave me here to die alone." Rachel's comment shifts the ground from the one of family relations that Susan wants to establish to that of science (and myth). While, as we will see in the section on the mother as scientist below, Susan Duncan attempts to construct them as compatible, Rachel does not. Indeed, in this scene, Susan's words are taken from the vocabulary of science, but the context is staged as a traditional family dinner, and her expectations of certain behavior on Rachel's part signal her wish to merge the logics of science with the social and behavioral trappings of family. Refusing to read herself as Charlotte's mother here, Rachel is motivated primarily, I would suggest, by her sense of being a hurt and abandoned daughter.

The revelation that Charlotte is cloned from Rachel's DNA as well as the discovery of chimera original Kendall bring to the fore the question of how motherhood should be understood specifically in relation to cloning. Is Rachel Charlotte's mother? Is Kendall Rachel's? Law scholar Kerry Lynn Macintosh suggests we take a functional approach to questions of family relations in cloning. For mothers, this seems to mean that to either have donated genetic material with the intention of becoming a mother (this alternative is not explicitly discussed by Macintosh) or to have gestated your partner's genetic double with the intention of becoming a mother, makes you a biological mother to that child. In terms of Gunnarsson Payne's framework, then, both the genetic and the epigenetic grammars are activated while we also recognize the emphasis that is put on intentions of motherhood from surrogacy narratives. This functional approach appears to me to be somewhat too dependent on traditional narratives of family in reproductive contexts that are anything but traditional or simple. It also presupposes a biologically based motherhood (genetic or epigenetic/gestational).

While genetic relatedness is seen as signifying sisterhood rather than motherhood as we will see in a section below, gestational motherhood, the acts of carrying and giving birth to a child, grounds claims to motherhood much more strongly in *Orphan Black*; it also resonates powerfully with many of its characters. The brief appearance of Sarah's and Helena's birth mother, Amelia (Melanie Nicholls-King), in the last two episodes of the first season illustrates well how much meaning these acts carry. Her birth mother is someone Sarah does not remember but has been "dreaming about [her] whole life" ("Endless Forms Most Beautiful," 1.10), and her appearance brings with it doubts about Mrs. S's motives and loyalties as Amelia seems to have evidence that Mrs. S is connected with Project Leda. Mrs. S, on her hand, warns Sarah to be careful with Amelia: "she didn't raise you" (1.10). With two mothers present, the narrative puts Sarah in a position where a choice seems to be required, as if there can be only one mother. The appearance of the birthmother also changes another relationship, that between Sarah and Helena. At this point, Helena is still trying to kill her fellow clones. Amelia reveals that she and Sarah are twins, telling her story of agreeing to be a surrogate for the Duncans but fleeing once she realizes something of what they are doing, giving one baby to the church, and one to the state (the foster system).

Sarah's dream of the love of a biological mother does not resonate with Helena. For her, brought up abused and taught to hate herself and how she was made, the mother who gave birth to her and abandoned her cannot be loved or forgiven. Helena kills her by stabbing her in the abdomen, saying: "You gave me to them. You let them make me this way" (1.10). Her words primarily seem to refer to the abuse she has been through, but they can also be read as evoking the complicity of the surrogate mother in the reproductive experimentation that created the clones. Certainly formed by her abusive upbringing, Helena also appears to believe that a present mother would make impossible a relationship between her and Sarah. She kills her mother to avoid having to be a daughter and to make it possible for her to become a sister.

Being a mother in *Orphan Black* is not about providing—or finding—origins. It is not an identity defined by genetics, even if the process of gestation and the act of childbirth come across as powerful mothering experiences. Motherhood is troubled, but also empowered, by being somebody's daughter, and as we will see below, something, perhaps, that you need to deserve.

Motherhood Deserved

If biological or genetic relatedness in not sufficient as a basis for a claim to motherhood, then what is? How do you qualify as mother in the narrative? A mother in *Orphan Black* appears to achieve validity and acceptance mainly through her wish—and to some extent her ability—to protect children. The most fervent protector of children in the series is, perhaps unexpectedly, Helena. As Staci Stutsman notes in passing in "The Unruly Clones: Tatiana Maslany's Unruly Masquerades in *Orphan Black*," "Helena's transition to sympathetic relates to her demonstration of maternal love" (94). The first sign of "maternal love" that we see is in relation to Kira when Helena is still under the control of religious fanatic Tomas. Helena abducts Kira from her home, but Kira follows her willingly, appearing to perceive Helena as unthreatening. Helena quickly forms a bond with the child and lets her return home. Helena's wish to protect Kira is clearly expressed in her subsequent interactions with Tomas (Daniel Kash) ("Entangled Bank," 1.8 and "Unconscious Selection," 1.9) and is one the main motivators for her rejection of his teachings and of his use of her as a weapon against her fellow clones. But Helena's protectiveness is not limited to Kira; in fact, her "maternal love" is to a great extent expressed precisely as protectiveness. At the home of Henrik Johanssen (Peter Outerbridge), the leader of a religious cult that call themselves New Proletheans, Helena connects with a little girl, smiling and sticking her tongue out. This girl is slapped by one of the women, a midwife (Kathryn Alexandre), and told off for not instantly obeying, distracted as the girl is by her interaction with Helena. The midwife then turns to Helena, smiling. Helena pushes her up against a doorframe: "There was a woman in convent like you. You touch her again, and I will gut you like a fish" ("Things Which Have Never Yet Been Done," 2.9). Johanssen's daughter Gracie (Zoé de Grand'Maison) witnesses this, and what she sees makes her reconsider her previous view of Helena as a monster. Helena's protectiveness renders her not only maternal, but more human in Gracie's eyes. The reference to the convent is telling; Helena's experience of abuse as a child is both a source of her violence, and a source of her protectiveness toward children. A similar, but more extreme, situation occurs in Season 3, when Helena, who has been staying with Alison and Donnie (Kristian Bruun) and bonded with their children, hears a drug dealer and his crew threaten the children. "Did you threaten babies?" she asks and, approaching them, menacingly: "You should not threaten babies" ("Insolvent Phantom of Tomorrow," 3.9). She proceeds to kill them.

Helena, then, is redeemed from the position of villain to a great extent through her maternal protectiveness. That protectiveness is also the defining feature of her own biological motherhood, and her pregnancy plays an important role in the narrative from the end of Season 2 to the series finale. As one of two clones who can conceive, she could be read as a natural mother, someone who cancels the need to formulate motherhood as something that has to be constructed and reaffirms it as something naturally given. However, Helena conceives through IVF and under anything but "normal" circumstance. She does not initiate the IVF procedure, which begins with her eggs being harvested without her consent and while she is drugged, but from the moment she learns about the existence of her fertilized eggs, the protectiveness that characterizes her interactions with children asserts itself. Helena, then, primarily enters the role of motherhood through a fierce protectiveness. As soon as she learns of their existence through Gracie, her "babies" become her main priority. She also identifies with them; they are like her, because in her mind they are made like she was: "He [Henrik Johanssen] will take my babies and put them inside me like how I was made." She voluntarily returns to the Proletheans to be impregnated: "Take me to my babies" ("To Hound Nature in Her Wanderings," 2.6).

Alison is clearly less fierce than professional killer Helena; nevertheless one of her first lines is telling Sarah, "How dare you show your face in front of my children?" ("Instinct," 1.2). Coming from someone who is introduced as a stereotypical suburban soccer mom, her ferocity is surprising. Her protectiveness is initially primarily about protecting her children from finding out that their mother is a clone. Her particular maternal identity as the suburban, well-groomed mother with a perfect home and well-behaved children—

in short, her idea of normalcy—is incompatible with her clone identity. She holds on almost fiercely to what she sees as normal motherhood, even when her own actions and the new relationships she builds within her clone family make this form of normalcy untenable. As she slowly comes to terms with this, her protectiveness becomes less destructive, less a matter of control.

Sarah is also already a mother at the opening of the series, a mother not fit to care for her child. As she explains to Alison, she "came back to fix things. Be a real mum to Kira" (1.8), but her understanding of what that entails evolves over the series. Initially, she intends get some money together, take Kira, who's been living with Mrs. S, and run. But as Mrs. S bitingly remarks the first time we see her with Sarah, "New clothes and a Jaguar do not a mother make" ("Variation Under Nature," 1.3). Motherhood, then, is not something simply inherent, and it is not made up of the outer trappings. Sarah increasingly appears to share Mrs. S's view that motherhood needs to be deserved. Her long fight to be a mother to Kira is characterized by her attempts to protect Kira. Her successes are measured by Mrs. S's recognition of Sarah's ability to do that, and her failures are marked by Mrs. S regaining or reclaiming control of Kira. But keeping Kira safe is not only a matter of keeping her out of the grasp of Neolutionists, the people now running the Leda project. It is equally a matter of learning to put the child's needs first and, importantly, to form a stable relationship; an aspect of motherhood that Sarah struggles with. Her desperate fight against the corporations that own her DNA and seek to control her life is ultimately about making a space where she can become "a real mum to Kira." For Helena, Alison, and Sarah, motherhood is something they grow into over the course of the series, rather than something that is inherent in them as the result of biological or legal motherhood, and even if these processes of becoming a mother are very different, they all center on protectiveness.

Siobhan Sadler (Mrs. S) is the most grounded mother figure in the series, and also, not incidentally, somebody with a violent past and a habit of fighting for what is important to her. Combining motherliness with deadly force, offering tea while concealing a gun behind her back, her role as protector is unquestionable. When the character Paul Dierden (Dylan Bruce), then currently employed by Dyad, tries to figure out where her loyalties lie, asking, "Who does Siobhan Sadler answer to?" her answer is simple: "I'm a mum, aren't I? If you think you're taking Sarah back, you'll have to kill me" (2.6). Her background bears her out—she has shown herself capable both of violence and of self-sacrifice, leaving England for Canada to keep Sarah and her foster-brother Felix (Jordan Gavaris) safe. "The forces against us grew beyond my grasp until I did what any mother would do. I gathered my children, and I left" ("Transitory Sacrifices of Crisis," 3.2).

As is clear from Mrs. S's comments above, mother as protector also activates ideals of self-sacrifice so common in stories of good mothers. While the violent content of the series sets the stage for extreme sacrifices, feminist (middle-class and white) discourses on motherhood often emphasize sacrifice in other, milder terms. The opening of the first episode of Season 3 neatly juxtaposes these different ideas of sacrifice. It begins with Helena dreaming of perfect suburban motherhood, an idyllic baby shower barbecue with the lyrics "Wouldn't it Be Nice" playing in the background. This scene is replaced with her reality, abducted and locked in a cramped box. While the suffering mother who is seen to willingly sacrifice herself for her child does so in contemporary western imagination in a suburban context where sacrifice involves, perhaps, giving up career and hobbies, the juxtaposition of that image of maternity with that of the pregnant, confined, and tortured Helena desperately trying to survive can be read in two ways. The immediately apparent reading is as a forceful critique of the position from which giving up certain privileges in seen as sacrifice, exposing white, middle-class motherhood anxieties as expressions of privilege. In another reading, however, the juxtaposition validates that fear. Motherhood *is* confining; it robs women of agency, reduces us to animals. When her discovered pregnancy later in that episode saves Helena from continued torture, this very salvation signals the extent to which she is reduced to a womb, a "carrier" as the Brightborn cooperation in Season 4 call the women who are impregnated with genetically manipulated embryos. I think these two readings can—perhaps must—coexist. Motherhood as a confining, selfhood-consuming experience for women, including white, middle-class women, needs to be addressed, while simultaneously recognizing the privileged position that makes it possible to overlook the many more tangible ways in which motherhood can be part of oppressive patriarchal structures.

While good mothers in *Orphan Black* appear willing to do anything to protect children, it is important to note that this does not make them victims or selfless, long-suffering women. They protect through action; when they are controlled, they attempt to break free; when they are abused, they seek revenge. The circumstances of Helena's impregnation provide one example. A number of studies have shown that women undergoing IVF and women becoming mothers through surrogacy often emphasize suffering as something that makes them deserving of motherhood. These procedures are indeed painful, as is childbirth; what is interesting is the scripting of that pain as a sacrifice that entitles a woman to motherhood. In a rhetorical analysis of case histories of women who have received infertility treatment, published in American women's magazines such as *Good Housekeeping or Ladies' Home Journal,* Chloé Diepenbrock shows that the woman telling these stories "sends the message to her reader that her ability to endure such hardships is the mark of the true woman's desire to reproduce" (105). As mentioned above,

Helena has her eggs harvested in an abusive procedure, but the implantation of the fertilized embryos is voluntarily and does not appear particularly painful. However, when she discovers that Johanssen is the genetic father not only of the fetuses she is carrying, but also of the ones implanted in his daughter, and thus grasps the abusive context she is in, she does not accept either her own or Gracie's suffering as an inevitable part of maternal suffering. Instead she takes her revenge through strapping Johanssen to a gynecological chair, violently "inseminating" him, and then setting the place on fire. The image of Helena escaping, a tank with her frozen embryos in her hand, shows a woman willing to protect her children at all costs, but not willing to be the victim or to suffer unnecessarily.

Motherhood Made—The Scientist-Mother

As feminists such as Sandra Harding, Donna Haraway, Nancy Hartsock, Geneviève Lloyd and many others have demonstrated, science has long been coded as a fundamentally male endeavor, characterized by supposedly male properties such as rationality and emotional detachment. Scientists can be inscribed as fathers; indeed, expressions such as "the father of empiricism" or "the father of the small-pox vaccine" are inherent parts of a scientific discourse in which men conceive ideas that women—defined by their embodiedness—cannot achieve. This is true of the story of assisted reproductive technologies, too. The two fathers of the first test-tube baby, Louise Brown, are presented as physiologist Robert Edwards and gynecologist Patrick Steptoe, the two men who developed the technology and also delivered the baby. The mother, Lesley Brown, is of course read as a subject in a medical procedure, confirming the role of woman as biology and man as manipulator or controller of that biology. In *Orphan Black*, on the other hand, there are two female scientists clearly taking on roles as mother-scientists, Virginia Coady and Susan Duncan, both combining discourses of motherhood with discourses on science, to some extent in different ways.[3]

Susan Duncan first appears in the role of (adoptive) mother in Rachel's home videos, which Rachel watches obsessively. Smiling, loving, and, we are led to believe, now dead, Susan is a perfect contrast to the cold, corporate-scientific environment in which Rachel was subsequently brought up. But as the narrative progresses, Susan (re)appears as scientist, having left Rachel to be raised by the Dyad Corporation and gone underground in order to be able to continue her Leda research. She appears to have little doubt concerning her priorities, the greater good of humanity, and few qualms about the individuals sacrificed to reach this aim. In this sense, she conforms to traditional male scientific ideals rather than to ideals of motherhood. However, she repeatedly creates domestic settings and scenarios, and appears to expect the relationships that are supposed to exist within these settings. Two instances are the years of Rachel's early childhood represented in the home videos and the domestic environment she shares with Castor clone Ira, whom she has brought up and who is now her lover,[4] and to which she brings Charlotte and Rachel. This environment is where the dinner scene occurs where she informs Rachel of her genetic relationship with Charlotte. As we have seen, Rachel dismisses Susan as a failure, but Susan retorts, "You are the failure, Rachel. You carry my last name, and you are the biggest disappointment of you all" (4.3). Rachel, then, disappoints in her capacity as daughter, and Susan, consequently, is disappointed as mother. But it is clearly a motherscientist who is disappointed. Rachel's failure in Susan's eyes is her inability to remain emotionally detached both from her fellow clones and from Susan; Rachel's resentment, anger, and jealousy are all exposing the incompatibility of the two discourses Susan wishes to reconcile. But she, too, vacillates between the two roles, at times showing something close to regret, as when she apologizes to Rachel for what she calls her "detachment": "I wanted to be your mother, but it was necessary to cut the cord" (4.3). Rachel, however, cannot accept Susan's excuses, and she attempts to kill her (a knife in the abdomen, like Helena's murder of birth-mother Amelia), claiming that she is doing what she was raised by Neolution to do—she is the daughter the scientist-mother's choices has created ("From Dancing Mice to Psychopaths," 4.10).

If Susan at times appears torn between the two parts of her motherscientist identity, negotiating between them, Virginia Coady's character is rarely, if ever, conflicted. In contrast to Susan's expressed wish to be a mother, Coady tells Helena that the Castor clones "came to [her] when they were very young" and continues, "The irony of it. I never wanted kids. I didn't think it was for me. Next thing I know, I've got more than I can count" (3.2). Neither does Coady create the domestic settings in which we often see Susan. Her statement about the Castor clones, however, would seem to imply a form of motherhood, and she often talks about protecting her boys. As we have seen, protectiveness is highly valued as an expression of motherhood in the series, and Helena initially appears to respect Coady's actions precisely as expressions of protectiveness. But when Coady's willingness to sacrifice individual Castor clones for the greater good becomes apparent, Helena loses that respect, and Coady's employment of motherhood comes across as cynical, parodic. Helena expresses this in her typical blunt manner: "You say you love boys, but you lie. You're a shit mother" ("Newer Elements of Our Defense," 3.4). Her final role in the series as jailor-midwife firmly casts her as the antithesis to the values that are central to motherhood in the series—the protection of children and, as we will see below, female solidarity—as she intends to use the newborn to prolong the life of a sick, old man, the god-wannabee P.T. Westmorland (Stephen McHattie). Coady dismisses Helena's pleas not to take her babies like Coady has let Westmorland take her Castors, that the babies need her: "I know who you are. Dumped at birth. A killer. [...] What kind of mother could you possibly be?" ("One Fettered Slave," 5.9). While this triggers Helena's self-loathing, her first priority remains protecting her unborn babies. When she cannot escape, she attempts to kill herself, refusing to be complicit the way she believed her birth-mother was, saying, "You will not be an experiment, too. I set you free ... my babies" (5.9). When revived, Helena instead attacks Coady, beating her senseless. She dismisses both Coady's judgment and her right to make it, echoing her earlier dismissal of Coady: "You are shit mother" (5.9). Creating or raising children in scientific contexts does not, then, a mother make in *Orphan Black*.

Motherhood Through Sisterhood

In contemporary western accounts of motherhood, mothering should take place within a family based on the romantic love between two, preferably heterosexual, people. As Stephanie Coontz notes in *The Way We Never Were*, the importance of romantic love to parenthood is a fairly recent and local construction and one which is not easily compatible with the discourse on motherhood as self-sacrificing, all-consuming love. In *Orphan Black*, the only family that can be read on these premises are the Hendrixes: Alison, her husband Donnie, and their two children, Gemma and Oscar (Millie Davis and Drew Davis). However, this nuclear family resists such reading; first, while there is certainly romantic love, Donnie was recruited as Alison's monitor before they were married, under the guise of a sociological research project in college, activating questions of control and objectification of women within marriage. Secondly, Gemma and Oscar are adopted children, highlighting the fact that romantic love (intercourse) does not equal reproduction in the manner of the uncomplicated traditional narrative of the happily-ever-after.

During Season 2, however, a possible recourse for Sarah to the normative, biologically based, heterosexual family is introduced with the appearance of dream-partner Cal (Michiel Huisman), Kira's biological father. The trajectory of Cal in the series is interesting. When he first enters what turns out to be his home, where Sarah, Kira, and Felix have broken in to hide, Sarah tells him, "I didn't come here for a father figure for my kid; I just needed a place to sleep" ("Mingling Its Own Nature with It," 2.3). This might have been her intention, but once he is present, his allure is clear, both as sexual partner and as father. When Felix wants them to leave, Sarah refuses; "Kira deserves something [...] nourishing for once, even just for a few days." Cal is thus granted temporary status as father and a nuclear family is presented as a temporary refuge from the violence and fear that, at this point in the narrative, have become everyday reality. Significantly, Felix, otherwise generally tolerant of unexpected additions to his family, leaves, telling Sarah, "There's no place for me here" (2.3). While the foster family he and Sarah belong to is flexible enough to accommodate difference of many kinds, the nuclear family unit appears to have no room for a gay foster brother. Cal remains, increasingly taking on the role as protector of Kira and, to some extent, of Sarah. A central scene opens with Sarah, Kira and Cal walking hand in hand—unequivocally conveying the idea of family ("Transitory Sacrifices of Crisis," 3.2). Cal is taking them to the house he's just bought, offering them a place to make their family permanent. The scene that plays out there neatly summarizes the main ingredients in this appealing family concoction. It shows them playing floorball, the scene overlaid with music and successfully merging the two discourses of parental and romantic love. This idyll is interrupted by a phone call for Sarah, her duties to her clone sisters calling her away. At first, Cal objects, asking her to stay. Sarah's insistence that she must go is rendered more acceptable to him when she adds, "You'd really do all this for us?" to which Cal responds, "Don't freak out. Kira is my daughter, too. I'd do anything for her." After Sarah kisses him, Cal lets her go, telling her to, "Go save [her] sister" (3.2). The simultaneous activation of romantic and parental discourses and the idea of them as mutually co-existing is present throughout their interaction, and Sarah's recognition of what Cal is offering enables him to recognize her familial obligations outside of the nuclear family constellation. As Sarah's duties to her sisters make her leave Kira, Cal takes Kira away to Iceland to protect her, and a family home becomes a possibility postponed. However, when Sarah joins Kira in Iceland, Cal is no longer there, and they are instead joined by Mrs. S and Kendall, replacing the heterosexual family unit with a family of women—daughters, mothers, sisters.

Helena also develops a love interest during Season 2 in Jesse (Patrick J. Adams), a tow-truck driver. Here, however, the biological connection of the traditional heterosexual nuclear family is absent—Helena leaves him to be impregnated with her fertilized eggs—and a family is never presented as a viable alternative, even though Helena tells Mrs. S with some emphasis that "[t]ogether, we will drive tow truck and make a home for our babies" ("A Community of Dreadful Fear and Hate," 3.7). Instead, Helena stays with Alison and Donnie for part of her pregnancy, trying hard to live up to the expectations on a pregnant woman, but eventually leaves to live in a tent in the woods. She may be pregnant, but it is clear that she is just as independent and self-sufficient as always, although at times seeking refuge with her sestras. Before taking off into the woods, she calls Sarah:

HELENA: I am having twins.
SARAH: Oh ... Meathead, that's huge. Are you okay?
HELENA: Yes, much okay. Because I know they will always have each other. Like us. But, *sestra*, can I say something?
SARAH: Yeah, yeah.
HELENA: I don't want them to grow up like me.
SARAH: Yeah, I get that feeling [4.3].

Their conversation conveys the sustaining quality of sisterhood, but it also expresses the hope that motherhood sustained by sisterhood can perhaps rescue your children from the fate of "becoming you." The importance of sisterhood to enable mothering, and of mothers to enable their daughters to become both sisters and mothers in their turn, is all expressed in the birthing scene that is the climax of the series finale. Sarah is remembering her own birthing experience and the presence and words of Mrs. S, "Look at me, honey, look at me, love" as Helena is saying that she can't go on, that she is too tired. Sarah keeps her gaze locked, echoing Mrs. S with force: "Look at me. Look at me. I'm right here. Okay, we're gonna do this together. You just keep looking at me, okay?" ("To Right the Wrongs of Many," 5.10). This intertwining of (biological and adoptive) mother, daughter, and sister in the same intense birthing scene is an effective and evocative way of demonstrating female relationships as sources of strength and motherhood as a communal experience.

At the opening of this text I claimed that clones do not have genetic mothers. Instead, we think of them as having genetic originals. As we have seen, the search for an original ends with a chimera, but the way in which Kendall is then discursively integrated in the extended clone family emphasizes further that "the Mother" as a necessary fixed point of family is not a given. Perhaps grammars of kinship can function even if the parts of family that make them up do not remain discrete and unchanging. Above all, perhaps "mother" does not need to inhabit the privileged position that makes her such a problematic figure for feminists. Evoking a controlling "bad mother," Kendall lashes out at Cosima, just after she's been found, "You're just a bad copy of me!" to which Cosima responds, "Yeah, we're kind of over the whole bad copy thing. It's way more accurate for us to call you older sister" (3.10). Helena unconcernedly goes on to combine sister with mother, calling Kendell "our original mother-*sestra*" (3.10).

The final scenes of the series show the *sestras* with all of their extended family, gathered at the Hendrixes' home. Men are present, in the roles of brothers, friends, lovers, sons, even husbands. But the primary relationship that sets up Alison's small garden as the space Sarah has been trying to create, where she can be a "real mum to Kira" (1.8), is that of sisterhood. Thrown into her old bad habits by the loss of Mrs. S, this space anchors her again.

Sharing their perceived failures and inadequacies, the *sestras* are not only validating each other's experiences of mothering; they are moving mothering firmly out of the nuclear family, anchoring it in sisterhood rather than romantic love. Thus *Orphan Black* offers hope, albeit perhaps on the level of the individual and the community rather than of society, hope of experiencing motherhood as both inter-dependence and independence.

NOTES

1. In fact, Felix (Sarah's foster brother) finds his biological half-sister through a DNA-match made by an online company in Season 4.
2. Not incidentally, one of the most contentious aspects of donor insemination is the question of the right of anonymity for donors. A child's right to know its genetic parents is often considered something of a moral or perhaps psychological imperative.
3. The appearance of P.T. Westmorland as demi-god patriarchal creator at the end of Season 4 displaces the women scientists, positioning them as his handmaidens rather than mother-scientists. While his appearance makes the clone-club's final victory more obviously a matter of young women taking down the patriarchy, I find the apparent narrative need for this male mastermind criminal somewhat depressing. The creators of the series also appear to have been unhappy with the way Westmorland comes across in the series, at least judging from the way they have Coady explain his role in the tie-in book *Orphan Black: Classified Clone Reports: Confidential*. She calls Westmorland their "beard" whom she and Susan used "for cover" but who "started to believe in his own myth" and is now "in [their] way" (DeCandido 157).
4. That Susan, apparently unconcernedly, takes on both the role of mother and that of lover to Ira, and our consequent reading of their relationship as incestuous, further emphasizes that Susan is unable to mother well, that her attempt to take on the role of mother is fundamentally flawed.

WORKS CITED

Bassin, Donna, Margaret Honey, and Meryle Mahrer Kaplan, editors. *Representations of Motherhood*. Yale UP, 1994.
"By Means Which Have Never Yet Been Tried." Writ. Graeme Manson. Dir. John Fawcett. *Orphan Black*. Season 2, episode 10. First aired 21 June 2014.
Coontz, Stephanie. *The Way We Never Were: American Families and the Nostalgia Trap*. BasicBooks, 1992.
DeCandido, Keith R.A. *Orphan Black: Classified Clone Reports: Confidential*. Harper Design, an imprint of HarperCollinsPublishers, 2017.
Diepenbrock, Chloé. "God Willed It! Gynecology at the Checkout Stand: Reproductive Technology in the Women's Service Magazine, 1977–1996." *Body Talk: Rhetoric, Technology, Reproduction*. Edited by Sally Gregory Kohlstedt, et al., U of Wisconsin P, 2000, pp. 98–121.
"Endless Forms Most Beautiful." Writ. Graeme Manson. Dir. John Fawcett. *Orphan Black*. Season 1, episode 10. First aired 1 June 2013.
"Entangled Bank." Writ. Karen Walton. Dir. Ken Girotti. *Orphan Black*. Season 1, episode 8. First aired 18 May 2013.
Franklin, Sarah. *Biological Relatives: IVF, Stem Cells, and the Future of Kinship*. Duke UP, 2013.
"From Dancing Mice to Psychopaths." Writ. Graeme Manson. Dir. John Fawcett. *Orphan Black*. Season 4, episode 10. First aired 16 June 2016.
Gunnarsson Payne, Jenny. "Grammars of Kinship: Biological Motherhood and Assisted Reproduction in the Age of Epigenetics" in *Signs: Journal of Women in Culture and Society*, vol. 41, no. 3, 2016, pp. 483–506.

"History Yet to Be Written." Writ. Graeme Manson. Dir. John Fawcett. *Orphan Black*. Season 3, episode 10. First aired 20 June 2015.
"Insolvent Phantom of Tomorrow." Writ. Russ Cochrane. Dir. Vincenzo Natali. *Orphan Black*. Season 3, episode 9. First aired 13 June 2015.
"Instinct." Writ. Graeme Manson. Dir. John Fawcett. *Orphan Black*. Season 1, episode 2. First aired 6 April 2013.
Macintosh, Kerry Lynn. "Human Cloning and the Family in the New Millennium." *Families—Beyond the Nuclear Ideal*, edited by Daniela Cutas and Sara Chan. Bloomsbury, 2014.
"Mingling Its Own Nature with It." Writ. Alex Levine. Dir. TJ Scott. *Orphan Black*. Season 2, episode 3. First aired 3 May 2014.
"Natural Selection." Writ. Graeme Manson. Dir. John Fawcett. *Orphan Black*. Season 1, episode 1. First aired 30 March 2013.
Neumann, Erich. *The Great Mother: An Analysis of the Archetype*. 1st Princeton paperback edition, Princeton UP, 1972.
"Newer Elements of Our Defence." Writ. Russ Cochrane. Dir. Chris Grismer. *Orphan Black*. Season 3, episode 4. First aired 9 May 2015.
"One Fettered Slave." Writ. Alex Levine. Dir. David Frazee. *Orphan Black*. Season 5, episode 9. First aired 5 Aug 2017.
Raymond, Janice G. "At Issue. Reproductive Technologies, Radical Feminism and Socialist Liberalism." *Reproductive and Genetic Engineering: Journal of International Feminist Analysis* vol. 2, no. 2 (1989), www.finrrage.org/wpcontent/uploads/2016/03/Repro_Technologies_Radical_Feminism_and_Socialist_Liberalism.pdf.
"The Stigmata of Progress." Writ. Aubrey Nealon. Dir. Ken Girotti. *Orphan Black*. Season 4, episode 3. First aired 28 April 2016.
Stutsman, Staci. "The Unruly Clones: Tatiana Maslany's Unruly Masquerades in Orphan Black." *Journal of Film and* Video, vol. 68, no. 3–4, 2016, pp. 83–103.
"Things Which Have Never Yet Been Done." Writ. Alex Levine. Dir. TJ Scott. *Orphan Black*. Season 2, episode 9. First aired 14 June 2014.
"To Hound Nature in Her Wanderings." Writ. Chris Roberts. Dir. Brett Sullivan. *Orphan Black*. Season 2, episode 6. First aired 24 May 2014.
"To Right the Wrongs of Many." Writ. Renée St. Cyr and Graeme Manson. Dir. John Fawcett. *Orphan Black*. Season 5, episode 10. First aired 12 Aug 2017.
"Transitory Sacrifices of Crisis." Writ. Aubrey Nealon. Dir. John Fawcett. *Orphan Black*. Season 3, episode 2. First aired 25 April 2015.
"Unconscious Selection." Writ. Alex Levine. Dir TJ Scott. *Orphan Black*. Season 1, episode 9. First aired 25 May 2013.
"Variable and Full of Perturbation." Writ. Karen Walton. Dir. John Fawcett. *Orphan Black*. Season 2, episode 8. First aired 7 June 2014.
"Variation Under Nature." Writ. Graeme Manson. Dir. David Frazee. *Orphan Black*. Season 1, episode 3. First aired 13 April 2013.
"The Weight of This Combination." Writ. Graeme Manson. Dir. David Frazee. *Orphan Black*. Season 3, episode 1. First aired 18 April 2015.
Wiegman, Robyn. "Intimate Publics: Race, Property, and Personhood." *American Literature* vol.74, no.4, 2002, pp. 859–85.

Motherless Bad Girl/ Bad Girl Mother

Naturalizing and Essentializing Motherhood in Orphan Black

LAINE ZISMAN NEWMAN

Introduction

> **INT. SUBWAY CAR:** *Sarah Manning sleeps on a subway, bleary eyed, with loud music in her ears and dark makeup beneath her eyes. "Huxley Station!" The announcer's voice jolts her in her seat: "Shit!" She wakes up, more than a little rough around the edges. A young girl looks over, her head resting on her mother's shoulder. Her mother glares, unblinkingly and unashamedly maintaining eye contact with Sarah and marking her disapproval of the abrupt curse. Sarah apologizes, casting her eyes to the window. The train pulls up and Sarah exits to the platform* ["Natural Selection," 1.1].

A singular, brief, and seemingly inconsequential exchange of glances between a mother's disapproving gaze and the show's protagonist, Sarah Manning (Tatiana Maslany), opens the premiere episode of *Orphan Black*. In this moment, it is not simply that Manning is being seen, but that she is being seen as out of place, as Other. Like the mother glaring back at her, our gaze consumes Manning too, though perhaps more with intrigue than disapproval. We are drawn to her through the way she repels others. The mother moves her daughter away ever so slightly, and we are compelled to move towards. Sarah Manning is captivating in her disheveled state, but she is quite clearly *not* the conventional figure of maternal grace and caring (she appears to be, in these opening moments, a little bit of a mess). As she emerges at her station, her short skirt and high boots further cue to us that Sarah Manning is a "Bad Girl." Brought up in the foster care system, Manning is presented as the quintessential rebellious woman whom we, as audience members, are driven to hold, support, and root for throughout the series. Within these first few moments, another character-defining reality begins to emerge, confirmed throughout the episode: Manning, with her smeared make up, foul language, and rough demeanor, is a young single mother, desperate to reconnect with her daughter.

As a popular science fiction series, filmed in Canada and produced by BBC America, *Orphan Black* is from the outset a valuable pop culture text for intersectional examination of privileged kinship structures and naturalized familial expectations. Despite its explicit feminist themes on autonomy of body-mind, *Orphan Black* perpetuates a prevalent patriarchal and sexist trope through Manning's story arch. She is the Bad Girl who can only find redemption by learning how to properly fulfill her presumed maternal duties. Applying feminist and queer theory to my analysis, this essay argues that although *Orphan Black* challenges essentialized readings of identity, it simultaneously upholds dominant gender expectations by depicting biological motherhood as a privileged redemptive practice. Though clearly distanced from our lived day-to-day experiences, the morals the series projects, particularly in relation to kinship, reproduction, and familial structures, offer ethical codes of behavior that reflect and extend normative ideals of family and a maternal imperative wherein women are only truly happy and humanized when they biologically reproduce.

Orphan Black is not devoid of feminist elements. Indeed, the direct reference to feminist theorist Donna Haraway's work in the episode titles for the fourth season makes evident the explicit intention to integrate feminist themes. The plot revolves around women who are constantly surveiled by technological implantations and monitors (typically white men), and battling to reclaim agency over their bodies. The *sestras*' explicit intellectual and physical strength, alongside their support and love for each other, is testament to the show's intended feminist undertones. However, the formulation of women's empowerment is nonetheless evidence of some exclusionary and essentialist tendencies, which work to naturalize gender performance and do not adequately attend to questions of difference.[1] What motivates many of the Leda clones (all played by Maslany), and conversely what scars them and leaves them wounded, evil, or damaged, is a direct result of how well they fulfill the role of mother, as well as their relationship to their own mothers. This archetype of the motherless mother is consistently portrayed as an ultimate and inevitable influence on the characters' development. It is all but inescapable, an instrumental force of essential determinism. In this way, *Orphan Black* can be read as a paradoxical cultural text: both empowering through its feminist articulation of women's agency and simultaneously problematic as it furthers stereotypical gendered expectations.

I begin this analysis by considering the ways in which motherhood is situated as redemptive and decode the impact of the absent mother trope, commonly iterated in media texts. Drawing on disability studies and queer theory, I then consider attribution of infertility to disease and the underlying implications of such a linkage. In the final section, I move from the Mother to the Child: an emblem of the future and a beacon of hope, possibility, and unexplained magic.

Returning Home: Redemptive Motherhood

> "All I know is I came back to fix things. Be a real mum to Kira."—Sarah, "Entangled Bank," 1.8

"Coming back" is the foundation of Manning's arrival. The very concept of returning implicitly points to the instincts that were already always there. It is not that Manning is learning to be a good mother, though we certainly see her in a state of becoming—but instead of this being positioned as a revelation, it is positioned as a return to a natural state, to the impulse and instinct to be good and to be present. From the outset of the series, it is evident that, of all of the clones, Manning is "special." Her role as mother is significant in the plot of the first season, as she attempts to regain access to her young daughter, and is further accentuated in the second season, when it is revealed that, due to a genetic anomaly, Manning and her twin sister, unlike the other clones, are able to procreate. Though there are consistent representations of non-biological motherhood in the series, it is biological motherhood that is conceived of as every woman's inherent objective and her noblest of destinies.

For Sarah, motherhood is redemptive, as it drives her away from a world of drugs and illegal activity, towards a no-less-violent world of protection and sacrifice. While the series demonstrates that one can simultaneously be a mother and maintain other priorities and responsibilities, it does so through an assumption that the maternal drive is the saving grace of womanhood: that the instinct to mother and ability to procreate are central to heterosexist gender actualization. Importantly, "The Mother," as figure and archetype throughout the series, is not depicted as necessarily virtuous, but instead as necessarily selfless. In a discussion of the representation of motherhood in *Harry Potter*, Margaret S. Mauk explains "a mother's love is not only presumed but valorized for its ordinariness, and as a result, readers assume that a 'good' mother will do anything for her child, regardless of any consequences" (130). The mother, Mauk explains, becomes a marker of morality despite the violence she may enact (130). This morality compass manifests throughout *Orphan Black* as well. Susan (Rosemary Dunsmore) and Virginia (Kyra Harper) are poor stand-ins for mothers, while Mrs. S (Maria Doyle Kennedy) and Sarah will put their children first. Putting them first often necessitates the infliction of pain upon others. The violent mother, however, is not seen as the villain, or the aggressor. She is justified in her protective stance, deemed implicitly to be defensive. In this way, redemptive motherhood is not to be equated with passivity, pacifism, or tranquility. On the contrary, in this series, and in other representations of motherhood in mainstream media, motherhood is a catalyst for justified violence in the name of family and kin. Unlike the "Bad Girl" or the villain whose actions may be selfish and uncaring, the violent mother is irrational with love.

As Mauk further explains, "political violence in the 20th century is reimagined to allow its scope to include the feminine and maternal. When virtuous violence is rendered as maternal, it is a defensive and reactive violence" (129). We may think here, too, of other series and media texts, in addition to Mauk's discussion of motherhood in *Harry Potter*. Bella endures her own physical demise for the sake of her unborn baby, risking her life, in the third installment of *Twilight* (2010); in the 2017 sci-fi thriller *Whatever Happened to Monday* (alternatively titled *Seven Sisters*), one sister puts her siblings lives in danger—resulting in most of their deaths—to protect her unborn children; and in the finale of *Aliens* (1986), Ripley (Sigourney Weaver) throws herself without hesitation into a battle to protect Newt, the orphaned child she takes under her care earlier in the film. Though all incredibly different media texts, these narrative arcs continually justify violence, death, and (self) destruction through a mother's need to secure the future of her children. Thus, a violent selflessness and aggression on behalf of one's children is deemed a gendered obligation, regardless of the cost. Karen Schneider notes, in attempting to "rescue and reassert the hegemonic family" in contemporary action-thrillers, "violence itself is the vehicle for both the hero's completion and the family's restoration; violence is required" (4–5).

Redemptive motherhood is exemplified through other characters as well. Unlike Sarah, whose return to motherhood may be attributed to being raised by a foster mother, Helena has nothing to easily "return" to. Her difficult life as an abused orphan hinders the conditions of arrival that enable Sarah to return to a perceived maternal state. Juxtaposed against Sarah's personae, a woman who simply lost her way, Helena is depicted as vicious, unkempt, irrational, and violent in the first seasons. Her outbursts are threatening and dangerous, as she brutally tortures and murders not only her surrogate mother, Amelia (Melanie Nicholls-King), but her "sisters" as well. We do not feel for her, but fear her. However, as the first season comes to a close, it is the presence of the Child,[2] an archetype I will shortly decode, that alters the tightly woven fabric of Helena's dysfunction. At the end of "Entangled Bank" (1.8), Helena is transformed from volatile to maternal through the touch of a child. After kidnapping Kira (Skyler Wexler) and dragging her into an alley, a single gesture from Kira, who places her hand on Helena's cheek, transforms Helena's character. A moment of humanity seeps through her eyes as she too is enthralled by the potential for motherhood:

> Kira: Helena?
> Helena: Yes, angel?
> Kira: What happened to you?
> Helena: [teary-eyed] I don't know.

Kira hugs Helena, embracing her kidnapper with the knowledge that she is not "evil" but damaged—detached from her humanity because of external forces. Something has happened to her to deprive and distance her from a natural maternal kindness. Through Kira's embrace, Helena's lips twitch and her arms shake as she navigates her own ability to return the gesture. Helena shifts from active to passive character: no longer able to determine what comes next, it is the child who takes the lead. Kira's next lines, "I should go home now," mark, not Helena's agentive relinquishing of power, but instead Kira's phenomenal ability to immobilize and subdue a violent creature by tapping into her own maternal instincts.

Somewhat similarly, Rachel in Season 2 and again in Season 5 kidnaps Kira and demonstrates in both instances brief and fleeting attempts to access her humanity. However, her infertility leaves her so yearning and unfulfilled that we see her abandon attempts to be kind or ethical behavior relatively quickly. Her strained and non-consensual encounters with motherhood are attempts to restore her sense of self and artificially produce what the heroines of the show seem to more naturally possess. Her continual search for what it means to be "real," to be human and to feel, is attached to her ability and desire to mother. It is as if the Child in her presence and the proximity of the Child will, in her mind, bring her closer to this objective. The childhood home video footage that Rachel watches repeatedly throughout the series replays this scenario as well. When Rachel watches and re-watches her childhood in her private screening room, she is not merely yearning for what was in the past, but what she so deeply desires in the future. Her liberation, humanness, and happiness exist within the remembered and imagined interactions between mother and child. I explore the relationship between redemptive motherhood and proximity in the following section.

A Necessary Orphan: The Absent Mother

> "You came to me an orphan. That's all you'll ever be."
> —Mrs. S, "The Antisocialism of Sex," 4.7

Whereas motherhood, as a symbol, identity category, and motivating narrative device, works to redeem women throughout the series, the absence of the biological mother is what necessitates such redemption. Even while motherhood is central to the plot of the series, the trope of the absent mother is equally influential. In a discussion on absent mothers in recent television series such as *Once Upon a Time*, *The 100*, and *Resurrection*, Rebecca Feasey notes that in current popular culture "the 'missing mother' trope not only continues, but has flourished since the emergence of quality teen drama, albeit within a more spectacular, fantastical and apocalyptic setting" (226). Importantly, Feasey's article focuses closely on the presence of the father as caregiver and the missing mother trope as a casual erasure of the mother's presence and influence. In many ways, *Orphan Black* responds to and resolves some of these stereotypical depictions of motherhood (and their absences). Contrary to the instances that Feasey analyzes, here mothers are not replaced by fathers, but by surrogate women—whether designated by the state, corporation, or chosen family. The absent, dead, or missing biological mother is not erased, but centralized. Her lack of presence shapes the identities and conditions the actions of her children. While seemingly responding to the erasure and deprioritization of the mother in sci-fi series, the consequences of the absent mother in *Orphan Black* perpetuate ideological gender norms that essentialize the role of woman through the duties of mother.

The necessary presence of the mother is a culturally specific representation, often universalized through media representations in the West. As Diana L. Gustafson points out in *Unbecoming Mothers: The Social Production of Maternal Absence*, "In pronatalist societies, in which becoming a mother is naturalized and reified, unbecoming a mother—the process of coming to live apart from biological children—is variously regarded as unnatural, improper, even contemptible" (qtd. in Kawash 9831). We learn to accept the good mother as necessarily present, as much as the transience or disappearance of the father figure remains unremarkable. While Sarah returns to Kira in Season 1, her presence and disappearance mark her stability and wellness. In her clearest state, not overcome or overwhelmed, Sarah prioritizes her daughter and is physically close to her. It is when she is furthest from herself, balancing on the edge of sanity and safety, that she furthers herself from her child, even if momentarily. Her mental wellness is marked by the proximity she maintains between her own body and her child's. Importantly, there are other instances when distance is maintained between Kira and Sarah that do not follow this pattern, most notably when Sarah sends Kira away to Iceland or to her father's cabin for her safety. Though these are actions which distance mother from daughter, I refer here to agentive movement of Sarah's body away from Kira to specifically mark how the physical maternalized body moves away from her biological kin when in distress.

In the introduction to *The Absent Mother in the Cultural Imagination*, Berit Åström notes the dead or absent mother-trope "transcend[s] historical and generic divisions" (1), made manifest throughout histories, cultures and forms (2). In *Orphan Black*, the impact of the absent mother and the consequences of this absence are reiterated through multiple clones' experiences and violent behaviors. Indeed, we may consider Helena's deadly anger and resentment towards Amelia, her "birth mother," for both her absence and her choice to surrender Helena to the Church. Somewhat similarly, in Rachel's characterization, we see that the assumed death of her parents altered her personality, from that of a young and happy child, to a cold and heartless villain. As the series continues and it is revealed that her mother did not die, but chose to be absent, Rachel's character is further complicated, though no less violent. The return of her mother replicates, to some degree, Amelia's return. The agentive choice for Amelia and Susan to leave their daughters has a traumatic impact on their children and on their own wellbeing, where both daughters inflict physical violence on the mothers that left them.

Though *Orphan Black* disrupts the conventional family unit through the feminizing of the family and the abstraction of the patriarch as unnecessary, supplementary, or even as dangerous, the woman's presence as mother is nonetheless by and large positioned as obligatory. Though centralizing women, this articulation of compulsory presence reinvigorates a Western ideal of motherhood that cannot be considered outside of underlying cultural, classist, and racialized critique. In discussions of Filipina migrant domestic workers, Samira Kawash notes, "Mothering is not essentially determined by presence; we must acknowledge that how and under what circumstances a woman chooses or is forced to leave her child matter tremendously" (983). Kawash goes on to note that this investment in presence shapes the image of what is deemed successful motherhood in the global North, affecting how it is viewed and experienced in the global South. Here too, the universalization and global presence of the clones conceals the cultural and racial specificity of the moral values projected. The oversimplification of idealized motherhood and the consequences endured by the absent mother (and her child) frame gendered norms as uncompromisingly universal.

Ultimately, the clones are all situated in some way as orphans; however, their experiences of mothers vary throughout the series, and we glean much about their characters through the presence or absence of these parental figures. For example, Alison's relationship to her mother, Connie (Sheila McCarthy), instrumentally affects how Alison relates to others and sees herself. Connie makes several appearances throughout the series, and we begin to understand Alison's neuroses and fear of failure through Connie's refusal to accept Alison's life choices, as she critiques Alison's husband and career goals. We do not hear of Cosima's parents until late in the series, in "Ease for Idle Millionaires" (5.5). Her background and upbringing are somewhat elusive, as is her own desire for motherhood (to be discussed shortly). It is at a somewhat uncomfortable dinner exchange with P.T. Westmorland (Stephen McHattie), Delphine (Évelyne Brochu), Susan Duncan, and Rachel Duncan that she first discusses her parents. Westmorland sits across from her at the table: "How are your parents, Cosima?" The question is posed almost as a threat, indicating surveillance and knowledge of familial history, alongside a soundtrack that is somewhat dire, cueing the audience to listen as we recognize that we have not yet heard of Cosima's upbringing.

> COSIMA: They are professors, and they live on a houseboat, so they are pretty remote. Anyways, but ... they are in love. And they love me. But, I haven't even told them I am sick. Cause if I did that, I would crack and I would have to tell them everything. I would have to tell them that I am a clone, and they would know that everything is a lie.
> WESTMORLAND: What a delicate balance you have: the clinical and the humane.

Cosima's well-adjusted demeanor, education, and drive are validated through her upbringing, and while her tone seems to imply neglect or distance between them, she is nonetheless quick to defend their relationships with each other. Though Cosima is sick, she is not maladjusted. She has a mother, and she is loved. Neither Alison nor Cosima seem to have perfect upbringings, and their experiences are not romanticized. However, in each case and throughout the series, the presence of the mother, or lack thereof, is a compelling and unwavering force on the clones. For those without an active motherly presence, the prescribed remedy is rewriting or perhaps rerouting familial narratives by filling the void of their mothers by becoming mothers themselves.

Inescapable Biology: The Genes That Matter and Normative Kinship

> "We may have been raised without familial bonds, but you, Ira, are my brother, and I'm beginning to believe that means something."—Rachel, "The Redesign of Natural Objects," 4.8

In the second season, it is not simply motherhood, but a woman's reproductive fertility which is portrayed as a woman's ultimate objective. The privileging of biological kinship is evident from the characters that remain unfulfilled by non-biological relations. Relatedly, infertility is paired with corporate control of the body, whereas fertility, for heterosexual women, marks liberation and choice (grounded invariably in the choice to pursue heterosexual motherhood). Through the series' plot developments, biological motherhood comes to represent not only the feminine ideal, but also utopic futurity and freedom. While the show may support unconventional kinship structures in some ways, it paradoxically devalues non-biological motherhood through the privileging of fertility.

We see this need and desire for biological motherhood not just in Sarah's narrative, but also through the struggles the other clones have with infertility. In Season 2, Rachel, as antagonist and villain, becomes increasingly obsessed with her own desire for motherhood, valorizing women's fertility and reproductive capabilities as a marker of human-ness and enacting violence motivated by a desire for biological children. After discovering that the clones are "barren by design" in Season 2, we are permitted access to Rachel's internal narrative through quick cuts from her imagined loss of control as she destroys her office, back to shots of her sitting motionless, clearly restraining her response. The pain is palpable as she recognizes her lack of control over her body and autonomy. The equation between a lack of autonomy and infertility pairs reproduction and fertility with desirable human gendered experiences, now articulated as intentionally out of Rachel's reach. Later, in Season 3, we witness the possibility of Rachel's redemption and humanity when she takes on the role of mother to Charlotte (Cynthia Gallant), a young clone who is introduced at the same time as it is revealed that Susan Duncan, Rachel's adoptive mother, is alive as well. Rachel's humanity grows in the moment she adopts the role of mother. Ultimately, this humanity is short-lived: Rachel, as villain, feels inadequately human because of her inability to reproduce her own child. Charlotte does not fulfill Rachel's desire to be a mother. This is most apparent later in the season when Rachel is willing to let Charlotte die to gain additional data on the clone disease, sacrificing Charlotte's well-being for the greater cause of furthering Neolution's science.

While there is an overt privileging of biological motherhood, the clones certainly demonstrate a kind of queer kinship marked by the adopted terminology of *"sestras,"* a development which signifies the clones' acceptance of and reconciliation with Helena after her violent introduction at the beginning of the series. Yet, even here, the family (though unconventional) is corroborated through shared genes. Though it is not a typical nuclear family formation, like other mainstream representations of kinship and heroism in popular culture, it comes to "[epitomize] love, support and safety" (Mauk 125). It is a family's love that perseveres and enables them to overcome. As Mauk further explicates:

> Using the family to create an essentialized morality presents cultural ethics not as constructs but as biological imperatives. This allows characters—and readers—to justify actions as moral without sufficient critical analysis. Furthermore, it allows agents who operate outside of this framework to be positioned as inherently immoral, unnatural, and inhuman [126].

It is not that infertile women are necessarily or inherently *bad mothers* in the series, but rather that they themselves problematically articulate that non-biological motherhood is not enough. It is their attitudes towards infertility and adoptive families that points to the idealization of biological motherhood in the series. Indeed, while Alison loves her children, in "From Instinct to Rational Control" (4.4), she expresses jealousy for Helena's fertility. Despite having two children of her own, she admits, "I just want to have my own baby." Two episodes prior, Felix (Jordan Gavaris) announces that he is looking for his birth family:

> FELIX: It's about me finding out who I am.
> SARAH: Me, S, Kira. That's your family, Fee.
> FELIX: No, that's your family. You're related to bloody everyone, including our foster mum. Go figure that.
> SARAH: You belong with us, Fee.
> FELIX: No, I belong on the dance floor ["Transgressive Border Crossing," 4.2].

Sarah's biological relationship to "bloody everyone" indeed situates her capabilities and heroism in her blood. The revelation that Sarah has been raised by biological family triggers a shift in the depiction of familial relations. Her newfound understanding of her genetic history brings her closer to a sense of self and family (indeed, she begins referring to Mrs. S more regularly as "mum" in this season). She is redeemed through her origin story and is positioned as whole: as a good mother. In part she gains this heroic status because of the battle she is in the midst of fighting, but also because her relationship to her foster mother now has biological underpinnings. This is not to denounce or trivialize Felix and Sarah's relationship. As foster siblings, their bond is centralized throughout the series. Yet, the quotation above is indicative of the simultaneous importance of non-biological relations and the privileging of blood relations. It is Felix here who pronounces the need to connect with his biological family as a means of finding out who he is. He positions biology as intrinsically connected to self, despite his undeniably close ties to his foster sister.

The association between non-biological motherhood and failed motherhood is also exemplified through Susan Duncan and Dr. Virginia Coady (Kyra Harper), who fail to keep their "children" happy or even breathing. Though Susan and Virginia continually privilege the success of Neolution's experiment over the very lives of their "children," the series does not entirely disconnect them from motherhood. Susan feels occasional, though fleeting, remorse for what she has done to Rachel; likewise, Virginia, in Mark's (Ari Millen) final moments of life, shows momentary humanity as she cries at the death of her last son, asking him about his future as she injects him with a poison that will ensure its impossibility. The writers make certain that we see Virginia as a mother in this instance as Mark utters his last words, "I'm so happy. Goodnight, Mom" ("One Fettered Slave," 5.9). Here, he reminds us that she is not only a scientist, not only a murderer, but also a failed mother.

So, it is not that these women are not mothers at all, but rather that they are incapable of fulfilling a loving and selfless maternal presence without a biological attachment to secure their instincts. Again, this is not to argue that all non-biological mothers fail in the series. Mrs. S is a continual source of strength and inspiration through all five seasons. Yet, her eventual biological connection to the genetic original of the clones does seem to privilege blood-relations.

In the scene following Mark's death by Virginia's hand, Helena further solidifies the privileging of biological motherhood as rightful motherhood. After being kidnapped by Virginia Coady and induced to labor, Helena pleas for her children's lives.

> HELENA: You let him take your babies, please not mine. They need their mother.
> COADY: Well that's just not true, Helena. You forget, I know who you are. Dumped at birth. A killer. You killed your own sisters. You stink, like an animal. What kind of mother could you possibly be? [5.10].

In this moment, we are asked to reflect on Virginia's motherhood, as she projects her dread and remorse over killing her son onto Helena's body. We believe, after Helena's fight to protect her unborn children, that she *will* be a good mother. Indeed, the implied response to Virginia's questions is answered in a scene later in the episode as Helena speaks to her still unborn children and chooses to sacrifice their lives, in the hope of evading a seemingly inescapably painful future, "You deserve better than me. You will not be an experiment, too. I set you free, my babies." In sacrificing their lives and refusing to allow them to be born into a life of captivity and experimentation, Helena makes one of the most difficult decisions a mother can make, but ultimately one we are meant to see as protective. In this moment, she tries to do what is best for her children, to care for them, and keep them safe in the only way she now can. Whether we feel she is misguided or not, we are driven to feel empathy for her as she questions, in those brief moments before giving birth, whether or not she could be a "good" mother.

I do not intend to create a monolithic theory of the series' projection of motherhood and gender essentialism. There are certainly characters and story arcs that deviate from the patterns I have identified thus far. However, even those characters that do not adhere to a reproductive imperative may in some cases further develop, rather than contradict, these theorizations. For example, through Cosima's characterization we see how biological motherhood and maternal instincts are portrayed as specifically a heterosexual imperative, upholding normative conceptions of a queer failure to fulfill and embody gender ideals. In the final episode of the series, Cosima hesitates to hold Helena's baby in a brief moment where we see her discomfort with children, as she admits, "Did you guys see how panicked I got when Felix handed me the baby earlier? Like, I am just not maternal at all" ("To Right the Wrongs of Many," 5.10). Cosima is the only primary clone not driven or plagued by the desire to embody and enact biological motherhood. In part, this constructs her as the most resistant to normative tropes of maternal imperatives. Indeed, Cosima is happy and healthy by the end of the series and does not seem to want children. However, moving beyond a simplistic reading of her character, we must consider her lack of maternal drive within the context of queer representation. While increasing visibility and presence for queer characters on screen, Cosima simultaneously propagates and extends myths of queer women as lacking in maternal desire. As I discuss in the following section, Cosima is not only an antithesis to the maternal, but also comes to demonstrate that such a positionality is dangerous: it is a disease necessitating intervention.

(In)fertility as Defect: Ableism and Conceptions of a "Cure"

> "Rachel, she's a failure, not a success. You are all barren by design."—Ethan Duncan, "Variable and Full of Perturbation," 2.8

When Rachel asks her adoptive father, Ethan Duncan (Andrew Gillies), why it is that Sarah, the unmonitored clone, is able to reproduce, Ethan responds that Sarah and Helena's fertility is a defect. While situating their ability as such within the realm of the Leda Project, infertility is positioned as a means of control and objectification. It is one component that precludes the clones from being fully human. The ethical treatment of infertility throughout the series extends beyond questions of autonomy to a significant, though perhaps less apparent positioning of infertility as inadequate womanhood or biological disability. The sterility sequence employed to "prevent ovarian follicles from maturing" had unintentional consequences, leading to unanticipated disease and risk of premature death. Infertility is grappled with not only through the Leda clones, but also the Castor clones' ability to sterilize women and the Prolethean's stance on reproduction and biology.

Linking infertility to disease and premature death and fertility to a "cure" universalizes and naturalizes womanhood on the basis of cisgender anatomical bodily functions. What does it mean to attribute infertility and sterilization to illness? How does such a turn valorize and promote the reproducing woman as the ideal and able-bodied woman? Eli Clare writes: "defectiveness justifies cure and makes it essential. [...] [It] wields incredible power because ableism builds and maintains the notion that defective body-minds are undesirable, worthless, disposable, or in need of cure. [...] The ableist invention of defectiveness functions as an indisputable justification not only for cure but also for many systems of oppression" (23). In *Orphan Black*, linking infertility to premature death and non-personhood reifies an association between fertility, health, and proper able-bodied personhood. Motherhood and fertility juxtapose the defective infertile body and are thus not only positioned as redemptive in a psychological realm, but also in a physical one. The very notion of a "cure" isolates some bodies as ideal and "natural" and casts others as defective and disabled. As Clare explains, "As an ideology seeped into every corner of white Western thought and culture, cure rides on the back of *normal* and *natural*. Insidious and pervasive, it impacts most of us" (14). The normalized body is valorized. It does not necessitate medical intervention, but instead is a catalyst for change and improvement. Sarah is not in need of a cure. Her ability to reproduce not only saves her from demonization and villainy, it also secures her health. It is not that the clones should avoid a cure; given that this disease is killing them, it is essential to the plot that they seek out a cure in order to maintain survival. What I want to highlight here is the way in which motherhood and reproduction are essentialized as characteristics of health and humanity. Dying prematurely is inextricable from infertile bodies.

While the series certainly centers the experiences of women and provides a potential resistance against the ways in which their bodies are constructed, commodified, and objectified by dominant patriarchal forces and corporations, it simultaneously naturalizes fertile women, deeming those infertile as at risk of being unfulfilled emotionally and physically vulnerable to illness. Counter to an alternative kinship structure of *sestras* (which at its core still relies on biology, though not reproduction), the centralizing of fertility itself reproduces patriarchal conceptions of essentialized gender roles.

The Future in the Child

> "Mommy, your sisters, I know how they feel sometimes.... Like ... Cosima, when she's sad. Helena, when she's lonely. Rachel's the angriest. There's even some I don't know.... I feel you, too, Mommy."—Kira, "Human Raw Material," 4.5

In *Orphan Black* it is not simply motherhood in the present that redeems the characters and offers hope; the presence of the child as extension of the mother (and as *future* mother) reaches beyond the now and predicates the possibility of a better, utopic future. Throughout the series, the Child (as character and archetype) is what saves the protagonist and her *sestras*. Though we begin by championing Sarah Manning, it is her non-clone child, Kira, who is the ultimate savior.

We see Kira's ability to save and redeem from the beginning of the series. Early on we see her pull her tooth and undergo surgery to donate bone marrow when the tooth does not suffice to help Cosima. Even more than helping the heroines of the story, she offers empathy to Helena and Rachel, humanizing their struggles beyond simplistically reading them as one-dimensional villains. As the series progresses, Kira's capacity to redeem others is extended through superhuman, unexplained abilities to access feelings and emotions. In "Human Raw Material" (4.5) Kira reveals that she is connected to all of the sisters, with knowledge of their whereabouts and feelings; beyond empathy and intuition, she also possesses a kind of biological telepathy. Through her "magical" superhuman abilities and her altruistic and virtuosic drive, Kira comes to both represent and physically embody the "Cure." Her selflessness and uninterrupted agentive offering of her body and genes (juxtaposed by the clones' forced, manipulated, and controlled bodies) provides hope not only in terms of a cure to defective bodies, but also a route to an alternative future: liberation from the science that created the clones.

In his well-known polemic, Lee Edelman positions the Child as the image of "futurity's unquestioned value" (4) and "the preeminent emblem of the motivating end [...] of every political vision as a vision of futurity" (13), not detached from political heteronormativity, but essential to its construction. The Child, as figure and not as individual, comes to represent and enact what is to come: a necessary drive towards futurity. He explains "the Child has come to embody for us the telos of the social order and come to be seen as the one for whom that order is held in perpetual trust. [...] [T]he image of the Child, not to be confused with the lived experiences of any historical children, served to regulate political discourse" (11). Arguably, Kira's unexplained abilities elevate her character from individual to figurative emblem. She represents the unexplained, unscientific, but hopeful future. Her powers and mysterious connections to the clones deviate from established scientific and social norms in this fictional world. We never quite understand how she connects with all of the clones' feelings—her empathy and ability to feel are beyond explanation. The Child can feel and see what we, and the clones, cannot.

Kira, unsurprisingly perhaps given my analysis thus far, is not only a daughter, but inevitably positioned as a future natural (read: non-clone) mother. In Season 5 it is revealed that Kira is so important to the science and institute because they intend to "fertilize over a thousand of her eggs and implant them in surrogates" ("Manacled Slim Wrists," 5.6). Kira will grow from Child to Mother rather seamlessly. In this way, Kira's character choices demonstrate that it is not that women (and more specifically mothers and maternalized women) should *not* offer of their physical bodies, but rather that they should not be compelled to do so by outside forces. That women's bodies may be the source of a cure and resources, and that they should feel a desire to donate and sacrifice them of their own accord is clearly applauded—there is a higher cause implicated in Kira's sacrifice of her body. She is taught to continually put others before herself as the quintessential manifestation of love and kinship, a form of selflessness which so often we attribute to the role of the Mother. As Kira donates her teeth, her bone marrow, and her safety, it becomes apparent that she is the Child for whom the future is constructed, but also the inevitable mother who will bear children to secure its arrival.

Importantly, Charlotte—the newest incarnation of the clones—is one of the only other recurring children who have a marked influence and presence in the series, as Alison's non-biological children are only briefly featured and are not fully formed in their character development. Charlotte fills a significantly different narrative role than Kira. She is not the Child as daughter, but rather, as an orphan herself, she signifies a continuation of a flawed and broken past (exemplified physically through her disability). Moved from monitor to monitor, her body, unlike Kira's, does not point us towards a redeemed future, but instead, through her lack of agency and continuing objectification, is a marker of stagnancy which Kira's presence works to combat. As a motherless orphan, directly cloned from Rachel Duncan, Charlotte, and the representation of her disabled body, suspend the future and bring us back from adulthood to childhood, as if endlessly looping time and stalling progress. Rather than looking at her and perceiving "child," the series continually instructs audiences to look at her and see: clone. She is situated as the antithesis of the Child-figure, an abelist representation, pointing to what is wrong with our histories and how it continues to implicate our current world. We quite literally know what Charlotte's future will look like, but through Kira, as simultaneous Child and future Mother, we are offered a glimpse of a better future, still on the horizon of experience, but increasingly brought to fruition through her selflessness and superhuman presence.

Conclusion: A Woman's Purpose

> "You're made to be able to do it."—Mrs. S, "To Right the Wrongs of Many," 5.10

In the epigraph above, Mrs. S reminds us that a woman's body is made to give birth and be a mother. She was, in fact, "made to be able to do it." This line, from the series finale, turns us towards purpose, towards actions deemed natural and normal. As Sarah guides Helena through childbirth, we cut to flashbacks of Mrs. S supporting Sarah as she delivered Kira into the world. The twin clones mirror each other as they enact and perform their gift of fertility. In this closing episode, the primacy of motherhood and the function of reproduction as a gendered imperative are stressed and centralized, perhaps more so than in any other singular episode. Mrs. S, as a non-biological mother to Sarah, might seem to complicate this privileging of biological reproduction, but we may also note how the proclamation and insistence that Sarah's body was made to do *this* is all the more poignant coming from her foster mother.

Blood takes a central role in marking familial bonds and validating kinship throughout this final episode. After invading Dyad to kill P.T. Westmorland, Sarah unknowingly arrives in the nick of time to save her sister, who has been induced to labor. It is only Sarah's blood that can save her sister. This is what connects the siblings and confirms their familial ties, despite the obstacles, violence, and past betrayals. This blood is the only thing that can save Helena. It is a literal manifestation and transfer of what is shared between them. Here, we may note similar patterns in other sci-fi and fantasy media texts. In *Harry Potter,* Lily Potter's love and sacrificial protection is transferred through Harry's blood—it is blood that mother and son share that saves Harry's life and protects him from Voldemort's curse. Similarly, in *Buffy the Vampire Slayer*'s Season 5 finale, "The Gift," it is a sister's blood that becomes the key to the survival of the next generation, as Buffy Summers (Sarah Michelle Gellar) sacrifices her own life in place of her sister (5.22). By utilizing familial blood as the linkage that saves and redeems, these series demonstrate the irreplaceable and necessary presence of biological and genealogical relations. The blood, which Helena lets from her body, is given as sacrifice towards what she deems to be a better future for her children. But it is her biological sister's blood that can save her, a validation of her need to survive for and with her children through their shared bodily experiences.

The final episode continues by further reinforcing the centrality of motherhood as a redemptive and necessary component of productive gender embodiment. Surrounded by children at Helena's baby shower, Sarah finally begins to grapple with the impact and aftermath of her own foster mother's death. She admits that she lied to her daughter about taking a high school equivalency test and laments: "I don't know how to be happy. There's no one left to fight, and I'm still a shit mom." Happiness is tied to mothering. Fighting was justified for motherhood, but, without an impending battle, Sarah is forced to be a mother on her own terms. Alison responds immediately with her own scenario of failed motherhood, of scaring her child; then Helena confesses that she, too, is a bad mother; and then Cosima admits her lack of maternal desire. Here, the women come together to empower and normalize the "bad mother," confronting the stigmatization that comes with questioning one's maternal instincts. But, at the same time, these scenes do little to dispel the essentialized position of heterosexual woman *as* mother. What connects the clones is not only their genes, not only their shared status as "orphans," but also their desire to conform to familial roles as matriarchs and their shared fear that they will not fulfill this given duty. They come together not to identify their independence and strengths apart from motherhood, but to lodge their strength directly within their identities as mothers.

Though the series explicitly addresses and attempts to dismantle the biological boundaries of familial structures, it increasingly founds kinship on the shared biology of the clones and the privileging of the fertile woman's body. While empowering the mother as hero and savior, ultimately, rather than reconfiguring reproductive futures, *Orphan Black* ends by reinforcing the happiness such futures will bring. Though the clones obtain a cure and relative emancipation from the corporations that created them, this is not a simple victory in a feminist struggle for autonomy, but a reinforcement of the idea that, when all is said and done, women will return to what they instinctually desire, what they yearn to perform: to be family, to be redeemed, to be a mother.

Notes

1. Here, we may also consider the representation of the clones as simultaneously singular and universal not only in terms of gender, but also other identity markers such as race. In casting the Leda clones, and most specifically Sarah Manning, as "every woman," the series projects the moral compass of the characters and their familial structures beyond the specificity of their make-believe world. The universalization of the clones in part occurs through the diversification of mother figures in a brief two-episode story arc wherein Sarah and Helena's "birth mother" is revealed to be Amelia, a black woman from South Africa. As Laura Harrison notes, "New reproductive technologies appear to offer an alluring promise of the deconstruction of racial difference via a postmodern explosion of the possibility that includes white children born of non-white parents" (262). Employing the role of the black mother figure to position the clones as global and omnipresent functions to neutralize and destabilize whiteness and privilege. We may ask here what it means for one body (particularly that of white actress Tatiana Maslany) to be every*body*? In addition to prioritizing particular forms of motherhood and belonging, how does light skin enable a mask of universality to embody what is deemed imperative to actualizing and fulfilling gender roles? The presence of the white clones' bodies as every*body* masks the ways in which by and large the cast of *Orphan Black* reproduces a homogeneous racially privileged and conventional white society.

2. Importantly, while I focus in on Helena's interaction with Kira here, this is not the first interaction we see with her and a child. Helena has contact with a little boy named Trevor (Jack Fulton) ("Effects of External Conditions," 1.4) when she enters his house in the middle of the night to tend to a stab wound. Here, too, Helena treats a child with affection, beginning a pattern through which we see the potential for the child to humanize the villain.

Works Cited

Ahmed, Sara. "A Phenomenology of Whiteness." *Feminist Theory* 8.2 (2007): 149–168.
Alien. Dir. James Cameron. 1986, 20th Century–Fox.

"The Antisocialism of Sex." Writ. Nikolijne Troubetzkoy and Graeme Manson. Dir. David Frazee. *Orphan Black.* Season 4, episode 7. First aired 26 May 2016.
Åström, Berit. "Introduction—Explaining and Exploring the Dead or Absent Mother." *The Absent Mother in the Cultural Imagination.* Palgrave Macmillan, Cham, 2017. 1–21.
"By Means Which Have Never Yet Been Tried." Writ. Graeme Manson. Dir. John Fawcett. *Orphan Black.* Season 2, episode 10. First aired 21 June 2014.
Clare, Eli. *Brilliant Imperfection: Grappling with Cure.* Duke University Press, 2017.
"Ease for Idle Millionaires." Writ. Jenn Engles. Dir. Helen Shaver. *Orphan Black.* Season 5, episode 5. First aired 8 July 2017.
Edelman, Lee. *No Future: Queer Theory and the Death Drive.* Duke University Press, 2004.
"Entangled Bank." Writ. Karen Walton. Dir. Ken Girotti. *Orphan Black.* Season 1, episode 8. First aired 18 May 2013.
Feasey, Rebecca. "Television and the Absent Mother: Why Girls and Young Women Struggle to Find the Maternal Role." *The Absent Mother in the Cultural Imagination.* Palgrave Macmillan, Cham, 2017. 225–240.
"From Instinct to Rational Control." Writ. Alex Levine. Dir. Peter Stebbings. *Orphan Black.* Season 4, episode 4. First aired 5 May 2016.
"The Gift." Writ. Joss Whedon. Dir. Joss Whedon. *Buffy the Vampire Slayer.* Season 5, episode 22. First aired May 22, 2011.
Gustafson, Diana. *Unbecoming Mothers: The Social Production of Maternal Absence.* Routledge, 2013.
Harrison, Laura. "Brown Bodies, White Eggs: The Politics of Cross-racial Gestational Surrogacy." *Twenty-first Century Motherhood: Experience, Identity, Policy, Agency* (2010): 261–275.
"Human Raw Material." Writ. Kate Melville. Dir. David Wellington. *Orphan Black.* Season 4, episode 5. First aired 12 May 2016.
Kawash, Samira. "New Directions in Motherhood Studies." *Signs: Journal of Women in Culture and Society* 36.4 (2011): 969–1003.
Mauk, Margaret S. "'Your Mother Died to Save You': The Influence of Mothers in Constructing Moral Frameworks for Violence in Harry Potter." *Mythlore* 36.1 (2017): 123–142.
"Natural Selection." Writ. Graeme Manson. Dir. John Fawcett. *Orphan Black.* Season 1, episode 1. First aired 30 March 2013.
"Newer Elements of Our Defence." Writ. Russ Cochrane. Dir. Chris Grismer. *Orphan Black.* Season 3, episode 4. First aired 9 May 2015.
"One Fettered Slave." Writ. Alex Levine. Dir. David Frazee. *Orphan Black.* Season 5, episode 9. First aired 5 Aug 2017.
"The Redesign of Natural Objects." Writ. Peter Mohan. Dir. Aaron Morton. *Orphan Black.* Season 4, episode 8. First aired 2 June 2016.
"Scarred by Many Past Frustrations." Writ. Alex Levine. Dir. David Frazee. *Orphan Black.* Season 3, episode 5. First aired 16 May 2015.
Schneider, Karen. "With Violence If Necessary: Rearticulating the Family in the Contemporary Action-Thriller." *Journal of Popular Film and Television* 27.1 (1999): 2–11.
"To Right the Wrongs of Many." Writ. Renée St. Cyr and Graeme Manson. Dir. John Fawcett. *Orphan Black.* Season 5, episode 10. First aired 12 Aug 2017.
"Transgressive Border Crossing." Writ. Russ Cochrane. Dir. John Fawcett. *Orphan Black.* Season 4, episode 2. First aired 21 April 2016.
The Twilight Saga: Eclipse. Dir. David Slade. 2009, Summit Entertainment.
"Variable and Full of Perturbation." Writ. Karen Walton. Dir. John Fawcett. *Orphan Black.* Season 2, episode 8. First aired 7 June 2014.
Whatever Happened to Monday. Dir. Tommy Wirkola. 2017, SND Films.

Hell and Back

Helena as Kore and Shaman in Orphan Black

JANET BRENNAN CROFT

"Every grain of wheat and every maiden contains [...] all its descendants and all her descendants—an infinite series of mothers and daughters in one. [...] [E]very mother contains her daughter in herself and every daughter her mother, and [...] every woman extends backwards into her mother and forward into her daughter."
—Jung and Kerenyi 153, 162

The myth of the descent of a goddess or heroine into hell and her return to the land of the living as an intermediary between the two realms is a central myth of the female experience, retold with variations in many cultures and resonating throughout many of the stories we tell. Among the most familiar goddesses and heroines associated with this mythic pattern are Persephone, Psyche, Eurydice, and Inanna, who, in their various ways and for various reasons, descend into hell, are transformed by what happens to them there and by interactions with gods and shadow-goddesses who serve as mentors or opponents, and either return to the world of the living with matured powers and abilities—or fail to return, unable "to pay an acceptable coin to Charon, guaranteeing safe return from death's blighted realm" (Edwards 15), and serve as a caution to others who would attempt this task.

This mythic pattern is of course a variation on the hero-journey as described by Joseph Campbell:

> All these different mythologies give us the same essential quest. You leave the world that you're in and go into a depth or into a distance or up to a height. There you come to what was missing in your consciousness in the world you formerly inhab-

ited. Then comes the problem of either staying with that, and letting the world drop off, or returning with that boon and trying to hold on to it as you move back into your social world again. That's not an easy thing to do [Campbell, *Power* 129].

What distinguishes this particular group of stories from the more general pattern is the female protagonist, the descent, encounters with the animus (in the form of an opposite-sex opponent or a rescuing hero) and the shadow-self (in the person of the mother or sister, either a false friend or a rescuer), and the type of boon brought back to the primary world (usually related to the restoration of the family).

While several of the other clones central to *Orphan Black* also have experiences that fit this model of descent into hell and return, I wish here to concentrate on Helena (Tatiana Maslany): the character who most dramatically exemplifies this pattern and whose thought processes are the most tied to religion, superstition, symbolism, and her own sense of special destiny. In her ongoing quest for family and for meaning, Helena makes descent after descent into hell, encountering evil kings, female false guides, and opportunities to save others. She is associated with angelic imagery (for example, Kira [Skyler Wexler] folds origami angels to represent her in "Variable and Full of Perturbation," 2.8), and her experiences enable her to serve as both an angel of death and a shaman.

Helena's first descents are passive or involuntary abductions, but increasingly she makes the descent on her own volition to save her *sestras*, a turning point I will argue is symbolized when she devours the scorpion Pupok, the externalization of her own self-doubts disguised as self-preservation. Her periods of imprisonment at the New Order Prolethean ranch and the Castor compound and her escapes are prime examples of the story pattern, and her disappearance and return in Season 4 and her arc in the fifth season grow from these experiences. Helena expands her role as avenging angel on behalf of her growing family of *sestras* and their mothers, brothers, spouses, her children and theirs and develops into a shaman and storyteller for the group.

Goddesses and Heroines

Let us first revisit briefly the four central stories of the goddess's descent that I want us to keep in mind.

Inanna

Inanna is the most ancient and powerful of these figures, the ur-legend of the female descent to hell (pun intended). Her story has come down to us in incomplete and fragmentary form. Inanna was the great Sumerian goddess of love, fertility, wisdom, and war and was associated with the planet Venus. Inanna goes to hell to visit her sister Ereshkigal, goddess of the underworld, instructing her servant Ninshubar to raise the alarm if she does not return in three days. As poet Kim Echlin has translated the story,

> The marriage bed was not wide enough for her.
> Heaven and earth were not wide enough for her.
> Inanna wanted to go to the underworld.
> She wanted the divine power of the underworld [50].

At each of the seven gates of hell, she is stripped of her ornaments or garments and their associated power and finally stands naked before Ereshkigal, but orders her sister off the throne and sits there herself. Ereshkigal "fasten[s] on Inanna the eye of death" (Wolkstein 60) and hangs her corpse on a hook. She is revived and rescued by helpers sent by her servant.

Inanna, on her return from Hell with the incorporated powers of her encounter with her dark sister Ereshkigal, brings back violence and terror, war and storms, to her people:

> Inanna was now a fierce warrior
> She walked through heaven and over earth.
> ....
> "I will fill the soaring mountain with terror.
> Let my holy games begin!"
> ....
> Inanna roared
> like thunder.
> She was drenched
> with blood [Echlin 66–67].

But in the end she incorporates this wild power and is praised as the protector and creator of her people.

Persephone

The myth of Persephone is also quite ancient, its oldest versions predating the establishment of the familiar Greek pantheon and forming, with the worship of her mother Demeter, the core of the Eleusinian mysteries. Kore (Persephone's name before her descent, simply meaning girl or maiden) is gathering flowers when she is abducted by Hades, god of the underworld. Demeter neglects her care of the earth and causes great suffering during her search for her daughter, and finally Zeus, who permitted the abduction, forces Hades to give her up. She is brought up out of hell to be reunited with her mother by Hermes and Hecate, figures of magic and spiritual guidance. But because Persephone ate six pomegranate seeds while in Hell, she must return there for six months out of the year as its queen.

And yet this is not entirely a punishment; she may very well have eaten the seeds intentionally, in spite of the story she tells Demeter, for as the queen of hell she becomes "powerful, autonomous, feared, and respected" (Agha-Jaffar 49), "free of domination by either her mother or her spouse" (51), and in fact her mother's equal (55).

Typically, this is interpreted as a myth about the origins of the seasons, or more broadly about the cycle of life and death, and the Eleusinian mysteries were concerned with the survival of the soul after death.[1] Because of Persephone's descent and symbolic death, she linked Olympus and Hades, and served as "the Mediatrix between two divine worlds" (Eliade, qtd. in Patterson 172).

Psyche

The myth of Psyche, told in its fullest form in Apuleius's 2nd century AD Latin novel *The Golden Ass*, is usually read as a metaphor for the soul reaching its full growth through the transforming power of love. Overshadowed by the familiar story of Psyche's search for her missing lover is the perhaps far older story of her relationship with her lover's mother, Aphrodite or Venus, who serves as a "Ruthless Mentor" (Frankel 5).[2]

In most versions of the original myth, Psyche is a mortal of goddess-like beauty. Eros, son of Aphrodite, falls in love with her and takes her away to his secret palace but visits her only in darkness. Eros flees to his mother after Psyche, prodded by her jealous sisters, takes a forbidden look at her mysterious lover, and Aphrodite takes vengeance on Psyche, separating her from Eros and leaving her alone and pregnant. Psyche realizes she must reach an accommodation with Aphrodite if she is to win Eros back. She humbles herself to the goddess, who sets her four impossible tasks.

The final task Aphrodite gives Psyche is to go to the goddess Persephone in the underworld and bring back a casket filled with one day's worth of her beauty. The danger in this ultimate task is that Psyche may not be able to enter Hades without losing her life in the process, and even if she makes it in alive, she might not be allowed to return to the land of the living. But she does find her way safely to Persephone and is careful to sit humbly on the ground rather than on the comfortable chair she is offered, and to eat nothing but a piece of common bread—knowing how Persephone was tricked by the pomegranate seeds (Apuleius 139). However, as Psyche is returning to the land of the living, she gives in to the temptation to take a drop of beauty for herself from the casket, and falls into a profound death-like sleep from which Eros must awaken her. Upon awakening, she is taken to Olympus, made immortal, married to Eros, and bears their daughter, Pleasure. In spite of, or perhaps because of, her disobedience to the final command of her mother-in-law and harsh mentor Aphrodite, Psyche is rewarded and elevated.[3]

Eurydice

The story of Eurydice is another one with many variants, the oldest perhaps recorded by Plato but popularized later by Ovid and Virgil. In the most familiar version, Eurydice is the beloved wife of the musician Orpheus. In an echo of Hades's abduction of Persephone, she is pursued by the god or shepherd Aristeus, bitten by a viper, and dies. Orpheus travels to Hell and plays his lyre so beautifully that Hades and Persephone relent and allow him to lead Eurydice back to the land of the living—with only the caveat that he must not look back at her until they both reach the upper world. At the last moment, fearing Eurydice is not really behind him (and in some versions of the tale, she is not—it is just an apparition), Orpheus turns to look at her, and Eurydice must return to hell.

Eurydice is the virtuous but entirely passive female who fails even to be rescued. Her descent into hell is involuntary; besides mourning her fate, she takes no active role in trying to escape, and whether she escapes or not is entirely up to the actions of Orpheus, whose story this really is. In some more cynical retellings of the tale, in fact, she nags him so much on the way out of Hades that he turns back and looks at her deliberately. As Janet Halfyard points out in a perceptive article on the Orpheus myth in *Buffy the Vampire Slayer*, however, it is possible for a heroine to play "a multifaceted role in relation to the myth," playing both the rescuing hero and the one who needs to be rescued at different points in the story (41); these "reversals and juxtapositions" of the myth thus become a commentary on success and failure, on the potential for salvific action and passivity within the same person (42).

Joseph Campbell interprets the myth of Inanna as the confrontation and assimilation of the opposite (*Hero* 89), and this is the mystery at the heart of all of these tales. Valerie Estelle Frankel asserts that the "descent was a desirable initiation made by female seekers of knowledge" in the ancient matriarchal traditions (124), in which she must face and confront her "dark sister," reintegrating her powers—that is, her own dark side, her shadow-self. And "[a]s teacher of independence, the evil stepmother [or other opposing older female] is essential to the story" (Frankel 38); as I noted earlier, as Aphrodite is to Psyche, she is the "ruthless mentor" who teaches the heroine to acknowledge and embrace the opposing shadow inside herself.

Helena: Season 1 and the Graphic Novels

Now let us finally turn to *Orphan Black*. Helena is one of a group of sister-clones called the Leda project (all played by Tatiana Maslany), bred by the shadowy Dyad Institute and its even more mysterious parent organization

Neolution as part of its project to secure immortality for the powerful elite of the world. Unlike their para-military brothers in the Castor project (all played by Ari Millen), cloned from the same original and brought up as self-aware, the Leda clones were carried by in-vitro surrogate mothers widely scattered around the globe and kept ignorant of each other—with the exception of Rachel, raised as self-aware by her guardian, Aldous Leekie (Matt Frewer), after the (supposed) deaths of the founders of the project, her adoptive parents Ethan (Andrew Gillies) and Susan (Rosemary Dunsmore) Duncan.

Helena is the biological (and mirror) twin of Sarah Manning, who is our main viewpoint character from the start of the series. Like Buffy the Vampire Slayer (Sarah Michelle Gellar), Helena is a deceptively fragile-looking petite blonde. Sarah and Helena's birth mother, Amelia (Melanie Nicholls-King), went into hiding when she grew suspicious of the couple who paid her to be their surrogate, had the children in secret, and gave Sarah up to be a ward of the state and her twin, Helena, to a convent in Ukraine. The Dyad Institute had long sought Helena, but was initially unaware of the twinning of the embryo and of Sarah's existence ("Unconscious Selection," 1.9), though Ethan Duncan did know there was a child "lost in the foster system" ("History Yet to Be Written," 3.10).

Helena's life in the convent was unpleasant enough to be considered a first descent into hell. She says, "When I was seven, the nuns said I had devils inside me" ("*Ipsa Scientia Potestas Est*," 2.5); they frequently disciplined her, and she developed a fiercely protective attitude towards other children. Episode 5.9 ("One Fettered Slave") reveals more of this back-story; she was caught witnessing the Mother Superior masturbating and was locked in a closet after the nun poured a gallon of bleach over her black hair. At the age of twelve, she was located and taken away by Maggie Chen (Uni Park), a double agent within the Dyad organization, and Tomas (Daniel Kash). Both were members of the fundamentalist Prolethean cult and indoctrinated and trained Helena to locate and kill the other Leda clones, telling her that she was the original and they were abominations. Watching her play with her doll house, Tomas says to the girl, "Tell me about the copies." She replies, "They walk the earth while the original is at home with God. I protect her from science devils" (5.9).

Maggie and Tomas are the king and queen of hell in this phase, playing good cop/bad cop games with her mind. In a frequently recurring phrase, Helena she is told that she is "the light," and the other clones are of the darkness. After her first kill, when she discovers that her victim shares her face, Tomas tells her, "You are the original…. You are the light" (5.9; see also Manson et al., part 2). This reinforces but also subverts the mythic pattern of seeking out and confronting the shadow-sister at the nadir of the descent into hell. Assassinating the shadow-sister from afar, destroying rather than learning from and absorbing her powers, is a fruitless path and prevents Helena from moving forward in her development. It is also noteworthy for the symbolism of light that Helena continues to bleach her dark hair long after the initial punishment ("Behind the Scenes: Hair and Makeup"; the dark roots are deliberate to show this), and often appears backlit with her wild hair like a halo.

The *Orphan Black* comic book tie-in begins after Chen and Tomas take her from the convent and reveals that Helena killed three of her sisters in Europe before the Proletheans moved operations to Canada (Manson et al., part 2). In the *Helsinki* comic, also a prequel, she kills at least one more (Fawcett et al., part 2).[4] Helena is an Ereshkigal looking at her many sisters with the eyes of death: "Dirty copies—they pervert His original. [...] I will cleanse them from this earth" (5.9). In the first television season, she has been stalking clone Beth Childs, the police detective who killed Maggie Chen and whose identity Sarah assumed after witnessing her suicide. In her first encounter with Sarah, Helena hesitates, sensing something different about her and refraining from killing her ("Variation Under Nature," 1.3). With this hesitation about killing Sarah, she starts to break away from the path laid out for her by the Proletheans and begin a more fruitful journey to understanding and reconciliation with her shadow-selves. Sarah, not so hesitant, stabs her with a piece of rebar.

Helena tracks Sarah to the home of her adoptive mother, Mrs. S (Maria Doyle Kennedy), meets Sarah's daughter, Kira, and then refuses to betray Sarah and Kira to Tomas. Sarah prevents Helena from killing Tomas when she turns on him, but Helena then kills their birth-mother for her part in Helena's tormented life, thinking she is finally destroying the queen of her hell: "You gave me to them. You let them make me this way" ("Endless Forms Most Beautiful," 1.10). "She separated us; she tore us apart," she justifies herself to Sarah, and begs, "Sarah, we make a family, yes?," but Sarah instead shoots her at point blank range.

Reading Season 1 from Helena's point of view, it is about Helena finding *her* shadow, Sarah. Helena begins to come to an acceptance of the humanity of the other clones, realizing she's been lied to and manipulated by Chen and Tomas and tracing it all back to Amelia and her fatal decision to give her to a convent. She must see her sisters *as* sisters and potential family, not abominable copies, to move on to her next phase.

Season 2: The Prolethean Ranch

Season 2 begins with Helena, who managed to drag herself to the hospital, being abducted by the breakaway New Order Proletheans, to whom

Tomas has gone for help and for whom she represents a golden opportunity to further their technologically-assisted breeding mission. Helena passively asks, "Who are you?" as the mysterious Mark (Ari Millen) wheels her out of the hospital; he answers, "Family" ("Governed by Sound Reason and True Religion," 2.2; this is doubly meaningful, as he is also her brother Castor clone).

Not all at the Prolethean ranch are willing to accept her as family. Gracie (Zoé de Grand'Maison), daughter of the group's leader, Henrik Johannsen (Peter Outerbridge), thinks her a soulless abomination, and Tomas thinks any child she would bear would be a monster—but Tomas is quickly disposed of by Mark, while Henrik proclaims, "It's a brand new day" (2.2). Helena is fed drugged food—a close-up on a half-eaten cluster of grapes evokes the image of Persephone's pomegranate seeds—and, while dazed, she is dressed in a wedding gown and ceremonially hand-fasted to Henrik, who then carries her down a long hall to the laboratory. The plastic veils part before them in a graphic representation of symbolic rape, "a death of girlhood" (Patterson 179), as Henrik prepares to harvest her eggs.

Helena awakens, tended by Henrik's wife Bonnie (Kristin Booth), the queen of this particular hell. Helena is still in her wedding gown, her feet bare and a ring on her finger. The architecture of the attic room where she is imprisoned is church-like, and her bed is an island in the middle of the floor. Grace later tries to suffocate her, but Helena overpowers her and runs. She stumbles upon the lab as she seeks a way out, the red edges of the plastic sheeting parting like labial folds, and, in a disorienting flashback, remembers what was done to her there.

She flees to Mrs. S's house, the one potentially safe place left to her, just in time to track Sarah from there to Rachel's vacant apartment. There she kills Daniel (Matthew Bennett), Rachel's monitor and bodyguard, who had been torturing Sarah there for the location of Kira. Horrified by the sight of Helena, still in her in her bedraggled wedding dress and carrying a knife dripping blood, Sarah cries out, "I shot you! You were dead!" Helena clings to her for comfort: "I need your help. Don't send me back. I was married. I think he took something from inside of me" ("Governed as It Were by Chance," 2.4). While Helena is now committed to Sarah as her true family, Sarah still needs further proof of Helena's loyalty, which Helena later hopes to provide by killing Rachel: "Rachel is problem. I fix problem." In talking her down from her sniper's nest overlooking Rachel's apartment, Sarah finally says, "You saved my life. You're my sister" (2.5).

A shot early in the next episode reinforces their new acceptance of each other, a restoration of family after an escape from hell: in their tent on the road to investigate a lead, they are shown curled up like a yin-yang symbol, dark and light as two mirrored parts of a whole ("To Hound Nature in Her Wanderings," 2.6; an image Amelia also used to describe the twins in her womb in 1.9). Helena has become another of the many people that Sarah "put[s] [...] under [her] wing," as her adoptive brother, Felix (Jordan Gavaris), describes it; when Sarah decides someone is family, she becomes their fierce protector and advocate ("The Weight of This Combination," 3.1). But they are soon separated again. Helena's budding romance with "Jesse Towing" (Patrick J. Adams) is broken up by a bar fight, and she finds herself being bailed out by Gracie, who has the perfect leverage to get her to return to the Prolethean ranch: "Helena, we want to take you to your children." "He stole my babies from me." "Your eggs. My father—he made them whole for you." Helena leaves willingly with Gracie and Mark; "Take me to my babies," she says (2.6).

Henrik implants some of the now-fertilized embryos in Helena's womb—but also, monstrously, in his own daughter Gracie. Monstrously, because the eggs were fertilized with his own sperm, as Gracie reveals to Helena in the infirmary afterwards. Helena and Gracie plan to escape but are caught by Henrik; in the ensuing struggle, Helena tells Mark and Gracie to run while she has Henrik down. Like her rescue of Sarah from the Dyad agent in an earlier episode, Helena is starting to rescue others from hell before escaping herself, a new pattern. Helena tortures Henrik gruesomely and fittingly with a cow inseminator, then burns down the ranch—a purification of a place of torment by fire. A beautifully framed Orphic moment closes out this particular descent into hell: Helena pregnant and triumphant, carrying the canister containing her remaining frozen embryos, looking back at the flames—rescuing all of her children, even those implanted in Gracie ("Things Which Have Never Yet Been Done," 2.9).[5] Mrs. S articulates a similar motivation later in another context, when she says "[...] I did what any mother would do. I gathered my children, and I left" ("Transitory Sacrifices of Crisis," 3.2).[6]

The final episode of the season closes with the "clone dance party" in Sarah's brother Felix's loft, a technical triumph of cinematography, but also deeply meaningful to the story. Helena is pregnant, on the run, anxious to search for her "boyfriend" Jesse—a very Psyche-like moment. But she is also finally being accepted as family—meeting clones Cosima and Alison, reuniting with Kira, and being grudgingly accepted by Felix. The clone dance party is a heavenly moment of "carnival": "liminal, [...] a moment of suspension between two states, of openness to transformation [...] a place of becoming in which differences diminish and commonalities matter" (Solnit 168–69). In this carnival moment, past conflicts are forgiven, and the family is restored. Helena even implies later that this party marked the moment when she stopped needing to ritually cut herself ("Let the Children and Childbearers Toil," 5.4).[7] But it only lasts a moment; Helena slips out in search of Jesse, having hidden the canister, but is abducted nearly as soon as she closes the door behind her ("By Means Which Have Never Yet Been Tried," 2.10). Her secretive habits have kept her from fully trusting her new-found sisterly bond and involving them in her plans, and thus she is imperiled.

Season 3: The Castor Compound

In the opening sequence of Season 3, Helena dreams of her baby shower. Her sisters are all there, healthy and happy, cooking her favorite foods and giving her presents. She wears a feminine pink dress and flowers in her hair, imagery of the Kore or maiden (Patterson 170)—but, like Persephone, she has been abducted to hell.

A scorpion crawls out of her dress, and she awakens to find herself trapped in a coffin-like box. This is the first appearance of the scorpion Pupok in the show, but the graphic novels reveal that Pupok has been a part of her life since childhood, appearing in moments of testing and self-doubt and externalizing a detached and calculating part of Helena concerned with self-preservation at all costs. In the *Orphan Black* comic, Pupok comments to Helena, "You like cages very much, yes? You spend a lot of time in them" (Manson et al., part 2). The scorpion is a multivalent symbol in mythology, representing both evil and protection from evil. Pupok's words in this episode point out the parallel to Psyche's story: "You're being tested again. This time you're carrying a child" (3.1).

Helena has again been betrayed by a mother-figure: Mrs. S has given her to the Castor project in return for the safe return of the kidnapped Kira by their parent organization, Topside. Sarah is now as fully committed to Helena as Helena to her; when she finds out about Helena, she rejects Mrs. S and makes Helena's recovery her primary concern.

At the Castor project's encampment, Helena encounters another queen of hell, Virginia Coady (Kyra Harper), mother-figure to the Castor clone group, who tells Helena, "Your family sold you out," but "[…] you're not expendable to me" (3.2). Her interest in Helena is, however, solely in the service of the mission of the Castor cloning project. She is looking for a cure for the fatal "glitches" her "boys" are experiencing. The deeper purpose of the Castor project is chilling: weaponized sterility, transmitted sexually by the male clones, to be used to slowly wipe out an enemy population over a generation or so; as revealed in the final episodes of Season 5, all in the service of wealthy, powerful elites bent on having the world's resources to themselves.

Helena manages to escape from her cell but is distracted by the plight of Parsons, one of the Castor clones being held for observation as he dies. He begs her to kill him. "We've both been abandoned by our families—left to suffer. I will make it go away," she promises and tenderly releases him. She confronts Coady as she is recaptured: "You say you love boys, but you lie. You're a shit mother!" ("Newer Elements of Our Defence," 3.4).

Sarah is also captured and placed in the adjoining cell, but Helena does not trust her, even though Sarah tells her about Mrs. S. When Helena gets another chance to escape, food is a part of the plan; in contrast to the pomegranate imagery of the poisoned grapes at the Prolethean ranch, here she uses a chewed bone to pick the lock in her first attempt, and butter to grease her way out the second time. There is also food imagery in her arguments with Sarah: "You want to be my sandwich? […] In Siberia, when planning escape, you take weak person with you. They are called 'sandwich' because you eat them" ("Scarred by Many Past Frustrations," 3.5).

Helena makes it out into the desert but is torn about leaving Sarah prisoner; finally, in one of her hallucinatory conversations with Pupok, she eats the scorpion, silencing the doubting, self-centered voice and turning back for her sister ("Certain Agony of the Battlefield," 3.6). As mentioned above, a scorpion can signify both evil and protection from evil. "Pupok" means "belly-button" in Ukrainian, and the omphalos or navel is a powerful mythic and shamanic symbol of the center of the world and of connections between worlds. Here Pupok symbolizes something central to the character of Helena—and is also voiced by Tatiana Maslany, cementing the identification. A similar image of devouring a scorpion-like creature, as a symbol for conquering, owning, accepting, and incorporating a darker part of one's self, occurs in the comic book series *Promethea*, in the February 2002 issue "Red Glare!"[8] Like Inanna, Persephone, and Psyche, and like Promethea, Helena has integrated the power of the underworld into her own being.

Though it is not Helena's doing this time (Paul Dierden [Dylan Bruce] set off a grenade with his last bit of remaining strength), the pattern established by the destruction of the Prolethean ranch repeats as once again a place of torment goes up in flames behind them as they escape. In Mexico they are met by Mrs. S, and Helena reconciles with her after threatening violence. Again, the escape from hell is followed by the re-formation of the family, as in other myths: "You can't have Sarah without the rest of her family, I'm afraid," Mrs. S says to her ("Community of Dreadful Fear and Hate," 3.7).

Helena is then placed with the Hendrixes—another family model, consisting of clone Alison, her husband, Donnie (Kristian Bruun), and their two adopted children, Oscar and Gemma (Drew Davis and Millie Davis). She helps make soap for their business, a symbolic action of self-purification, and also helps clean up a problem they are having with their drug-dealing sideline and the gang behind it, rescuing her canister of frozen embryos yet again and leaving a bloodbath behind her: "You should not threaten babies," she growls at gang leader Pouchy (Tony Cianchino), protecting Gemma and Oscar as well as her own unborn children ("Insolvent Phantom of Tomorrow,"

3.9). Donnie engineers a reunion with "Jesse Towing" for her in the final episode of the season. But it is not consummated, as Helena is called away to deal with Rudy, one of the Castor clones—as with Parsons, in the end, she serves as an angel of death to ease him gently, but with no forgiveness for his sins, out of his painful life (3.10).

Season 4: Hermit and Shaman

Season 4 marks an important new trajectory for Helena. At the beginning she lives in an uneasy equilibrium in the suburban Hendrix household, posing as Donnie's wife for pre-natal checkups and for an interrogation when the police connect the murders of the gang members to Alison's political campaign. Helena has a talk with Donnie in the fourth episode in which she realizes that Alison, whose sterility is a part of the Leda project design, is "jealous and angry, because me having babies and bringing the police." (Sarah and Helena are unique among the clones in being fertile.[9]) Sensitive to the stress she is placing on the Hendrixes, Helena buries the canister of embryos and leaves: "Little science babies, forgive me. I did not know to feed you liquid nitrogens. But your twins are in my belly, and when they are old, I will tell them all about you and our adventures" ("From Instinct to Rational Control," 4.4).

Her return in the ninth episode is full of shamanic imagery. She has been living alone in the north woods; we first see her rise, clad in furs, from a blind on the snow-covered forest floor, kill a deer, and carry it back to her camp with its round bough-covered hut and home-made altar. The crossbow she uses has Orphic echoes, as Halfyard points out in relation to Buffy's use of this weapon: "the bowed and pointed shape of [Buffy's] crossbow [echoes] both the bowed and pointed shape of Orpheus's lyre and indeed its physical construction as a strung wooden instrument" (Halfyard 43).

Helena phones Sarah to check in and, concerned about her evasiveness, returns just in time to save Alison and Donnie from being tortured and killed by a Neolutionist, neatly and efficiently shooting an arrow through his neck. Neatness and efficiency are important here. The Helena we have come to know has usually been either ritualistic or unrestrained in her violence, whether against her sisters or her enemies. Here we see her calmly assess the situation and take care of it with no fuss; no severed Barbie doll heads or stick figures drawn on the wall or self-mutilation as in her early days as an assassin, no torture or buckets of blood as with Henrik or the Pouchy gang; she has integrated her uncontrolled side and takes the Neolutionist down like a deer in the woods ("The Mitigation of Competition," 4.9).

Donnie and Alison have gotten in too deep and Helena pulls them out of hell. "[Helena] is our avenging angel," Alison says: "She saved our lives, she cleansed our sins with fire, we are forgiven, and I would lay down my life for that sweet little thing" ("From Dancing Mice to Psychopaths," 4.10). How exactly their sins were "cleansed with fire" we never find out, though it could have something to do with her disposal of the corpse of the Neolutionist, which is *not* added to the growing collection under the floor of the Hendrix garage.

Halfyard notes of Buffy the Vampire Slayer's long story arc that she makes multiple descents, taking her further down into hell, and eventually "come[s] back up along the chain [of descents] and rescue[s] everyone else" (45), as Helena is doing here: "it falls to her to bring people back when they are lost to the darkness" (47).[10] The female quest is often centripetal (Patterson 170), spiraling inward, but also must, at times, function centrifugally, spiraling outward in order to return the necessary boon to society; in this penultimate season Helena has taken an internal vision or spiritual quest while hidden from us and come back stronger, more focused, and able to spiral out, to act as an Orphic rescuer and shamanic guide to other characters.[11]

Season 5: Radiant and Transcendent Motherhood

In the first episode of the final season, the Hendrixes and Helena are tracked to their forest hide-out by a corrupt cop in Rachel's pay; Helena is badly injured in the fight which follows, a stick penetrating her abdomen and injuring one of the fetuses as she saves Donnie's life ("The Few Who Dare," 5.1). In the second episode we learn that her babies share Kira's remarkable ability to recover from injury. "Like Sarah, I make miracle babies," she says; realizing that she will be even more sought after by Neolution now, she runs to find a new place to hide ("Clutch of Greed," 5.2).

In an interesting twist, she shelters in a convent with Sister Irina (Eileen Sword), a nun who once protected her as a child in Ukraine. Aside from the fact that it is an unexpected place for her to hide, why the convent? It may seem like a return to her very first hell, but it is not hell anymore. Helena has a friend and ally here, she is protected rather than abused, she has a place with her *sestras*, and she is no longer an emotionally vulnerable child but a woman on the brink of motherhood. On a psychological level, Helena now has the shamanic power to move between realms. Upon her return to the upper world, Inanna incorporated the power of hell into herself. Psyche, too, gained power from her descent into hell; tasting the drop of beauty from Persephone's casket was part of her transformation from human to goddess. When Persephone herself makes her annual return to Hades, it is as queen, not as a terrified, abducted virgin. Helena, like Persephone, may find it empowering to "return to the underworld [...] to renew her status as queen of that realm" (Agha-Jaffar 49), in effect "assuming responsibility for her own healing and transformation" (54). Like her retreat into the woods, this is an inward journey she chooses for herself, rather than one she is forced to take. When Sarah visits her at the convent in episode four, it is a touching reconciliation; Helena's observation that Sarah's "heart is heavy" is an invitation to the confessional, and Sarah shares her worries about Kira with her twin, her "other self," and receives comfort and guidance in return. Like a shaman guiding others along the path, Helena prepares to communicate the lessons learned on her inward journey: she writes out and illustrates her story for her soon-to-be-born babies, telling of "my joys, my pain and sorrows, so they will walk a brighter path" (5.4), and in the end will share the story with her *sestras* as well.

Long-lost Gracie, who miscarried the child who was from the same group of fertilized embryos as the two in Helena's womb, tracks her to the convent and tells her that her husband, Mark, is dead, and she is alone in the world. But she has been sent to find Helena as the price for Coady to continue giving Mark the treatments that keep him alive. Helena reminds Gracie that she still has family—her unborn nephews—and Gracie shifts allegiances, lying to protect her, but the GPS on her phone gives them away. Gracie is executed and Helena captured ("Guillotines Decide," 5.8). Here Gracie plays the part of Psyche, seeking a boon from Helena/Persephone so that she may gain back her lover from Coady/Aphrodite. But Helena is not yet powerful enough to save Grace or protect herself.

Helena must descend into hell one last time. Taken by Coady to the old Dyad Institute basements, she will be forced into premature labor so that her umbilical cord blood can be harvested for P.T. Westmorland (Stephen McHattie), the man behind Neolution, who, in his impatience, sweeps through the plastic veiling around the birthing chamber in an echo of the rape imagery at the Prolethean ranch. When Helena begs her not to take her babies, Coady mockingly goads her: "What kind of mother could you possibly be?" Unable to escape, unwilling to allow her babies to be subjects for the next generation of Neolution experiments, Helena attempts suicide, reaching the very nadir of her many descents. But here, again, her relationship with her twin, Sarah, saves her; a direct transfusion of Sarah's blood, a viscerally physical representation of union with the shadow-sister, calls her back from the brink. The image of the two sisters connected by a slender tube of blood calls to mind Frida Kahlo's painting "The Two Fridas" (1939)—symbolic of the essential but vastly complicated unity of self and shadow-self.[12] Infused with Sarah's strength, Helena overcomes Coady, and they make their escape further into the basements (5.9)—sisters making the last descent further into hell together.

In the final episode Helena gives birth on the floor in a boiler room deep under the Dyad labs, "down here in the filth and garbage" as Coady says upon catching up with her, but as closely connected to the shamanically powerful earth itself as possible in her captivity. The scene not only intercuts with Sarah's memories of giving birth to Kira, but echoes the birth of Sarah and Helena themselves in a makeshift room in Wales ("To Right the Wrongs of Many," 5.10; Manson et al. §1).

More pertinent to our theme, however, is the long denouement of the episode in which loose ends are tied up, and the clones all must figure out "what to do with their freedom," as co-creator Graeme Manson puts it in one of the commentaries ("Clone-Centric"). Again, shamanic imagery abounds in our glimpses of Helena's life as a new mother. She lives with her twin boys in the Hendrix's semi-finished garage, a place redolent of death and secrecy (her fight to the death with Rudy; the site of bodies buried, dug up, desecrated, and buried again) and of sexual energy (Alison's passion for Donnie re-awakened by their shared crime, Helena's frustrated reunion with Jesse in a truck parked half-in, half-out of the garage). It is transformed into a place of light and life; angelic stick figures made of twigs and feathers dangle in the sunlight above the bassinets and recall Helena's hut in the woods, colorful art hangs on the walls, and the babies nap in hammocks suspended between sky and ground. This pole reaches down into the earth; death and passion are not erased but remain as a foundation for life. The adjoining enclosed garden is a *hortus conclusus*, an earthly paradise representing the skyward pole; it is open to heaven, but also grounded by the now-marked and tended grave of the "science babies." In this garden Helena's dream baby shower is re-created, but with a vastly expanded family and no hidden scorpion. Here the sisters are healed by sharing their feelings of failure as mothers, and Helena cements their bond by telling them all their own story from her book. Here, too, is where she finally names her babies—"It is time for you to take the names of real men"—Arthur and Donald, kingly names and role models to live up to.

Conclusion

According to Valerie Frankel's study of the heroine's journey in world mythology, in many of the stories she collects and interprets, "[t]he heroine's goal is to become a complete mother, resplendent with power. If her family is shattered [...] she cannot become whole without assembling the pieces. [...] [T]he heroine quests to create a family" (Frankel 145). While in stories and myths, motherhood and restoration of the family are often explicit goals, they can of course also be mythical metaphors for a woman's fully productive and connected life. But in Helena's case the quest is quite literal, and the final scenes of the last episode show Helena as a resplendent mother indeed. Helena's mission was to save and restore her shattered family, shattered in part though her murders of her own sisters for the Proletheans and her lack of knowledge that let her "science babies" die. Confronting and not killing her shadow/mirror/twin Sarah changed Helena's path; through her repeated descents into hell, she became the hero, shaman, and storyteller who could "make a family" out of her damaged and scattered kin.

In *Orphan Black*, the success of Helena and her sisters in finally taking down Neolution has truly global implications. As Lee Edwards observes of Psyche's descent to hell, "Like Prometheus, [Psyche] steals immortal secrets for humanity" (10). The Leda clones save the whole world, not just themselves, from the chilling elitist future envisioned by the Neolutionist project. "Stronger together" is the main lesson the series teaches; for some characters, and especially Helena, the strength they add to the group is a direct result of their own repeated, traumatic, and eventually deliberate and triumphant descents into hell.

NOTES

1. In some interpretations of the mysteries, it is thought that worshippers were shown Persephone's son by Hades, Brimos or Iacchus, and told "the goddess of death had borne a son in the fire" (Wasson et al., qtd. in Patterson 172)—the birth of a holy child out of death.

2. C.S. Lewis uses this story as the basis for his final novel, *Till We Have Faces*. Orual's relationship with the goddess Ungit explores this aspect of the tale.

3. As Lee R. Edwards points out, in patriarchal myth, "Heroines typically have sons, hostages to patriarchy, signs [...] that they have been incorporated again into an unchanged world" (13–14). Persephone, as we have seen, bears a son; Psyche, whom Edwards argues is a mold-breaking female hero rather than a heroine, has a daughter. There is a strong emphasis on the female line of descent in *Orphan Black*; though there are sound scientific reasons for it, there is also a mythic rightness to it. However, Helena bears twin sons in the end; a reference back to the Castor and Pollux myth, namesake of the male clone branch, as well as to Henrik Johanssen's god-complex.

4. The third series of comic books is an alternate-universe retelling in which Beth does not die.

5. The tie-in book *Classified Clone Reports* mentions that Helena also got the women and children out of the ranch before they could be harmed by the fire (DeCandido 80).

6. For more on the representation of mothers and mothering, see both Newman and Howell in this volume.

7. The angel wing cuttings began while she still had the blood of her first kill on her hands (5.9), but the habit of cutting in general might have begun even earlier, as she says she had done this since she was small. Helena does cut herself at least once after the dance party, when she finds a nail in her cell in the Castor encampment (3.5)—but this is at a point when she feels she has been betrayed by Sarah.

8. My thanks to David Emerson for this reference.

9. For more on the representation of infertility in *Orphan Black*, see Buckman, Bell, Bonnevier, Newman, and Wilson in this volume.

10. While Halfyard specifically references Willow (Alyson Hannigan) here as another Orpheus-figure, the statement is equally applicable to Buffy.

11. Note that in Season 5, Alison similarly goes on a voyage of self-discovery away from our view and from the other clones; she leaves in "Beneath Her Heart," 5.3, and returns

in "Gag or Throttle," 5.7, when she donates all her craft supplies to charity and turns to music instead.
    12. In fact, artwork referencing this painting was used in publicity materials for this episode.

WORKS CITED

Agha-Jaffar, Tamara. *Demeter and Persephone: Lessons from a Myth.* McFarland, 2002.
Apuleius. *The Transformations of Lucius, Otherwise Known As, the Golden Ass.* Robert Graves, trans. Farrar Straus & Young, 1951.
"Behind the Scenes: Hair and Makeup." *Orphan Black.* Season 2 Blu-Ray bonus feature. 2014.
"Beneath Her Heart." Writ. Alex Levine. Dir. David Wellington. *Orphan Black.* Season 5, episode 3. First aired 24 June 2017.
"By Means Which Have Never Yet Been Tried." Writ. Graeme Manson. Dir. John Fawcett. *Orphan Black.* Season 2, episode 10. First aired 21 June 2014.
Campbell, Joseph. *The Hero with a Thousand Faces.* New World Library, 2008.
_____, and Bill D. Moyers. *The Power of Myth.* 1st edition, Doubleday, 1988.
"Certain Agony of the Battlefield." Writ. Aubrey Nealon. Dir. Helen Shaver. *Orphan Black.* Season 3, episode 6. First aired 23 May 2015.
"Clone-Centric." *Orphan Black.* Season 5 Blu-Ray bonus feature. 2017.
"Clutch of Greed." Writ. Jeremy Boxson. Dir. John Fawcett. *Orphan Black.* Season 5, episode 2. First aired 17 June 2017.
"Community of Dreadful Fear and Hate." Writ. Sherry White. Dir. Ken Girotti. *Orphan Black.* Season 3, episode 7. First aired 30 May 2015.
Croft, Janet Brennan. "Psyche in New York: The Devil Wears Prada Updates the Myth." *Mythlore*, vol. 30, no. 3/4 (#117/118), 2012, pp. 55–69.
DeCandido, Keith R.A. *Orphan Black: Classified Clone Reports: Confidential.* HarperCollinsPublishers, 2017.
Echlin, Kim, and Linda Wolfsgruber, ill. *Inanna: from the Myths of Ancient Sumer.* Groundwood Books, 2003.
Edwards, Lee R. *Psyche as Hero: Female Heroism and Fictional Form.* Wesleyan UP, 1987.
"Endless Forms Most Beautiful." Writ. Graeme Manson. Dir. John Fawcett. *Orphan Black.* Season 1, episode 10. First aired 1 June 2013.
Fawcett, John et al. *Orphan Black: Helsinki.* Idea and Design Works, 2016. *Orphan Black*, vol. 2.
"The Few Who Dare." Writ. Graeme Manson. Dir. John Fawcett. *Orphan Black.* Season 5, episode 1. First aired 10 June 2017.
Frankel, Valerie. *From Girl to Goddess: The Heroine's Journey Through Myth and Legend.* McFarland, 2010.
"From Dancing Mice to Psychopaths." Writ. Graeme Manson. Dir. John Fawcett. *Orphan Black.* Season 4, episode 10. First aired 16 June 2016.
"From Instinct to Rational Control." Writ. Alex Levine. Dir. Peter Stebbings. *Orphan Black.* Season 4, episode 4. First aired 5 May 2016.
"Gag or Throttle." Writ. Renée St. Cyr. Dir. David Frazee. *Orphan Black.* Season 5, episode 7. First aired 22 July 2017.
"Governed as It Were by Chance." Writ. Russ Cochrane. Dir. David Frazee. *Orphan Black.* Season 2, episode 4. First aired 10 May 2014.
"Governed by Sound Reason and True Religion." Writ. Karen Walton and Graeme Manson. Dir. John Fawcett. *Orphan Black.* Season 2, episode 2. First aired 26 April 2014.
"Guillotines Decide." Writ. Aisha Porter-Christie and Graeme Manson. Dir. Aaron Morton. *Orphan Black.* Season 5, episode 8. First aired 5 August 2017.
Halfyard, Janet K. "Hero's Journey, Heroine's Return? Buffy, Eurydice, and the Orpheus Myth." *Reading Joss Whedon*, edited by Rhonda V. Wilcox et al., Syracuse UP, 2014, pp. 40–52.
"History Yet to Be Written." Writ. Graeme Manson. Dir. John Fawcett. *Orphan Black.* Season 3, episode 10. First aired 20 June 2015.

"Insolvent Phantom of Tomorrow." Writ. Russ Cochrane. Dir. Vincenzo Natali. *Orphan Black*. Season 3, episode 9. First aired 13 June 2015.
"*Ipsa Scientia Potestas Est*." Writ. Tony Elliott. Dir. Helen Shaver. *Orphan Black*. Season 2, episode 5. First aired 17 May 2014.
Jung, C.G., and Karl Kerényi. *Essays on a Science of Mythology; the Myth of the Divine Child and the Mysteries of Eleusis*, Princeton UP, 1969.
Kahlo, Frida. *The Two Fridas*. 1939. Museo de Arte Moderno, Mexico City.
"Let the Children and Childbearers Toil." Writ. Greg Nelson. Dir. David Wellington. *Orphan Black*. Season 5, episode 4. First aired 1 July 2017.
Lewis, C.S. *Till We Have Faces*. Harcourt Brace, 1956.
Manson, Graeme, et al. *Orphan Black*. IDW Publishing, 2015. *Orphan Black*, vol. 1.
"The Mitigation of Competition." Writ. Alex Levine. Dir. David Frazee. *Orphan Black*. Season 4, episode 9. First aired 9 June 2016.
Moore, Alan, et al. "Red Glare!" *Promethea* #18. America's Best Comics, 2002.
"Newer Elements of Our Defence." Writ. Russ Cochrane. Dir. Chris Grismer. *Orphan Black*. Season 3, episode 4. First aired 9 May 2015.
"One Fettered Slave." Writ. Alex Levine. Dir. David Frazee. *Orphan Black*. Season 5, episode 9. First aired 5 Aug 2017.
Patterson, Nancy-Lou. "*Kore* Motifs in *The Princess and the Goblin*." *For the Childlike: George Macdonald's Fantasies for Children*, edited by Roderick McGillis, Scarecrow Press, 1992, pp. 169–182.
"Scarred by Many Past Frustrations." Writ. Alex Levine. Dir. David Frazee. *Orphan Black*. Season 3, episode 5. First aired 16 May 2015.
Solnit, Rebecca. *A Paradise Built in Hell: The Extraordinary Communities That Arise in Disasters*. Viking, 2009.
"Things Which Have Never Yet Been Done." Writ. Alex Levine. Dir. TJ Scott. *Orphan Black*. Season 2, episode 9. First aired 14 June 2014.
"To Hound Nature in Her Wanderings." Writ. Chris Roberts. Dir. Brett Sullivan. *Orphan Black*. Season 2, episode 6. First aired 24 May 2014.
"To Right the Wrongs of Many." Writ. Renée St. Cyr and Graeme Manson. Dir. John Fawcett. *Orphan Black*. Season 5, episode 10. First aired 12 Aug 2017.
"Transitory Sacrifices of Crisis." Writ. Aubrey Nealon. Dir. John Fawcett. *Orphan Black*. Season 3, episode 2. First aired 25 April 2015.
"Unconscious Selection." Writ. Alex Levine. Dir TJ Scott. *Orphan Black*. Season 1, episode 9. First aired 25 May 2013.
"Variable and Full of Perturbation." Writ. Karen Walton. Dir. John Fawcett. *Orphan Black*. Season 2, episode 8. First aired 7 June 2014.
"Variation Under Nature." Writ. Graeme Manson. Dir. David Frazee. *Orphan Black*. Season 1, episode 3. First aired 13 April 2013.
"The Weight of This Combination." Writ. Graeme Manson. Dir. David Frazee. *Orphan Black*. Season 3, episode 1. First aired 18 April 2015.
Wolkstein, Diane, and Samuel Noah Kramer. *Inanna, Queen of Heaven and Earth: Her Stories and Hymns from Sumer*. Harper & Row, 1983.

Living in the Panopticon
Resistance to Surveillance in Orphan Black

BRANDI BRADLEY

In the final season of the groundbreaking series *Orphan Black*, in an episode titled "Clutch of Greed," Felix Dawkins (Jordan Gavaris) looks out of the window of his foster mother's house to the surveillance vans across the street and tells his foster sister, Sarah (Tatiana Maslany), "It's like we're in a bloody Panopticon" (5.2). Oh, Felix. You've been living in the Panopticon for some time now.

Orphan Black is a story about women under the microscope. This BBC series, which concluded its fifth and final season in August 2017, used a biopunk plot and a neopunk protagonist to take the viewer through the struggles of a group of clone women against the institution that created, studied, monitored, controlled, and attempted to destroyed them. Time after time, the protagonist Sarah slips from their grasp and rallies other clones to resist this system. The structure of the institutions within the series closely resembles the Mettray, a prison system Michel Foucault analyzes in *Discipline and Punish: The Birth of the Prison*, a panopticon-style penal colony for delinquent children which corralled orphans into family factions and employed surveillance to ensure complacency. This structural parallel to the Mettray in the series can instill within the viewer a sense of paranoia, helplessness and a feeling of being watched.

In the text, *Discipline and Punish: The Birth of the Prison*, Foucault examines the structure of "highly hierarchized groups" (293) within the prison to mold and shape its occupants. This method of a prison structure theorized a space of reform, ensuring prisoners would conform to societal norms. Foucault explains, "[The chiefs and their deputies] were in a sense technicians of behaviour: engineers of conduct, orthopaedists of individuality. Their task was the produce bodies that were both docile and capable" (294). The Mettray used observe-and-report strategies to ensure their prisoners modeled appropriate behavior. Docility is accomplished by these systems of observation and prioritizing inclusion over isolation: not only spaces of awareness of surveillance, but also cultivating a desire to be among the observers.

The creators of *Orphan Black*—John Fawcett and Graeme Manson— chose a narrative structure that slowly introduces the viewer to the inescapable structures of power which mold and form these individuals. The slow narrative progression widens the scope of the viewers' awareness and the characters' reality and reveals the supposed futility of their resistance. Foucault observed that a structure which utilized constant awareness of surveillance and small group bonding ensured passive prisoners. *Orphan Black* presents characters whose passivity is nurtured in ignorance of their surveillance. Their resistance is triggered when each discovers the lack of control they have over their bodies and their existence. Foucault's design does not account for familial bonds being stronger than institutional commitment. Neither Foucault nor the *Orphan Black* institutions—led by P.T. Westmorland (Stephen McHattie), the Duncans, and the Dyad Institute—account for the *sestra* or the *sestra*-ally bond being strong enough to overthrow their overseers.

When *Orphan Black* begins, Sarah has isolated herself from family. She left her child in her foster mother's care before disappearing for almost a year. She returns in hopes of becoming a better mother and finding enough money to give her child a good life. In an attempt to steal several thousand dollars from assuming her dead double's identity, she learns that she is a clone. The narrative unfolds to reveal multiple enemies: the Dyad Institute which created her; the Proletheans, a religious cult with multiple sects who at first attempts to destroy the clones and then later wants to harness the reproductive capability of Sarah and her estranged twin/clone assassin Helena (all the female clones are played by Maslany); Castor, a military operation which created a series of super-soldier male clones (all played by Ari Millen); and finally a seemingly immortal man—P.T. Westmorland—looking for the secrets of eternal life. As this narrative progresses and unfolds its mysteries, it also reveals the structure of the prison which holds these characters. The viewer is offered a small scope from which to view this world, and, episode by episode, the scope widens, and the viewer is able to see more of the power system which inhibits the characters. This is not a narrative with one evil villain to face, but systems—international corporations, conservative religions and scientific organizations—to dismantle. However, until the viewer and the characters get the full view of their prison, they cannot begin to tear it down.

In order to acclimate the viewer into this world, the narrative begins by showing Sarah asleep on a train. Sarah is an orphan who was raised by her foster parent, Mrs. S, aka Siobhan (Maria Doyle Kennedy), with her foster brother, Felix Dawkins. When Sarah returns to the city, her first action is to make a phone call to Mrs. S to ask when she will be able to see her daughter, Kira (Skyler Wexler). Mrs. S denies this request because Sarah has been missing and incommunicado for almost a year, and Mrs. S labels her unfit to be a mother. Sarah's transgressive motherhood[1] is often used against her. The narrative does not hesitate to introduce the power dynamics of Sarah's family. Mrs. S is the dominant elder figure in their family, always presenting herself as the alpha. In the prison of the Mettray, prisoners were organized into families "composed of 'brothers' and two 'elder brothers'" (Foucault 293). Like the Mettray families, Mrs. S is in the position of both granting rewards and punishments. She decides when and if Sarah can see her daughter.

Once Sarah steals Beth's identity, she also finds herself responsible for the obligations of her dead double's family. Beth's extended family consists of her live-in boyfriend, Paul (Dylan Bruce), and her detective partner, Art (Kevin Hanchard). Paul and Beth had been fighting because their relationship was dissolving. Art and Beth's relationship had been tense because of a civilian shooting they were attempting to cover up ("Natural Selection," 1.1). Sarah's dual life here requires her to assume multiple roles for multiple people. With Sarah's foster family, she has to prove she is a changed person—an upstanding, stable mother for Kira. However, with Beth's family, Sarah has to maintain the illusion that she is Beth—an upstanding police officer and the perfect girlfriend. If Sarah can't maintain her image as Beth, she won't be able to access the thousands of dollars she is stealing from Beth's bank account. She plans to use the money to flee with Kira. If she can't maintain her image with Ms. S, she loses access to Kira. Sarah must transition through multiple female roles—career woman, girlfriend, mother, daughter—in order to please her multiple families.

In the process of appeasing these families, Sarah becomes further immersed in the mystery of her double and discovers yet another *sestra* family that she must appease. Sarah meets two of her biological identicals—Cosima and Alison—who inform her that she is a clone, and the clones are being murdered. At this point of the narrative, the members of the families have acted as obstacles as opposed to enemies: Mrs. S won't allow Sarah access to her daughter, Cosima demands Sarah retrieve evidence, and Alison won't offer Sarah any information outside the cover of darkness. All these demands prohibit Sarah from obtaining what she wants, but none of these obstacles place her in danger. However, now that the families have been established, the narrative can now reveal that the clones *are* in danger. Sarah is burdened with helping her *sestras* in order to protect them. In an effort to persuade Sarah, Cosima insists, "Look, we are your biological imperative now" ("Variation Under Nature," 1.3). Considering this character has been introduced as an orphan, the sudden appearance of a family who shares genetic material and is in mortal danger must be alluring to Sarah.

The introduction of an adversary also reveals the faction of the *Sestra* Army. Foucault explained how the Mettray also organized its prisoners into military-style factions: "each family, commanded by a head, was divided into two sections, each of which had a second in command; each inmate had a number and was taught basic military exercises; there was a cleanliness inspection every day, an inspection of clothing every week; a roll-call was taken three times a day" (Foucault 293). Alison mobilizes like a soldier: she keeps a weapon with her at all times, dispenses information on a need-to-know basis, and trains herself in tactical support. Beth trained Alison in defense and weaponry and, until her suicide, led the *Sestra* Army. Alison would have been the default leader of the *Sestra* Army after Beth killed herself; however, Sarah asserts her dominance by smacking Alison in the face and is deemed the leader ("Variation Under Nature," 1.3). After the shift in power, Alison becomes second-in-command. Both Alison and Sarah enlist in the *Sestra* Army because they both claim they feel the responsibility of needing to be prepared to protect their children ("Variation Under Nature," 1.3). The *Sestra* Army is designed to ensure the protection of the clones and the children of clones. The arrangement of the *Sestra* Army, like the army faction in the Mettray, facilitates discipline while also enhancing the opportunity for bonding. As the series continues, the members of the army faction shift, but Sarah maintains her role as leader and is eventually christened Athena, the goddess of war, by her brother Felix ("Guillotines Decide," 5.8). Sarah leads the resistance.

However, the *Sestra* Army is not only concerned about the sniper who is murdering clones, but the narrative also reveals that the *Sestra*s are undergoing secret medical experiments as they sleep. Sarah discovers this fact and learns that within the clone's family systems exists a built-in monitoring system. Foucault observed a system of monitoring and observing of inmates embedded in the Mettray "families," explaining that, "Heads or deputy-heads of 'families,' monitors and foremen, had to live in close proximity to the inmates; their clothes were 'almost as humble' as those of the inmates themselves; they practically never left their side, observing them day and night; they constituted among them a network of permanent observation" (Foucault 295). The monitoring system accomplishes two objectives: the monitors model "good" behavior and report "bad" behavior, and, as noted above, "[t]heir task was to produce bodies that were both docile and capable" (Foucault 294). In order to maintain docile and capable bodies within the families, the clones have been assigned monitors. Delphine (Évelyne Brochu) is assigned to Cosima, Donnie (Kristian Bruun) to Alison, and Paul to Beth, but Sarah replaces Beth. When the *sestras* become self-aware, not only of their existence but of their monitors, the dynamics of the relationships change. When Sarah realizes that Paul is Beth's monitor (and, through her assumption of Beth's life, her own) she utilizes that intimacy to feed him the information she wants him to pass along to his superiors. When Cosima realizes she is being monitored by Delphine, she asserts that knowing she is being watched will situate her in the power position: "Well, if we're gonna get past our monitors, we have to engage" ("Parts Developed in an Unusual Manner," 1.7). However, it seems that Foucault does not account for day-to-day interaction creating an emotional bond. He does not consider that developing affections between the watchers and the watched could motivate the monitors to rebel against the institutions.

In the world of *Orphan Black*, monitors are almost always lovers, which creates the assumption that lovers are not loyal. The monitors are instructed to become romantic interests, ensuring day and night observation. This requires the monitors to become intimate with those whom they are watching. Paul, who was being blackmailed by Dyad with information regarding his war crimes, could not fake his connection enough to fool Beth. Paul wouldn't fully commit to Beth, nor would he terminate the relationship. Paul was only fulfilling the parameters of his mission by watching Beth spiral further into depression and drug abuse. Because of his orders to ensure that the subjects make their own decisions, he is not allowed to break up with Beth, pushing her to initiate the breakup. She doesn't, calling him a coward ("The Collapse of Nature," 4.1). Their standoff presents individuals incapable of disengaging but also incapable of allowing each other the intimacy required to create a more powerful bond. At this point, Paul's relationship with Beth is a job, and he is only pretending intimacy, while Beth holds people at a distance to protect herself, a survival strategy from her abusive childhood. Because Sarah assumed Beth's life, Paul stays in the relationship and eventually develops an emotional attachment to Sarah. His affection for her tests his allegiance. Sarah knew intimacy from being raised in a chaotic but loving household, and her performance of intimacy with Paul is more convincing than Beth's best attempt at real intimacy. With Beth, his loyalties remained with the Dyad Institute, but, with Sarah, his instinct is to keep her protected despite his orders. When the institute learns that Sarah has been impersonating Beth, he is instructed to bring her to them. However, Paul informs Sarah that she is in danger and should run (1.7). Eventually, he sacrifices himself for her safety, blowing himself up in order for Sarah to escape her military base prison with Helena ("Certain Agony of the Battlefield," 3.6). Paul did not love Beth, but he did love Sarah enough to sacrifice himself. It seems the key to forming bonds which overthrow the institution is an intimacy which feels genuine.

The question of loyalty consistently challenges Delphine and Cosima's relationship. Cosima allows herself to be seduced by Delphine in order to feed Dyad false information. Delphine claims to work for Dyad only to protect Cosima. In order to achieve their complementary goals, they must continually keep secrets and seemingly betray each other. In the final season, Delphine resides inside P.T. Westmorland's compound, under his tyrannical thumb, in order to find a cure for the autoimmune disease which eventually kills the clones and has afflicted Cosima. When they are reunited, she reminds Cosima that she "promised to protect her" ("Ease for Idle Millionaires," 5.5). In *Discipline and Punish*, Foucault is quite focused on the system which trains the inmates within the system but does not account for the concern for each other's safety and security which could manifest by creating these bonds. By foregrounding Delphine's concerns for Cosima's safety, the show illustrates how the individual can supersede the faceless institution.

Early in the series, the clones accept the logic of assigning a monitor to each of them. Cosima explains to Sarah that, as a scientist, if she were in charge of an experiment on the scale of their creation, "I would put an observer close to the subject, you know, somebody to keep tabs and, and, and accumulate data" ("Conditions of Existence," 1.5). The monitoring system works as long as the clones were kept ignorant of the surveillance. Before they were self-aware, the subjects were docile in ignorance; however, once the clones became aware of their monitors, they responded with paranoia, weapons training, and denial. This is different from what Foucault observes in the Mettray. Those prisoners are aware from the beginning that they are part of a penal system, and they are being watched. He maintains that surveillance maintains the prisoner's docility: they won't misbehave because they know they cannot get away with any infraction without being punished. On *Orphan Black*, the clones only resist when they recognize they are part of a system. The rationale the series provides for the clone's ignorance is the legality of the experiment and the concern over tampering with the results. Paul is instructed that his function is to observe, and, "As long as your subject makes her own choices, there are no wrong decisions" ("Variations Under Domestication," 1.6). The implication is that ignorance will ensure the clones do not revolt.

While Cosima and Sarah learn to keep the upper hand with their monitors, Alison does not. Instead of growing closer to her monitor and using this information to her advantage, she has trouble determining who is watching her, and it causes her to act irrationally. The emotional breakdown of her placement within the Panopticon is clever considering the panopticon-like nature of living in suburbia. The Panopticon is, in Foucault's assertion, a perfect prison. In *Discipline and Punish*, he explains that this style of prison acted as the opposite of the medieval dungeon, "or rather of its three functions—to enclose, to deprive of light and to hide—it preserves only the first and eliminates the other two" (Foucault 200). The prison was built with a tower in the middle, providing the ability to view the inside of each cell while the prisoner can never view who is watching them. It creates this illusion of being watched at all times, all sins visible: "Full lighting and the eye of a supervisor capture better than darkness, which ultimately protected. Visibility is a trap" (Foucault 200). *Orphan Black* also utilizes lighting as iconography, filming most of Alison's scenes in the daylight or under the activation of motion detector security lighting. This character is associated with the security of visibility, but also the prison which that visibility provides. Suburbia—with its neighborhood watch organizations, security systems, and nosey neighbors—has been transformed into the panopticon of the 21st century.

Alison is most offended by the "betrayal" of being spied upon. Obsessed with the possibility of her monitor being her husband, she searches through his belongings and installs a camera in her bedroom. Here the narrative opens the scope to show the viewer the panoptic nature of Alison's everyday life and the irony of her irrationality. In "Variations Under Domestication," Alison hosts a potluck, despite keeping her husband tied to a chair in her craft room. She refuses to cancel the event, rationalizing to Sarah, "It's my turn" (1.6). Canceling was not an option for her. Her neighbors roam about her home, asking questions and commenting on her nervous behavior, while her husband is bound and gagged in the basement. In this episode, she is the center of a judging community, much in the same way Foucault describes how the Panopticon watchtower would work. "The judges of normality are present everywhere. We are in the society of the teacher-judge, the doctor-judge, the educator-judge, the 'social worker'-judge" (Foucault 304). However, Alison's paranoid and violent reaction against her potential monitors is actually the opposite of the system which Foucault observes in the Panopticon. He notes the anxiety of being watched is associated with anonymous observers, and "the more numerous those anonymous and temporary observers are, the greater the risk for the inmate of being surprised and the greater his anxious awareness of being observed" (Foucault 202). Alison is comfortable with her numerous observers, because she can control what they see. However, the idea of a singular personal observer beyond her control activates her paranoia, because it takes the idea of being watched beyond a common thought experiment. To each of her potential monitors, she points out the invasion of privacy of being watched, both by her husband and best friend. She was not being observed *en masse* like everyone else in Baily Downs; she was being specifically singled out and spied upon. Not only does the idea of a single focused observer fuel her paranoia, but it leads her to irrational and violent behavior. First, to her husband Donnie, whom she smacks with a golf club, after which she comments, "But I whacked him, and it felt so good" (1.6). When Alison suspects her neighbor Aynsley (Natalie Lisinska) of being her monitor, she seduces Aynsley's husband then fights her in the street. Eventually, in an attempt to bully a confession from her, Alison watches Aynsley's scarf become caught in a garbage disposal and allows her "monitor" to be strangled to death ("Endless Forms Most Beautiful," 1.10). This is not a docile body, but a violent body of defiance. Alison's refusal to be watched leads her to eliminate watchers by any means necessary.

In "Entangled Bank," Felix comments that Alison's irrationality is rooted in a loss of a "fake happiness" (1.8). Alison was so accustomed to her constant observation that she was oblivious to it. Despite her wrath over the idea of being watched, Alison's primary demand throughout the series is how she wants her "life back." She wants to go back to her ignorance: ignorance of her biology, surveillance, and *sestras*. Alison likes her panoptic cage because it is a prison for which she understands the rules. She knows she is being watched by her neighbors but feels a security in the fact that she can watch as well. Not knowing who watched her and when she was being watched fueled her paranoia and despair. Later, when Donnie confesses his role as her monitor and the accidental murder of Dr. Aldous Leekie (Matt Frewer), his confession reveals how he was approached to monitor his then-college girlfriend for a sociology experiment and had been in the dark in regard to the clones. For Alison, this assures her that their relationship, marriage, and intimacy had not been a Dyad Institute construct and that, in a time of crisis, Donnie chose Alison over the institution. The shared secret of Donnie's involuntary manslaughter of Dr. Leekie—and the garage burial—gave them an opportunity to bond. With this information, Donnie and Alison usher in a new era of their marriage, one in which they work as fully transparent partners instead of adversaries cloaked in mystery.

Unmonitored by the Dyad Institute, Helena was still subject to monitoring, in her case by the self-appointed monitorship of Tomas (Daniel Kash), a member of a religious group who views the clone experiments as against God's will. Acting as guardians, Tomas and the Proletheans specifically trained Helena to kill her clone *sestras*. She was raised ignorant of her parentage but somewhat self-aware. Tomas told her that she was "the original" from which all others were copied. However, her self-awareness came with abuse, isolation, and a sense of superiority. She was "the original" but Tomas referred to her as an abomination. He gave with the right hand and slapped it away with his left. Tomas's control over Helena, instilling within her a superiority over the other clones, led to the murder of multiple clones, but the systematic abuse also led to a fragmented identity which rebelled as soon as she met

Sarah. She was easier to control when he convinced her she was isolated, singular, and better than the others.

In the war against the Leda clones, Helena was an excellent soldier. She was a sniper, performed field surgery on herself when injured, gathered information on the *sestras* to use against them, was adept at fighting and escaping tense situations, and—on all levels—a stone-cold killer. She is both family faction and army faction. She's a specimen so dynamic, even Dyad director Dr. Leekie cannot help but comment on it: "[They] trained a clone to kill clones. Brilliant, really" ("Unconscious Selection," 1.9). Foucault's assessment of the Mettray implies that punishment on the prisoners by the prisoners was the intended order: the deviant polices the deviant. The factions impose this hierarchy to ensure that one inmate possesses a position of superiority to justify imposing punishment. The inmates become the jailers. Foucault ponders what might motivate one to impress this authority of the punisher on others and what allows others to be punished. In *Discipline and Punish* he explains, "The theory of the [social] contract can only answer this question by the fiction of a juridical subject giving to others the power to exercise over him the right that he himself possesses over them" (Foucault 303). Helena is introduced as the agent of justice, as "the original" from which the clones were created. She is raised with a mission, to eliminate her copies from the world. She has carved scars into her back into the shape of angel's wings. She refers to the clones as sheep, occasionally baaing at them. Cosima, through analyzing Helena's knife (and weapon of choice), explains, "[I]f you were a messed up, abused loner whose faith compels you to belong and somebody that you trusted told you that this was the way to redeem yourself in the eyes of God," and Sarah responds, "Yeah, I might become an angry angel, too" ("Effects of External Conditions," 1.4). Sarah and Cosima recognize how this combination of isolation and religious ideology created a being which would take extreme action to be redeemed. Helena's social training by the Proletheans created a monster.

For Helena's crimes, Sarah has to be the one who brings Helena to justice. Once Helena separates herself from the Proletheans—choosing Sarah over Tomas—she is no longer bound to any conventions of obedience but instead chooses a family whom she will be loyal. When Helena stabs their birthmother Amelia (Melanie Nicholls-King), who had placed Sarah and Helena in separate foster systems, Helena explains it is because "She separated us. She tore us apart" (1.10). Helena believes that she is free to do as she wishes, dispensing justice as she sees fit. She is unconcerned with possible consequences because she believes Sarah will never hurt her, that their biological connection will protect her. She explains to Sarah, "Scientists made one little baby, and then we split in two [...]. So I cannot kill you, sister. Like, you could not kill me. Sarah, we make a family, yes?" (1.10).

Unfortunately for Helena, the risk of Sarah allowing her unpredictable twin to live outweighs the connection of their biology, and Sarah shoots her. Here, Sarah is confronted with the question of nature over nurture and who to protect. She and Helena, separated at birth, had not the time or opportunity to develop the fully bonded connection necessary for her to choose Helena over her foster family. In their climactic fight at the end of "Endless Forms Most Beautiful," Sarah's response to Helena is, "I've already got a family" (1.10). Sarah is Helena's only family. However, Sarah has cultivated relationships with Felix, Mrs. S, her daughter, and the other *sestra*s. In this instance, nurture wins.

But what viewers are presented is the possibility that Helena cannot be killed. She comes back swinging each time, except now to the aid of her *sestra*s. After recovering from the multiple gunshot wounds inflicted by Sarah, she flees the Prolethean colony and rescues Sarah from being sliced open by a Dyad goon. When the police come close to discovering Helena and her involvement in the death of a local drug dealer, she hides in the woods—draping herself in the hides of rabbits, raccoons, and deer—only to emerge in time to rescue Alison and Donnie from being murdered by Evie Cho's (Jessalyn Wanlim) henchmen ("The Mitigation of Competition" 4.9). When Helena is introduced, she is an enemy, but, as the narrative progresses, she is eventually and reluctantly accepted into the *Sestra* Army, taking on the task of protecting the clones, Kira, Alison's children, and her own "science babies." Helena's cause is no longer in the service of an institution, but the family she cultivated. She happily dishes out justice for her *sestra*s.

Proctors of justice on *Orphan Black* are limited to clones within the soldier faction: Beth, who killed Prolethean Maggie Chen (Uni Park) before her suicide; Helena, with numerous clone killings and her birth-mother Amelia; Alison, who, through negligence, kills her neighbor Aynsley; and Sarah, who shoots Helena. They feel justified in their actions because they operate in a system within a society that is not monitored by society. The clones are part of an illegal experiment, which means they cannot rely on the police to regulate justice. Again, Foucault notes a system outside of the social contract within the Mettray. The prisoners governed justice themselves because the incarceration system "gives a sort of legal sanction to the disciplinary mechanisms, to the decisions and judgements that they enforce" (Foucault 302). Within the Mettray, the primary tools of justice were to severely punish minor offenses before they become major ones through "confinement to one's cell; for 'isolation is the best means of acting on the moral nature of children'" (Foucault 294). He described the cells, where, upon the walls, black letters warn, "God sees you" (Foucault 294). This act of isolation and surveillance inflicts a sense of being ostracized but never alone. Foucault sees this as societal training: to be alone but also to be watched and judged by your actions.

The show, on the other hand, sees *being watched* not as a reason to change, but as a reason to perform according to the watcher's expectations, until one is ready to fight.

Additionally, the show indicates that one cannot fight back in isolation. Isolation is used on Helena when she is punished by Tomas. She is locked in a cage for protecting Sarah from him. Helena alludes to this type of repeated punishment when she explains her upbringing in the convent. When Tomas locks her in the cage, he also strips her of her superiority over the other clones, claiming, "You're no better than they are!" (1.9). Later in the scene, she holds a gun between Tomas and Sarah. He proclaims Helena is the original clone and the rightful mother to Sarah's daughter, Kira. Sarah pleads that Tomas likely will lock Kira in a cage. The idea of going back into the cage, or seeing anyone else be punished in this way, leads Helena to turn her back on her guardian. This type of struggle with the abuse one suffers as a result of the power structure is not remarked upon in Foucault's assessment of the Mettray in *Discipline and Punish*. Within the family systems, "The essential element of its programme was to subject the future cadres to the same apprenticeships and to the same coercions as the inmates themselves: they were 'subjected as pupils to the discipline that, later, as instructors, they would themselves impose'" (Foucault 295). The implication of this is reminiscent of a hazing ritual, where one must suffer in order to gain power. In this situation, all Tomas's promises of power—motherhood and superiority—are not strong enough to subject one to the same methods of discipline she experienced as a child. The family factions in the Mettray composed the inmates into groups of at least three. A revolt against a family head would require the support of the other members of the family. If Helena had been charged with power over another in her family system, she might be more hesitant in overthrowing her guardian. Instead, her previous isolation allows her to adapt her loyalties to her new family more easily, allowing her to fully join the resistance.

Rachel, on the other hand, is the clone who never abandons her sense of superiority and initially rejects any resistance against the institution which imprisons her. Much like Alison, Rachel enjoys her cage. It provides her the most power. The subjects within the Mettray were aware of their placement within the prison system, many of them orphans who were given up by their families. Rachel, too, is an orphan within a system. She has always been aware of her biology, raised by doctors and scientists within the Dyad Institute. The intention was to create a child "unfettered by tradition" (1.9). Rachel rises from scientific subject to program director of the Dyad, never leaving the constraints of her prison. Foucault explains in *Discipline and Punish* that, at the Mettray, students are often cycled through the prison systems: "The carceral network does not cast the unassimilable into a confused hell; there is no outside. [...] In this panoptic society of which incarceration is the omnipresent armature, the delinquent is not outside the law; he is, from the very outset, in the law, at the very heart of the law" (Foucault 301). Rachel was not trained in any other area. Dyad produced not only her routine but also her identity. Rachel, as the self-aware clone, convinced herself that she is superior to the others, and, when they challenged that superiority, she struggled to accept that she was just as much a product of the institutions the rest of them.

Rachel has more power than all the other clones: she holds a prominent position within the Dyad Institute, she has money, she chooses her monitor; however, she can never be freed from Dyad. She was created by Dyad, was raised by the institution under constant surveillance, was educated by them, and ultimately worked for them. Foucault notes this institutionalized employment only funnels individuals from one institution to the next. "Careers emerged from [the carceral], as secure, as predictable, as those of public life" (Foucault 300). She's a domesticated cat in a power suit. Unlike Helena, who chooses her *sestras* over dominating a comrade, Rachel can't wait to assert her superiority over the others. This could be because, when Helena thinks of family, she thinks of a sister or equal, which is evident when Helena insists on getting to know Sarah in Season 1. But when Rachel thinks of family, she thinks about having a baby, something which she can control and over which she can assert her superiority.

Rachel is the clone with the most power but also the one with the most insecurity. Her jealousy of Sarah's ability to produce children unfolds in a chilling scene of Rachel drinking a martini, watching videos of herself as a girl, and manically laughing and crying. Rachel wants a child but only because she wants something she can control. Her childhood, career and all relationships are dictated by the Dyad Institute.

Rachel's rebellion occurs when she is placed in the same inferior position of the other clones. After suffering an injury, Rachel is imprisoned on an island with Susan (Rosemary Dunsmore), her mother and the scientist from the original Leda project. While there, she discovers that her biological material was used to clone Charlotte (Cynthia Gallant), a girl who also lives on the island with them. Rachel is upset that she was not part of the decision-making process. Her mother tells her that their purpose is "in service of the greater good" to "create a more perfect human being" ("The Stigmata of Progress," 4.3). Rachel is being persuaded that the sacrifice is justified with a promise of glory and the service to humanity. Rachel's autonomy is not even important to her mother; she is merely biological material which could help create more biological material, which leaves Rachel vulnerable to Westmorland's false promises of autonomy. Susan tells Rachel, "Charlotte was cloned from you" over dinner one evening, in the same tone that one would comment, "The chicken is free range" (4.3). This type of disruption of familial connection isolates Rachel further and strips her of her superiority, pushing her to fight, not for the *sestras* but for a power position at Dyad. She believes she is entitled to a position as leader of the institution. Everyone Rachel has ever valued—her parents, Ferdinand (James Frain), the institute which raised her—never valued her back. She never developed an intimacy with anyone and, eventually, her only allegiance was to herself.

Her one truly rebellious act is her affair with Ferdinand, a Topside executive who plots with Rachel about destroying all the clones and fleeing together to a tropical island. Their sexual dynamic is one of power-plays: dominant and submissive. When she betrays him by feeding confidential information to the *sestras* instead of allowing Ferdinand to use it to "build a dynasty," he attempts to strangle her but is impotent to her power over him (5.8). In the bedroom, she is the powerful one, but she knows that outside the bedroom she would always be at his mercy. She would have been trading one jailer for another. That was not freedom. Her decision to aid the *sestras* was not one of unity, but one of self-preservation.

In the end, left without a prison and without a purpose, Rachel is also without the *sestra* connections that the others forged. By asserting her superiority over them at every turn and placing her faith in the institution which made her promises of freedom she never received, she was left alone once that institution was dismantled. At the end, the *sestra*s are gathered in Alison's backyard in celebration of Helena's boys, but Rachel is on the other side of the house, waiting covertly in an Uber for Felix. She hands him the list of the remaining clones all over the world so Cosima can cure them of the autoimmune disease they are all susceptible. When Felix tells her that he won't be inviting her inside, she tells him it's fine because "the last thing I want to do is see another face like mine" ("To Right the Wrongs of Many," 5.10). Rachel is outside the family as well as the institution now, still isolated, uncertain how to proceed. Having spent a lifetime alone but under the watchful eye of Dyad, it is possible that Rachel will never know how to live without being watched.

A viewer may wonder if the *sestras* would ever accept Rachel into the fold. Helena was murdering them, but she was forgiven of her sins because of her shifting attitude from superior to united. The fan favorite culmination of this acceptance and forgiveness is the dance of the clone *sestras* at the end of Season 2 ("By Means Which Have Never Yet Been Tried" 2.10). Rachel's repeated betrayal of the *sestras* means forgiveness would be determined by whether Rachel could stop acting superior long enough to develop an intimacy with them absent of the all-seeing eye of Dyad. While the institutions within this program mimic Foucault's observations of the penal systems in France, his observations are just that. Because he did not write about how to overthrow these systems, readers of his work could feel helpless. *Orphan*

Black presents the familiar systems of family obligations, panopticon neighborhoods, and justification of cyclical abuse, but offers a solution: stop the cycle by uniting and resisting. Soon after the series concluded, in October of 2017, women were witness to real-life allied resistance. The trending Twitter hashtag #metoo, started by activist Tarana Burke in 2006 (Ohlheiser) and spurred by actress Alyssa Milano's viral tweet in October 2017 (@Alyssa_Milano), created a worldwide awareness and conversation regarding the vast numbers of women who had experienced sexual assault and sexual harassment in the home and workplace. Women spoke out against consistent sexual harassment in the entertainment industry, the food industry, journalism, and music. They named names and called for the resignations of once powerful men. This #metoo awareness has led to the Time's Up Legal Defense Fund (*Time's Up*) designed to raise money to provide legal funding and support for victims. During the 2018 Golden Globe awards, supporters wore all black clothing and Time's Up pins, signifying a commitment to change the old Hollywood systems of keeping women docile, compliant and silent (Buckley). This was not a movement instigated by institutions, but through human connection: individual women publicly expressing awareness and empathy.

Looking at Foucault's structure, one can see how he and other institutions underestimate the human connection of their subjects. His text does not consider what would happen if those subjected to abuses of power rallied together. The victory of a resistance does not rely on whether those in power at the institutions are willing to concede, but whether those under the thumb of those institutions are willing to unite and fight. What *Orphan Black*'s weekly viewership could have learned, and what women in 2017 began to realize, is that taking down corruption is not up to the institutions choosing to change, but individuals who band together in solidarity with their *sestras*.

Note

1. For more on Sarah as a "Motherless Bad Girl/ Bad Girl Mother," see Laine Zisman Newman's essay in this collection.

Works Cited

@Alyssa_Milano. "If You've Been Sexually Harassed or Assaulted Write 'me Too' as a Reply to This Tweet." *Twitter*, 15 Oct. 2017, 4:21 p.m. twitter.com/alyssa_milano/status/919659438700670976.

Buckley, Cara. "Powerful Hollywood Women Unveil Anti-Harassment Action Plan." *The New York Times*. 1 Jan 2018.

"By Means Which Have Never Yet Been Tried." Writ. Graeme Manson. Dir. John Fawcett. *Orphan Black*. Season 2, episode 10. First aired 21 June 2014.

"Certain Agony of the Battlefield." Writ. Aubrey Nealon. Dir. Helen Shaver. *Orphan Black*. Season 3, episode 6. First aired 23 May 2015.

"Clutch of Greed." Writ. Jeremy Boxson. Dir. John Fawcett. *Orphan Black*. Season 5, episode 2. First aired 17 June 2017.

"The Collapse of Nature." Writ. Graeme Manson. Dir. John Fawcett. *Orphan Black*. Season 4, episode 1. First aired 14 April 2016.

"Conditions of Existence." Writ. Karen Walton. Dir. Grant Harvey. *Orphan Black*. Season 1, episode 5. First aired 27 April 2013.
"Effects of External Conditions." Writ. Graeme Manson. Dir John Fawcett. *Orphan Black*. Season 1, episode 4. First aired 20 April 2013.
"Endless Forms Most Beautiful." Writ. Graeme Manson. Dir. John Fawcett. *Orphan Black*. Season 1, episode 10. First aired 1 June 2013.
"Entangled Bank." Writ. Karen Walton. Dir. Ken Girotti. *Orphan Black*. Season 1, episode 8. First aired 18 May 2013.
Foucault, Michel. *Discipline and Punish: The Birth of the Prison*, 1995. Vintage, 2009.
"Guillotines Decide." Writ. Aisha Porter-Christie and Graeme Manson. Dir. Aaron Morton. *Orphan Black*. Season 5, episode 8. First aired 5 August 2017.
"Natural Selection." Writ. Graeme Manson. Dir. John Fawcett. *Orphan Black*. Season 1, episode 1. First aired 30 March 2013.
Ohlheiser, Abby. "The Woman Behind 'Me Too' Knew the Power of the Phrase When She Created It—10 Years Ago." *The Washington Post*, 19 Oct. 2017.
"Parts Developed in an Unusual Manner." Writ. Tony Elliott. Dir. Brett Sullivan. *Orphan Black*. Season 1, episode 7. First aired 11 May 2013.
"The Stigmata of Progress." Writ. Aubrey Nealon. Dir. Ken Girotti. *Orphan Black*. Season 4, episode 3. First aired 28 April 2016.
Time's Up. Time's Up Legal Defense Fund, 2017, www.timesupnow.com. Accessed 24 Aug. 2018.
"To Right the Wrongs of Many." Writ. Renée St. Cyr and Graeme Manson. Dir. John Fawcett. *Orphan Black*. Season 5, episode 10. First aired 12 Aug 2017.
"Unconscious Selection." Writ. Alex Levine. Dir TJ Scott. *Orphan Black*. Season 1, episode 9. First aired 25 May 2013.
"Variation Under Nature." Writ. Graeme Manson. Dir. David Frazee. *Orphan Black*. Season 1, episode 3. First aired 13 April 2013.
"Variations Under Domestication." Writ. Will Pascoe. Dir. John Fawcett. *Orphan Black*. Season 1, episode 6. First aired 4 May 2013.

"My story is an embroidery"
Representing Trauma Within the World of Orphan Black

ALYSON R. BUCKMAN

Imagine walking out into the world and coming face-to-face with someone who looked just like you—then watching that person remove her shoes, put down her purse, and walk in front of an oncoming train. That moment of self-recognition is immediately followed by self-obliteration. But you are a tough woman; you have been through a great deal in your 28 years of life, including the violence of an abusive relationship, a criminal lifestyle, growing up in foster care and moving around regularly, and having at least one abortion and a child on your own. You are a grifter; you can handle it, and you might as well make the most out of the opportunity afforded by that abandoned purse. In attempting to squeeze all possible resources out of that opportunity, though, you gradually get caught in a mystery in which you see yourself yet again, witness the obliteration of the self again, and then are confronted with a self who tries to kill you. Eventually, you, Sarah Manning, learn you are sister to 274 female clones (Ledas) and an unknown number of male clones (Castors) created by Neolution through Projects Leda and Castor, the Dyad group, Topside, and the military. You and a core group of self-aware Ledas work together to discover your shared history, research a cure for the fatal genetic disorder shared by 99 percent of the Ledas, retake ownership of your bodies, and destroy the corporate, religious, and military cabals intent on subduing, wielding, and/or eliminating groups of Ledas and Castors.

In the course of the series, one or more clones suffers the following: murder; suicide; parental abandonment; threats to or injury of their children; being spied and reported upon; threats to themselves, their friends, and their families; seeing friends, family, and fellow clones die through suicide, violence, or their shared disease; repeated penetration of their bodies without their consent, including medical testing without their knowledge, implantation of microrobots able to kill them remotely, through attempted extraction, and/or through switching on particular genes (such as those activating the disorder), and implantation of devices which allow others to spy upon them; violent extraction of said devices; kidnapping, imprisonment, and torture; stabbings and shootings; involuntary "marriage"; and verbal, physical, and mental abuse throughout their life span. In considering the diverse subjects implicit within this quick summary and listing of experiences within the series, the first common element noted throughout well may be trauma, with individualism, communal ethics, and corporate and government law, religion, science, and funding emerging as additional elements; several of these are addressed within this anthology. From such a list, one might also note the importance of form and genre as well as gender and the construction of identity to an analysis of representation of trauma within the series. The conclusion of the series offers a means of pulling all these pieces together and illuminates the necessity of storytelling and community to post-traumatic growth and healing from trauma.[1] Through form and hybridity of genre and through the representation of gender, identity, and trauma within the series, *Orphan Black* emphasizes agency, community, and storytelling as modes of healing and resistance.

Form and Genre: "...many beginnings and no end"[2]

The melodramatic, serial story demands regular traumatization of its characters, especially female characters: they must suffer for the audience, engaging regularly with emotional extremes. As an ensemble of characters—if not of actors[3]—relief from suffering for one character generally overlaps with the renewal of stress for another, continuing the audience's investment in suffering and minor resolution. Full resolution cannot be attained until the end of the series, although particular threads may be resolved, such as the mystery of the origin of the clones.

Serial melodrama is accompanied by elements of the female gothic: unknown origins; entrapment; mystery; suspicious and brooding romantic partners; strange and alien spaces; fear; morbidity; and unsafe domiciles with doors that lock from outside.[4] The gothic in general privileges traumatic experience, keeping its protagonists far from safety and comfort. Ellen Moers specifically privileges audience fear in her definition of the gothic, arguing this fear relates not to Plato's notion of *katharsis* but to physiological arousal:

"to get to the body itself, its glands, muscles, epidermis, and circulatory system" (90). Steven Bruhm links the gothic to a "politics of pain" (*Gothic*) and the difficulty of representing trauma ("The Contemporary"). In his dissertation on the subject, Eric Brownell connects his study of the gothic with cultural trauma, in keeping with James Berger's assessment of the connection between late 20th-century cultural patterns and the representation of trauma (571–572), although Brownell focuses most of his attention on mid-20th century gothic texts; the latter argues the genre relies upon the interdependence of past and present and the shattering of identity (2), subjects which will be discussed shortly in relation to *Orphan Black*. The confusion of the relationship between heroine and predecessor in gothic fiction—the omnipresent portrait of the deceased woman who often controls the gaze and psyche of characters through the mystery she represents (Brownell 2–3)—has its analog in the confusion between self and other represented by the clones, discussed further later in this essay, as does Brownell's claim that gothic narratives "simultaneously critique (and connect) public and domestic forms of oppression" (3), although the clones act not as scapegoats for repressed cultural trauma—or, at least, not solely as such—but as avatars of resistance to Western politics of domination and subordination, whether it be through the realms of law, religion, the corporate world, domestic spaces, science, or even the cosmetics industry.[5] Such confusion is enabled in part through the construction of woman as cipher in gothic fiction, as per Sedgwick, and as absent presence; mothers, if known, may vanish and other women act as substitutes. The names act as ciphers as well, in this case through the eponymous "Orphan Black." The typical situation of female characters in Western stories is acting as ciphers or blanks, responsible for launching the action but unimportant as persons in their own right; this is yet another element of Laura Mulvey's theory of the gaze, discussed below, but also is a part of such texts as Joseph Campbell's *The Hero with a Thousand Faces*, in which women act as temptation, goddess, or reward but not as agent and subject. However, experience enables women within the gothic and within the world of *Orphan Black* to become subjects (Sedgwick 255–270). Although the text does situate the women within mythology (through Leda, the swan, and Castor, among others[6]) and stories of goddesses (see Felix's art show and his naming of the clones as, for instance, Hestia, Goddess of Hearth and Home; Athena, Goddess of War; or Metis, Goddess of Wisdom and Deep Thought, "Guillotines Decide," 5.8), the women are more complex than most of these stories.

Both the gothic and *film noir* regularly overlap with detective stories, as is the case here: the clones must investigate the mysteries of their formation, biology, and the ways in which they are controlled in to gain agency. Violence, alienation, isolation, ambivalence toward authority, urban surrounds, and morally uncertain protagonists connect the series to *film noir*. (One might also argue for the presence of the *femme fatale* as represented by both Sarah and Rachel.) Significantly, though, the women are investigating themselves rather than an outside, masculine force investigating what they represent; although men are also part of the investigation, they never become dominant in determining the meaning and origins of the women. In her work on the male gaze, Laura Mulvey discusses the ways in which woman as mystery often becomes a fetish object, wherein audience pleasure is found through the male representative of law and order determining female guilt and responding to it with either punishment or forgiveness; the examples she uses include Alfred Hitchcock's *Vertigo, Marnie,* and *Rear Window,* among others, and she illustrates how audiences are asked literally to see through the main character's eyes due to the use of subjective camera: his gaze—it generally is a male gaze—becomes our own.[7] In *Orphan Black,* the gaze of representatives of law and order—police officers, government and military representatives—is turned back on them; authority is interrogated and often found guilty (generally of collusion with Neolution). When subjective camera is used, it generally links the gaze of audience and camera to that of the clones, although at times we see through the surveiling eye of the government, military, corporation, or Neolution; our identification, however, remains with the clones and their families unless the audience actively is defying the structures of identification.[8] While often subjected to nefarious corporate tactics, including the designation of themselves as property, i.e., literally objects, through the bar codes placed in their DNA, the Ledas (all played by Tatiana Maslany) remain subjects and agents in determining their meaning and plan of action; while one might argue they still are objects of the gaze in their representation of normative, culturally attractive, and sexual female bodies (see Dani Howell and Laine Zisman Newman in this collection, for instance), they simultaneously act as agents of their own destiny rather than relying upon Paul (Dylan Bruce), Art (Kevin Hanchard), Cal (Michiel Huisman), or Felix (Jordan Gavaris) to save them. The symbolic—the world of phallogocentrism, which "works better," Sarah K. Donovan writes, "when women and mothers are silent and unacknowledged contributors" (136)—is aligned with the forces of patriarchy quite explicitly through, especially but not solely, the figure of John Mathieson, aka P.T. Westmorland (Stephen McHattie). The Ledas self-determine what they "mean" and what they will become rather than their mystery being penetrated and made meaningful by male subjects, although certainly the latter attempt to secure their own meaning for the Ledas. The clones actively build their own herstories from bits of information gathered through a variety of sources: scientific, military, corporate, and familial. One field is unable to contain all the necessary information to building meaning. The mystery genre in general requires investigators to work with "confused, fragmented testimonies" (Hamilton 17) and make meaning from them in a process similar to working with trauma (15–17, 19); building their history and knowledge requires similar tasks from the clones, and it also is an act through which they assert their subjectivity.

Gender: "The future is female!"[9]

Narrative form and function coalesce with gender to help us understand the traumas undergone by the Ledas and their healing from it. Reproduction, for instance, is at the heart of several of the Ledas' traumatic experiences. While many women experience physical and emotional trauma before, during, and after delivery, especially black women,[10] and many women are infertile (about 10 percent, or 6.1 million, of American women ages 15–44 have difficulty initiating or maintaining a pregnancy),[11] the particulars of reproductive trauma within the world of *Orphan Black* set it apart. Not only are 272 out of 274, i.e., 99 percent of, female clones infertile, but they also were designed this way; although it is not stated explicitly, the male clones, i.e., the Castors (all played by Ari Millen), seem to be infertile as well, especially since the result of intercourse with the Castors is sterility in their female partners.[12] It is Helena and Sarah who are "failures" in their ability to reproduce, in an inversion of popular Western thought regarding reproduction. The cultural emphasis on women's "natural" ability to give birth successfully[13] results in both female mortality and the sense that a woman isn't a "real" woman within our culture if she is infertile; *Orphan Black* subtly interrogates this notion through this inversion. "How is it," asks Rachel, "the unmonitored tramp [Sarah] was successful?" "In her fertility?" Professor Ethan Duncan (Andrew Gillies)[14] responds, surprised, "Ha! Rachel, she's a failure, not a success. You are all barren by design." The camera cuts back and forth from her composed, seated self to a visualization of her inner anger, sweeping items off her desk and yelling gutturally. Rachel declares to him, "It's time we begin fixing your mistakes" ("Variable and Full of Perturbation," 2.8). Much of her anger at Sarah (and Helena) seems to come from their ability to reproduce, to be exceptional when Rachel felt herself the only exceptional clone, and to meet cultural mandates of "real" womanhood through reproduction.

The reproductive system is used to control the clones from the beginning: their reproductive systems are constructed as a fail-safe, which is responsible science in designing a prototype. This is one of several examples of these women being denied the fundamental right of control over their own bodies. What has not yet been discussed in this essay is that these women are further traumatized by their own bodies through the violence of a disease that begins, ironically, in the reproductive system; it is ironic because cloning is a reimagining of reproduction, a dis-ease (natural and/or symbolic) with natural reproduction. Beginning in the uterus and traveling into the lungs, then the sinuses, mouths, and lips, this disease debilitates the women, causing fatigue, unconsciousness, and bleeding from the vagina, nose, and mouth. They have trouble breathing, and the coughing which ensues creates more bleeding. The control imposed upon clone bodies within a patriarchal, corporatocratic world creates sterility, infertility, and death. The relegation of control to the reproductive system in female and the cerebral cortex in male clones is significant as well in that women often are aligned with the body in Western culture while men are aligned with the mind and civilization. Helplessness, fear, and debilitation are invoked by these disorders, emotional responses encouraged in treatment of the clones and ones connected to the experience of trauma (van der Kolk xi-xvii; Hunt 18; Herman 34).

The inability to have children is an explicit psychic wound for Rachel and Alison; their longing for children and their jealousy of Sarah and Helena's motherhood is apparent from the moment they learn these two are able to conceive, though Alison quickly discards this negative reaction[15]; later, we will learn from Donnie (Kristian Bruun) that he and Alison repeatedly attempted *in vitro* fertilization (IVF) treatments in their quest for a child of their own biology. When Alison attempts to get information from Portia Grossman (Lindsey Connell), someone whose IVF journey was parallel to their own, about the Brightborn Clinic, the tears that well up in her eyes are not merely part of her disguised interrogation ("From Instinct to Rational Control," 4.4). Rachel, on the other hand, repeatedly attempts to take Kira (Skyler Wexler) for her own and to punish Sarah and Helena for their fertility. While taking their eggs (and those of Kira, Sarah's daughter) certainly would be useful to continuing cloning experiments, Rachel's hostility towards these two especially is connected to her jealousy and her continual comparison of herself with other clones, to which she admits and which is apparent in several scenes, including the one nearly fatal to Susan Duncan (Rosemary Dunsmore): "Oh, Rachel. For all the joy and insight your sisters have given me, for every Sarah, every Cosima, I regret making you" ("From Dancing Mice to Psychopaths," 4.10). This is when, of all possible times, Rachel chooses to attempt matricide. While Westmorland's inserted visions of the dead swan help push her towards attacking Duncan, there is a clear path which leads to it from Rachel's own psyche. Rachel has attempted for so long to hold herself superior to her sisters—something Helena is encouraged to do as well by the priest, Tomas (Daniel Kash), calling her the "original" from which the others are made as abominations—but the ground keeps slipping out from under her belief, much to her resentment and ultimate humbling in the final episodes.[16] (Here we see also the text's refusal of a hierarchy of value for any reason in relation to the clones.)

The forced intrusions upon the bodies of Kira, Helena, and Sarah in the interest of gaining their offspring and eggs relates as well to Rachel's pursuit of approval and affection from father figures, initially Ethan Duncan, then Aldous Leekie (Matt Frewer), and, finally, John Mathieson/P.T. Westmorland. (She even calls Ferdinand [James Frain] "Daddy" during their kinky sex play.) First, she is traumatized by the abandonment of her parents, which makes her eager to please authority figures and, second, she is so invested in her fairy tale that she can be a person when her sisters cannot, that she can gain subjectivity in a world in which she is an object of science, she believes Westmorland's fiction that he always thought of her as a daughter ("Gag or Throttle," 5.7) and will emancipate her. Many of the women in this series function as models of the ways in which women have attempted to fit within a patriarchal world, and Rachel is a model of the woman who is a co-conspirator, hoping to gain power even as she takes it from other women in the service of the father. Note, in the example cited earlier, that she uses language used to contain/control/shame female sexual agency within patriarchal rape culture, calling Sarah a "tramp." Mathieson resorts to similar tactics when he degrades Rachel, attempting to shame her by saying he knows how she "touch[es herself] in the shower, where [she] think[s] it's clean" ("One Fettered Slave," 5.9); she only "thinks" it's clean—obviously, as a woman pleasuring herself, she cannot be clean: she is dirty, degraded. Rachel is interested in gaining her own power—a consequence of feeling out of control as an official lab rat, abandoned by her adoptive parents—and will do so by any means possible ... at least until she learns it is impossible within the world of Westmorland/Mathieson and Neolution. Her sense of helplessness and her objectification is visualized through a flashback close-up on her picking at her fingers behind her back as she is introduced as science object and asked her property tag number (5.7), and it is verbalized by Mathieson in "One Fettered Slave" (5.9) when he speaks of his intimate knowledge of her insecurities and actions. Mathieson knows about Rachel's masturbation and her nail picking because he has inserted his vision (literally and symbolically) within her and without her consent, rendering her even more of a tool for his will; her decision to pluck out her robotic eye/camera in order to defy her own objectification and Mathieson's will appropriately follows her return of Kira, drugged, to her mother rather than having Kira's eggs harvested for Mathieson. These are her first acts in solidarity with her sisters and against patriarchal, corporate control. Significantly, this is when she begins to find the personhood and freedom she has sought; we will discuss the gaze and the mirror further shortly, subjects with which Rachel's eye is entwined.

Trauma and Being in the World: To "Gag or Throttle" (5.7)

As suggested above, traumatic events disrupt the integrity and autonomy of the self, invading, injuring, and defiling it. One no longer feels control over the self. Traumatization influences a person's sense of what Martin Heidegger called "being-in-the-world." Learning one is a clone, of course, would be the first element to cause a crisis in one's sense of self; if we follow Jacques Lacan's theory that the mirror stage[17] is fundamental in human identity development, to suddenly be confronted with a mirror of the self which is not a mirror but another location of the self with a separate relationship both to the Imaginary and the Real could wreak havoc with the psyche. As philosopher Jeremy Heuslein asserts, "[Sarah's] identity begins to unravel and respin itself" (76). The simplest questions to be asked would include: Are we the same or are we different? Are we whole or fragmentary? Are we "we" or are we "you and I"? How are you separate from me?[18] To be confronted with one's self and then to see that self step in front of a train is traumatic not only as an act of witnessing but as an act of identification with that self and its annihilation.

Sarah takes this even further in assuming Beth's life: she symbolically and literally annihilates her own self by substituting Beth's body for her own in order to cut ties with her former life and boyfriend, the drug dealer Vic Schmidt (Michael Mando). She has her foster brother, Felix, identify Beth's body as that of Sarah Manning and suppresses her own identity in attempting to mimic that of Beth, including her interactions with Beth's live-in partner, Paul Dierden, and Beth's partner on the police force, Art Bell. She studies Beth's accent, mannerisms, hair, and clothing through video recordings left behind in Beth's home and performs Beth.

Helena's identity also comes into question when she is confronted with her clone/twin, Sarah. These two are the only explicitly textual twins within the show[19]; they are carried by the same surrogate mother, Amelia (Melanie Nicholls-King), who then gave one to the church and one to the state to try and protect them. They are raised without knowledge of each other, and, already abused by the nuns within the order, Helena fell into the hands of Proletheans within the church, religious extremists who believe that genetic manipulation only should occur through God's will. Tomas and Maggie Chen (Uni Park), the Proletheans who discover her, act from within the church and brainwash her to kill her fellow clones, whom they term "abominations." They deceive Helena in order to use her as a tool, telling her she is the original from whom the other clones were made; she is responsible for the death of multiple clones, including one within *Orphan Black: Helsinki* (Fawcett et al.)

and three within *Orphan Black* (Manson et al), the first graphic narrative prequel. However, when Helena attempts to kill Sarah, she is brought to a halt by a sense of recognition stronger than that felt with the other clones. She begins to disobey Tomas and, in refusing to bring him Sarah and Kira, is caged by him as punishment. She saw the other clones as a false, inferior reflection of herself, and, with each murder, carved more feathers of the angel wings in her back; as an avenging angel, she sought annihilation of the perverse mirror, what one might call the uncanny in Sigmund Freud's terminology. With Sarah, she perceives the mirror as a mirroring of the same, which contributes to her rebirth as *sestra* ("sister" in several Slavic languages) rather than murderer.[20] Sarah calls her, "my twin, my other self" ("Let the Children and Childbearers Toil," 5.4). Interestingly, it is discovered that Helena's organs are a literal mirror of her clone sisters: her organs are on the opposite side, called *situs inversus*, from typical organ placement, otherwise known as *situs solitus*.

While we see Helena and Sarah come to a recognition of the self within the mirror—two selves, separate but replicated—Rachel, who has repudiated the mirror version of herself, comes to recognition through the implantation of the vision of another within herself. When Rachel taunts Sarah over the loss of her eggs, Sarah, with the help of Kira and Cosima, is able to fight back with a pencil and stab out Rachel's left eye. Rachel's vision, symbolically, is defective; she is unable to see the similarities between herself and her sisters.[21] She then gains a bionic eye through which she gets flashes of the death of a swan which represents the Ledas, prompting her, in part, to stab Susan Duncan and seek out Westmorland; when she does not cooperate, she receives electric shocks through the eye. Later, she will discover that the eye functions as a surveillance tool of herself; her gaze (and soul) has been subordinated to that of Westmorland in a literalization of the male gaze. It is through her realization that she must re-vision herself and the other clones that she chooses to rip out the bionic eye, return Kira to her mother, and positions herself against Neolution and its assorted cabals. She finally recognizes the clones as an iteration of herself and asserts their combined humanity.

The traumas experienced by the clones damage their sense of self in relation to others. Herman argues, "The traumatic event thus destroys the belief that one can *be oneself* in relation to others" (53, original emphasis). Rachel and each of the other women—Alison, Beth, Cosima, Sarah, Helena, Rachel, Kira, M.K.—feel a sense of helplessness and fear, key elements of trauma (van der Kolk xi–xvii; Hunt 18; Herman 34), as they realize they are trapped by others. Cosima, Sarah, Helena, Rachel, and Kira all wind up locked in enclosed spaces at *least* once while others determine their fates. Sarah and Helena are locked up and strapped down multiple times, generally with the threat of bodily invasion in front of them. Beth feels helpless and trapped as well, duped by Evie Cho (Jessalyn Wanlim) and told by Cho and Duko (Gord Rand) that, unless she killed herself, Neolution would kill her sisters ("The Scandal of Altruism," 4.6). And so she walks in front of a train, beginning our portion of the story. Traumatized persons feel cut off from life, feeling isolated, abandoned and alienated, and thus "feel that they belong more to the dead than to the living" (Herman 52); suicide is a regular unfortunate outcome of PTSD. In this case, Beth is not only traumatized but pointed toward the train by Neolution. Sarah is on the cusp of suicide as well in "The Antisocialism of Sex" (4.7), rejected and blamed by her foster mother, Siobhan Sadler, for Siobhan's mother's (Kendall Malone's [Alison Steadman]) death at the hands of Neolution. Felix, luckily, goes in pursuit of her and brings her home. Helena and Cosima are locked up for going against patriarchal mandates: Tomas puts Helena into a cage for not following his dictate to kill Sarah, and Westmorland/Mathieson cages Cosima, saying, "Cosima can rot" ("Manacled Slim Wrists," 5.6) for protesting his treatment of his first test subject, Yanis (Andrew Muselman), and resisting his dictate to put a bullet in Yanis' head. In addition to being caged by Tomas and shackled at one point by Sarah, Helena is betrayed by Siobhan, abducted, and caged by Castor for experimentation; caged by the Proletheans so that her eggs can be harvested, inseminated, and returned to her womb (and that of Gracie [Zoé de Grand'Maison]); and abducted, strapped down, and her pregnancy induced by Neolution while being verbally abused. This verbal abuse and her sense of hopelessness for her children in the hands of Neolution leads to her attempting suicide as well: she hopes to save her children from the paths of the other clones and herself, but she is saved by Sarah.

Rachel also is made to feel helpless. One of the first signs for Rachel that Westmorland/Mathieson does not hold her in the esteem he claims is when he takes her to meet Virginia Coady (Kyra Harper) and then announces Coady will be examining her, including a gynecological exam, without her consent or choice. To have her body penetrated without her permission is a violation of Rachel's rights as a human being, just as it is for the other clones. Sarah is under an even worse threat when she is strapped down for an oophorectomy without her consent. Dyad plans as well to impregnate her in the future, with or without her consent ("By Means Which Have Never Yet Been Tried," 2.10). Sarah's body is penetrated later (or perhaps simultaneously) by the implantation of a robotic worm in her mouth, designed to trigger the disease which plagues her infertile sisters, and again by Rachel when she stabs Sarah in the leg in Season 5. Such repeated invasions of the body signal the series' affinities with horror, the gothic, and the abject as well as its commitment to traumatization of its characters.

However helpless they feel, they ultimately fight back, which is essential to their sense of agency. Cosima sets the Neolutionist followers against her own Dr. Frankenstein (Westmorland/Mathieson), Helena (in one example) sets the Prolethean farm on fire, Sarah repeatedly takes initiatives against Neolution, and they all bring Neolution down together. Alison often is used as a pawn throughout the series; her most violent revolt against this is when she believes Aynsley (Natalie Lisinska) to be her monitor: she allows Aynsley to die as her scarf gets caught in the garbage disposal. Prior to this, when she believes her monitor to be Donnie, she hits him with a golf club and tortures him with her hot glue gun. She feels violated and betrayed, and this leads her to manslaughter rather than suicide. Rachel fights in her own way as well, though her anger is directed toward her sisters rather than those responsible for her situation; it may be a result of her own self-loathing and internalized misogyny, masked by her assertion that she is superior to her sisters. It seems she has no qualms over killing her fellow clones. She is responsible for the death of the first clone to fall sick with their disease, killing her so that her body might be studied and a cure for herself produced (remembered in 5.7; occurs prior to Season 1); she also attempts to kill her own adoptive mother (4.10) and looks forward to Sarah's reproductive mutilation (2.10). In the canonical *Orphan Black: Helsinki* graphic novel and *Orphan Black Classified Clone Reports*, Rachel is responsible for pushing for the annihilation of clones in Poland, Germany, Denmark, the Netherlands, Finland, and the Czech Republic by Ferdinand, a cleaner, in large part due to her jealousy of Veera Suominen's relationship with Ethan and Susan Duncan, her parents.[22] In the series, Rachel attempts to set a Helsinki-type event into play within her own clone cohort, calling in Ferdinand to kill her sister clones and their friends and families ("The Weight of This Combination," 3.1). By destroying the other clones, she destroys herself and re-enacts her parents' abandonment.

As stated, implicit within trauma is a disruption of the link between self and world. As Herman writes, "Traumatic events destroy the victim's fundamental assumptions about the safety of the world, the positive value of the self, and the meaningful order of creation. [...] Trauma forces the survivor to relive all her earlier struggles over autonomy, initiative, competence, identity, and intimacy" (51–52); as described above, discovering one is a clone could do the same. Repeated violence, the constant threat of annihilation (whether internal or external to the self), incursions upon the physical body, and a sense of general helplessness as well as one's own imbrication in violence and the need for secrecy (i.e. a lack of communication) destroy one's sense of identity and relationship to the world and others and continue the traumatization. Involvement in or witnessing violence toward others, including the death of others, destroys one's sense of self, meaning, and safety (Herman 51–52) and is another element of *Orphan Black*'s trauma. Helena's original mission of killing the other clones creates an existential crisis in her as she begins to question Tomas' narrative after recognizing her twin's humanity.

Sarah's witnessing of both Katja Obinger and Beth's death and fear for her own life ("Natural Selection," 1.1) clearly has a deep effect on her beyond the way it represents a death of the self, just as witnessing Kendall's death affects Cosima (4.6). Both are shaken, with Cosima sinking to the ground, sobbing, and Sarah screaming "shit!" repeatedly (1.1) and later refusing to tell Felix why she has (Katja's) blood on her face ("Instinct," 1.2). Watching her daughter get hit by a car also traumatizes Sarah as well as Kira ("Entangled Bank," 1.8).

Trauma inscribes itself upon the body through mental, emotional, physical, and physiological reactions. It also may be visibly, physically inscribed upon the body as a result of the violence done to it. M.K., *aka* Veera Suominen, *aka* Mika, survives the destruction of the Duncan lab and is the only survivor of the Helsinki clone group, and her trauma is imprinted on her body through the scarring of her face from burns as well as on her psyche. She notes, to Ferdinand, that "you killed six of my sisters. Murdered thirty-two of our friends and loved ones" (4.4). About Niki, her "only friend," she seethes, "You gassed her family. You burned her alive" (4.4; see also *Orphan Black: Helsinki*). In the televised scene with Ferdinand, she is projecting pictures and newspaper articles on the wall of Beth's living room; as she tallies his crimes the newsprint is projected on her burnt face, creating a doubled inscription of the event. She is so traumatized (understandably so) by these events that she hides behind a sheep's mask,[23] goes by two of the letters of her property tag (3MK29A) rather than her given name, and acts as a secretive recluse, fearing someone will betray her and/or give away her location as she works against Ferdinand and Dyad. She becomes multiple in order to hide herself even as she works against Dyad and Topside; Jennifer DeRoss suggests she contains clone multitudes.[24] Helena's carving of angel wings in her back with a razor in recognition of her allegedly righteous murder of fellow clones illustrates her traumatization and its inscription on her body; she carves Tomas's narrative into her back, and the pain provides her a sense of control over her situation and relief from her confusion. Kira, like Helena, later will mutilate herself through cutting to rid her body of its indeterminacy. Sarah's attempt to take on Beth's identity, discussed above, also functions as an embodiment of trauma as she seeks rebirth, forgetting, and dissolution of the relationship with Vic even as she attempts to reconnect with Kira, Felix, and Mrs. S.

Each of these clones attempts to either forget what they have done and seen, gain revenge for it, as in the case of M.K., or, at least, come to terms with it. In the scene noted above, M.K. attempts to immolate Ferdinand in what he calls a "revenge fantasy" (4.4). In addition to her self-mutilation, Helena re-enacts the penetration of her own body upon the body of Prolethean leader Henrik Johanssen (Peter Outerbridge) ("Things Which Have

Never Yet Been Done," 2.9); she also seeks retribution against Siobhan for her betrayal to Castor ("Community of Dreadful Fear and Hate," 3.7). Alison, Rachel, and Sarah use alcohol and drugs to become numb, and Cosima uses marijuana to relax and gain relief from pain; Sarah also uses partying and sex, and Rachel engages in sexual domination with Ferdinand for the illusion of control. Rachel additionally enacts vengeance for any slight against her, real or imagined, including Sarah's incomprehensible fertility. Sadly, this latter drive towards eliminating her sisters precludes her inclusion in the end community even after she finally understands that her existence depends upon that of her sisters. The drive to re-enact one's own trauma through vengeance repeatedly is shown to be regressive and contributes to the continued effects of said trauma within the series. Communication, reflection, and community are shown to be the only effective means of moving forward, as has been observed in studies of trauma resolution.

Healing from Trauma: "They're never going to have to go through everything we did"[25]

The simultaneous desire to talk and refusal to do so characterizes trauma and is the "central dialectic of psychological trauma" (Herman 1); intimacy is both rejected and desired (Herman 52; Henry 66). "The ordinary response to atrocities is to banish them from consciousness. Certain violations of the social compact are too terrible to utter aloud: this is the meaning of the word *unspeakable*" (Herman 1, original emphasis). This dialectic occurs within the series but is not limited to the need to keep secrets from those outside of the Clone Club. A few such examples follow: Alison and Donnie fail to communicate their own, individual, traumatizing manslaughter of others until they cannot go further without doing so; finally being open and honest with each other strengthens their marriage and affords them greater resiliency. Donnie's inscription of a heart in the wet cement covering Leekie's corpse—"I've always wanted to do that," Donnie comments, to which Alison responds, "I have never been more attracted to you than I am right now" ("Things Which Have Never Yet Been Done," 2.9)—is one of the sweeter moments of the show and illustrates the importance of honest communication. Helena admits to Sarah that she cut herself as a child through adulthood but was able to stop once her sisters accepted her (5.4); Janet Brennan Croft in her essay in this volume convincingly identifies the clone party in 2.10 as that moment. The identity of Siobhan's mother, who also is her husband's killer, is a revelation even to her two foster children since she has not discussed it with them. Helena won't tell Art what the Proletheans took from her (her eggs) in "Governed as It Were by Chance" (2.4), and, as previously stated, Sarah won't tell Felix why there is blood on her face after Katja is killed (1.2). M.K. initially keeps herself separate from the other clones aside from delivering quick warnings; she is there to help them, but she does not ask for help herself, and she refuses bonding out of fear of continued loss and betrayal. She begins to see herself as person again through Beth, who calls her "Mika" affectionately, re-asserting her humanity, but then Beth is lost to her, and she reverts to her own dehumanization. Finally, M.K. begins to enact intimacy once more with the other clones, surprised that they do the same, but this ends in her self-sacrifice for Sarah as she recognizes the danger posed by Ferdinand to Sarah as well as the rapid advancement of her own expiration date through her illness. Like Beth and, momentarily, Sarah, she also is tired of internal and external fights and her own pain, and she uses her own resignation towards her fate for the good of the group.

As we see in the case of M.K., isolation makes overcoming trauma far more difficult and maintains the sense that one is not a part of the world, often with tragic consequences. While Jennifer DeRoss makes the compelling case in her essay in this volume that M.K. is bound to the other clones, physically she generally remains separate. The clones are at their most vulnerable when they feel isolated and helpless, and we see this in several of the characters beyond M.K. Helena is manipulated into killing her sister clones because of the dehumanizing abuse she suffered as well as her isolation and ignorance of reality; her isolation in the Castor camp also encourages her to believe the lies Coady tells her. That she is imprisoned in the Castor camp at all is, in part, due to her sneaking away from the clone party; since she did not tell anyone she was leaving, she isolated herself and discovery of her absence took longer.[26] Rachel's abandonment by her parents is linked to her repeated attempts at gaining power, generally at the expense of others and especially at the expense of her sister clones. She learns to identify with her oppressors rather than against them, resisting community with those like herself. While Beth engages with Cosima, Alison, and M.K., she also keeps herself separate; she has realized the man she loves, Paul, is not in love with her, and investigating the clone mystery wears on her and threatens her sense of self and bonds with the other clones, although she commits suicide in part to protect them. Maslany states, "She's not like the other clones, where they sort of reach out to each other. She sort of peels herself away in a way that … that her separation is, sort of, her ultimate demise" ("Inside *Orphan Black*: 'The Collapse of Nature,'" 4.105). Sarah repeatedly attempts to accomplish tasks on her own, avoiding reliance on others; however, her plans work best when others are working in concert with her. Rachel and Dyad/Neolution soon learn to separate Delphine (Évelyne Brochu) from Cosima; Cosima's time on the island, alone, is when she is at her most vulnerable, and it is the first time we hear her speak of her own parents. Trauma leads to the desire to separate oneself from others out of shame, guilt, doubt, and a sense of inferiority (Herman 52–53), and it leaves one vulnerable.

Connections to community, communication, and a sense of agency lead to relief from trauma, while impulsivity and isolation, conversely, are linked with suffering (Herman 58, 133). Through community, survivors rebuild the capacity for "trust, autonomy, initiative, competence, identity, and intimacy" (133); Dr. Janina Scarlet argues meaningful connections with others lead to better mental health. Reliable safety, mourning and remembering, and the re-establishment of everyday life are essential to healing as well (Herman 156). We see these elements throughout *Orphan Black*. As is common in serial drama, especially those uncertain of renewal, *Orphan Black* maintains the large arc mysteries but wraps up much of season-long arcs by the end of each season. Three out of five of the seasons end with some momentary peace in the season finale, establishing momentary safety, reflecting upon what they've been through and who they have lost, and celebrating in somewhat mundane fashion, whether it be a dance party, a celebration at Bubbles, a momentary reunification of Sarah with Kira, or a baby shower.[27] In order to heal and to return the social order to normalcy, survivors must both remember *and* speak the truth about their trauma. When the truth is finally recognized, survivors can begin their recovery and engage in post-traumatic growth, creating meaning from trauma (Scarlet). It is notable that, near the end of the last episode, Helena brings her journal out. Entitled *Orphan Black*, it details what they have been through and how they have bonded. "It's story about my *sestras*. I call it *Orphan Black*. […] My story is an embroidery with many beginnings and no end. But I will start with the thread of my *sestra* Sarah, who stepped off a train one day and met herself" (5.10). The last bit of the finale concerns Delphine and Cosima traveling around the world curing the other clones, ridding them of their disease even if they were unaware of it. Community, sisterhood, communication, and normalcy end the series and enable the healing of the clones, even Rachel, who provides the names of her sister clones in order that they may be cured.

Near the beginning of the essay, I briefly mentioned elements of genre which contribute to the representation of trauma within the series. While serialized melodrama and the elements of the gothic maintain the production of trauma (whether physical or emotional), elements of the detective story/*film noir* enable healing. Finding out who did what to whom and why is a central generic element of the series as the clones, functioning as *de facto* detectives, investigate the multiple layers of involvement by corporations, the government, the military, and religion in their lives. In keeping with the other generic elements mentioned early on, the detective element of *Orphan Black* also supports the traumatic narrative: violence is a given in the detective story. However, healing is vital as well. The detective, argues Cynthia Hamilton, functions as a sort of therapist to survivors of trauma, enabling their voices, listening to their stories, and becoming a witness to them. Through the narratives the detective assembles in order to understand survivors, s/he helps to process the event, allowing the survivor to move forward. This therapeutic role may overwhelm the detective, creating problems for her/his own interpersonal relationships and, potentially, a sense of helplessness. The "confused, fragmented testimonies" mentioned earlier are made meaningful, resulting in a "healing narrative" (15–17, 19). As a result, the text also illustrates the process by which we make meaning and the ways in which we can take control of our narrative; the traumatization, therapeutic process, and recovery of the detective(s) enables hope for healing, survival, and agency in the face of disempowerment (21). For Hamilton, these stories ultimately function as liberatory fiction for readers, interrogating the structures of power and (hi)story surrounding survivor and detective(s). Here we link again to the larger culture of which these traumatic stories are a part: the trauma victim "calls for an interrogation of the dynamics of history … [and] stands as witness to the culpability of those in power and to the dangerous ideology that would naturalise or vindicate the actions of those responsible for inflicting the trauma" (16).

Valuing, recovering, and telling our stories; seeing the personal as political; and forming community are central to feminism as well. The mid–20th century and beyond has seen the recovery of past and present female scientists, artists, authors, and others by feminist scholars in order to understand that others have come before us, and we are not alone. This is why Alice Walker went "In Search of Our Mothers' Gardens," linking her own story and creative endeavors to those of Zora Neale Hurston. It is why, in part, *Hidden Figures* is such an important story in retelling the story of women—Katherine Jonson (Taraji P. Hanson), Dorothy Vaughan (Octavia Spencer), and Mary Jackson (Janelle Monae)—central to the first crewed trip to the moon in the 1960s. It is the rediscovery of Ada Lovelace's central role as a 19th-century mathematician to the development of the computer. These are only a few of the connections women can make to facilitate their own sense of being in the world. Understanding that our personal stories are political, as Sara Evans did in 1979, enables agency as well, allowing us to connect our personal experiences with an understanding of relationships of power.

Orphan Black, although science fiction at heart, places itself within the real world and a real history. While Neolution goes further than actual science has and did so earlier than the advancements in cloning in our world—at least to anyone's knowledge—action occurs in a world that includes Darwin's theory of evolution, eugenic experimentation, gene therapy, and the cloning of animals as well as landmark cases such as Citizens United, which considers corporations to function as people. The personal gets tied to the public world; the separation of public and private, developed alongside industrialization, no longer has meaning as the corporate world enters the bedrooms of these women and patents their DNA. Susan Duncan and Virginia Coady work with the less-talented but male, white, and wealthy John Mathieson to build the myth of P.T. Westmorland and Neolution due to sexism within the world of science, subordinating themselves to his ego and quest for youth since it allowed them to use their minds, however devoid of ethical principles or nurturing they were. Hinted at in the series but explicitly stated in the Cormier files, Mathieson was, according to Coady's account, Coady and Duncan's "beard. [...] [I]t's not like women were allowed to be scientists back when we started. Hell, we're barely allowed to be now in the oh-so-enlightened twenty-first century. [...] The man whose money and whose gender allowed two brilliant women to do their work without the patronizing looks and the obnoxious comments and the dismissive memos" (DiCandido 157). Henrik Johanssen functions as a similar sort of engagement with the contemporary Western world: he is a eugenicist who wants to promulgate his own (white) vision of human improvement upon the world, reiterating the white supremacist, Nazi, fascist leanings of the Western world. Like Mathieson/P.T. Westmorland, his vision of the future is a reiteration of the same in its emphasis on a white, male hierarchical vision. The series illustrates the trauma incurred by such visions.

Orphan Black creates a liberatory, unified narrative out of fragments, much as the clones construct meaning from the fragmentary elements provided by Professor Ethan Duncan in his copy of *The Island of Dr. Moreau*. Really, it is a fragment of a fragment they decode since the book and their copy of the book is lost to them, and they are left only with a nursery rhyme. Sarah's early role as detective (impersonator) and the involvement of Art as partner enables resources and protection for the clones, just as Cosima's investigation of the science simultaneously weaves an origin story for the clones as well as one of healing. All of the clones act as therapists to each other, witnessing their trauma, testifying to it, and strengthening their sisterhood. As a liberatory fiction, *Orphan Black* interrogates corporate, religious, military, and governmental power as well as the ethics of identity in its representation of trauma. It establishes the need to not only act as a witness to trauma but also to build community, heal, and tell our stories as the clones tell theirs. The future is still female.

Notes

1. In her essay on Helena in this collection, Janet Brennan Croft argues that Helena becomes "hero, shaman, and storyteller" and, with her sisters, saves the world, partly through her repeated descents into hell.
2. "To Right the Wrongs of Many," 5.10.

3. The male and female clones are each played by one actor, respectively: Ari Millen and Tatiana Maslany.
4. For more on the female gothic, see, for instance, Cynthia Wolff, Eve Kosofsky Sedgwick, and Ellen Moers.
5. Krystal brings us much needed comic relief in her theories of conspiracies and power plays within the cosmetics industry. She refuses to see Sarah as a clone sister and, while being just so very wrong about events, manages to put together some very good information on her own. And the cosmetics industry is, it turns out, involved, if only as providing delivery systems for Neolution's projects. See note 13 for more on Krystal.
6. For more on the uses of mythology in *Orphan Black*, see Janet Brennan Croft in this collection.
7. There is no space herein to discuss either the complexities of Laura Mulvey's work nor the many critiques her work has received. Teresa deLauretis was one of the first to pose a challenge to Mulvey's work, arguing that it reinforced gender binaries. bell hooks has also discussed the ways in which audience members can resist the gaze of the camera and look elsewhere.
8. Art, Beth/Sarah's black, male partner, is one of the few authority figures worthy of trust, and he becomes an honorary member of the family as a result of his care for the clones and their families as well as his clear integrity.
9. "To Right the Wrongs of Many," 5.10. On February 6, 2017, Hillary Clinton made her first public comments after she lost to explicit misogynist Donald Trump in the 2016 presidential race. Addressing the MAKERS women's empowerment conference, she argued, "Despite all the challenges we face, I remain convinced that yes, the future is female" (Kelley). "The future is female," while used by Clinton then and during her campaign as well as in the final episode (August 2017 release) of *Orphan Black* (in what seems to be a direct homage to Clinton, although it is put in the mouth of John Mathieson, a man similar to Trump in his misogyny and narcissism, who is mocking Sarah in his seeming defeat of the Leda clones), was originally coined by the Greenwich Village lesbian feminist bookstore Labyris, which put the slogan on t-shirts to fund their activist literary enterprise (Mettler). The slogan also shows up earlier in the show, worn, for instance, on a t-shirt by Hellwizard (Calwyn Shurgold) as he DJs Felix's art opening (5.8).
That the show is purposefully interacting with such moments as Clinton's speech is made explicit in the Season 5 behind-the-scenes shorts; for instance, in the bonus "Inside *Orphan Black*: Ease for Idle Millionaires," Maslany reflects, "The focus of that episode was about patriarchy, and where you fit in that system, and how do you fight it and how do you fight from within it.... It was really, uh, interesting dynamics especially with what was going on. I think Trump had literally just been, um ... just won, like that week. And then we got the script and it was like, "Oh, God, we're talking about this...'"
10. Notably, NPR's series on maternal death illustrates the ways in which sexism and racism in medicine is responsible for maternal death, since nurses and doctors often do not listen to women, especially black women, about their own bodies; as a result, elements like pain and bleeding—indicators that something is going wrong—often are ignored (Martin and Montagne, "Black"). Serena Williams is the most notable example of such racism and sexism; the tennis champion experienced blood clots, something to which she is prone and about which she is therefore very informed, after the birth of her daughter in September, but the nurse refused to listen to her concerns, arguing she was confused from labor medications. The doctor performed an ultrasound, but of her legs rather than her lungs. Williams persisted in self-advocacy and finally received lifesaving treatment (Salam). For more on gestation-related trauma, see Ellison and Martin; Martin and Montagne, "Many"; Martin and Montagne, "Black"; and Martin and Montagne, "U.S. Hospitals,"; see Martin and Montagne, "Black," for more on black gestational trauma.
11. See "Infertility" for figures on U.S. infertility rates.
12. While sexual and gender difference is accepted as part of the lives of the Ledas—Cosima is lesbian, it is hinted that Sarah is queer, and Tony is transgender, for a few examples—the Castors are markedly heterosexual, although this is tied to the hostile sexual imperative given to them by the military: testing out the Castors as sexual weapons to subdue

populations through illness and infertility. The aggressive, punitive, sexual construction of the Castors clearly is linked to other elements critiquing compulsory heteronormativity and patriarchy within the series.

13. According to Martin and Montagne, "many of the mistakes that lead to maternal death stem from a medical system that bases care on the idea that it's rare for a woman to die in childbirth. It's a system where funding and resources are directed mostly at saving babies" ("U.S. Hospitals").

14. Rachel's adoptive father and head of the cloning project for its first several years with his wife, Susan. After making it clear they (Susan and Ethan) wanted to be permanent, autonomous parents for Rachel, Aldous Leekie set their lab on fire, and they fled, abandoning Rachel. They were presumed dead for over two decades.

15. Still, Helena notes that Alison is "jealous and angry because me having babies..." in "From Instinct to Rational Control" (4.4).

16. Tatiana Maslany specifically addresses Rachel's desire to hold herself above the other clones and the ways in which she must come to terms with her equality with her sisters in "Inside *Orphan Black*: Gag or Throttle," concluding: "she isn't that special thing that she thinks she is."

17. In the mirror stage, the infant discovers their own separateness from the mother figure through the reflection of their self as a discrete entity; it also denotes understanding one's relationship to both the Imaginary and the Real. Buket Akgun also connects the clones to the mirror stage.

18. Philosopher Gregory Pence argues that questions about one's origin would be of the most interest upon learning one is a clone (165–166, chapter 14); while this author clearly disagrees about which questions would be most vital, dependent upon the conditions under which one learned one was a clone, certainly originary questions plague all of us—otherwise ancestry.com and DNA testing would not be so popular right now!

19. The *Orphan Black: Helsinki* graphic novel also features a set of clone twins, Fay and Femke, although doubt is expressed in regard to whether they actually are twins.

20. The initial encounters, i.e., the shock of recognition, between the other clones in the core group—Cosima, Alison, Beth, Mika/Veera, and Katja—take place offscreen and thus cannot be factored into this analysis. Krystal, another clone whom the core group encounters, refuses to acknowledge Sarah as a clone; she refuses the reflection of the mirror as a reflection of the same. "Oh, this is what you think I look like?," she asks Art and Felix. "Okay, are you, like, blind? 'Cause this girl looks nothing like me. Like, first of all, my tits are way bigger. And, secondly, even if you could drag a comb through that hair, she's like a seven on a good day, and I've been told I'm a ten." A few moments later, when Sarah asks a question, Krystal responds, "I'm sorry, who are you again?" Sarah responds, "I'm Sarah. I'm your clone." "Right, whatever" (4.10). Although she is attacked by Castors and comes face-to-face with her self, Krystal resolutely follows her own narrative. Although I have suggested here that the clones are a reiteration of the self, a mirror, they are individual personalities; we get a diverse representation of womanhood through these clones which makes it even more empowering since neither a unitary ideal of womanhood nor biological determinism are privileged.

21. Within Western culture, the eye often symbolizes a window to the soul as well.

22. While this information about the source of Rachel's annihilating anger comes in one of Veera's nightmares in the graphic narrative, the dreams of the clones often are insightful, accurate, and/or prophetic. The *Orphan Black Classified Clone Reports* confirm Rachel's responsibility for Helsinki (4). Jennifer DeRoss argues, in her essay in this volume, that Veera is responsible for taking away Rachel's innocence about her identity as a clone, inciting Rachel's fury.

23. This is fitting, since the first successfully cloned animal was Dolly the sheep; Fawcett and Maslany both discuss this allusion in the behind-the-scenes commentary "Inside *Orphan Black*: Transgressive Border Crossing" (4.106). M.K. uses the mask not only to comment upon the reduction of herself and her sister clones to animals but also to cover her embodied trauma. Interestingly, in the aforementioned short, Maslany suggests the clones' faces function as masks since "all the clones have the same face."

24. See DeRoss, "Sheeply Empowerment," in this volume.
25. "To Right the Wrongs of Many," 5.10.
26. Thank you to Janet Brennan Croft for this additional example of isolation.
27. Bronwen Calvert briefly discusses these momentary respites as well in her essay in this anthology.

Works Cited

Akgun, Buket. "'[S]omeone Else Sometimes': Down the Rabbit Hole and Through the Looking-Glass in *Orphan Black*." 47th Annual Popular Cultural Association/American Culture Association Conference, San Diego, California, U.S.A., 12–15 April 2017. https://www.academia.edu/33848891/_S_omeone_else_sometimes_Down_the_Rabbit_Hole_and_Through_the_Looking-Glass_in_Orphan_Black_

Anzaldua, Gloria. *Borderlands/La Frontera: The New Mestiza*. 3rd edition, Aunt Lute Books, 2007.

Berger, James. "Trauma and Literary Theory." *Contemporary Literature*, vol. 38, no. 3 (1997), pp. 569–582.

Brownell, Eric. "Gothic Heroines and Cultural Trauma in 20th Century Literature and Film." Dissertation, University of Minnesota, 2015. conservancy.umn.edu/bitstream/handle/11299/170948/Brownell_umn_0130E_15758.pdf;sequence=1.

Bruhm, Steven. "The Contemporary Gothic." *The Cambridge Companion to Gothic Fiction*. Cambridge UP, 2002. 259–276.

_____. *Gothic Bodies: The Politics of Pain in Romantic Fiction*. U Pennsylvania P, 1994.

"By Means Which Have Never Yet Been Tried." Writ. Graeme Manson. Dir. John Fawcett. *Orphan Black*. Season 2, episode 10. First aired 21 June 2014.

Campbell, Joseph. *The Hero with a Thousand Faces*. Princeton UP, 1973.

Cantor, Joanne. "The Media and Children's Fears, Anxieties, and Perceptions of Danger." *Handbook of Children and the Media*. Edited by Dorothy G. Singer and Jerome L. Singer, Sage, 2012, pp. 215–229.

Croft, Janet Brennan. "Hell and Back: Helena as Kore and Shaman in *Orphan Black*." *Orphan Black: Sestras, Scorpions, and Crazy Science*, edited by Janet Brennan Croft and Alyson R. Buckman, McFarland, 2018.

DeCandido, Keith R.A. *Orphan Black: Classified Clone Reports : Confidential*. Harper Design, an imprint of HarperCollinsPublishers, 2017.

De Lauretis, Teresa. "Oedipus Interruptus." *Alice Doesn't: Feminism, Semiotics, Cinema*, Indiana UP, 1984, pp. 83–95.

DeRoss, Jennifer. "Sheeply Empowerment: An Analysis of M.K.'s Reappropriation in *Orphan Black*." *Orphan Black: Sestras, Scorpions, and Crazy Science*, edited by Janet Brennan Croft and Alyson R. Buckman, McFarland, 2018.

Donovan, Sarah K. "Not Why but Who." *Orphan Black and Philosophy: Grand Theft DNA*, edited by Richard Greene and Rachel Robison-Greene, Kindle ed., Open Court, 2016, pp. 127–139.

Eisenstein, Sergei. "A Dialectic Approach to Film Form." *Film Form: Essays in Film Theory*, Edited and translated by Jay Leyda, 2nd edition, Harcourt, 1969, pp. 45–63.

Ellison, Katherine, and Nina Martin. "Nearly Dying in Childbirth: Why Preventable Complications Are Growing in U.S." *National Public Radio* 22 Dec. 2017. www.npr.org/2017/12/22/572298802/nearly-dying-in-childbirth-why-preventable-complications-are-growing-in-u-s.

"Entangled Bank." Writ. Karen Walton. Dir. Ken Girotti. *Orphan Black*. Season 1, episode 8. First aired 18 May 2013.

Evans, Sara. *Personal Politics: The Roots of Women's Liberation in the Civil Rights Movement and the New Left*. Vintage, 1979.

Fawcett, John et al. *Orphan Black: Helsinki*. Idea and Design Works, 2016. *Orphan Black*, vol. 2.

Fiorenza, Elisabeth Schüssler. *But She Said: Feminist Practices of Biblical Interpretation*. Beacon, 1993.

_____. *Wisdom Ways: Introducing Feminist Biblical Interpretation*. Orbis, 2001.
"From Dancing Mice to Psychopaths." Writ. Graeme Manson. Dir. John Fawcett. *Orphan Black*. Season 4, episode 10. First aired 16 June 2016.
"From Instinct to Rational Control." Writ. Alex Levine. Dir. Peter Stebbings. *Orphan Black*. Season 4, episode 4. First aired 5 May 2016.
"Gag or Throttle." Writ. Renée St. Cyr. Dir. David Frazee. *Orphan Black*. Season 5, episode 7. First aired 22 July 2017.
"Governed as It Were by Chance." Writ. Russ Cochrane. Dir. David Frazee. *Orphan Black*. Season 2, episode 4. First aired 10 May 2014.
"Guillotines Decide." Writ. Aisha Porter-Christie and Graeme Manson. Dir. Aaron Morton. *Orphan Black*. Season 5, episode 8. First aired 5 August 2017.
Hamilton, Cynthia. *Sara Paretsky: Detective Fiction as Trauma Literature*. Manchester, 2015.
Heidegger, Martin. *Being and Time*. 1927. Translated by Joan Stambaugh. SUNY P 2010.
Henry, Vincent. *Death Work: Police, Trauma, and the Psychology of Survival*. Oxford UP, 2004.
Herman, Judith. *Trauma and Recovery: The Aftermath of Violence—From Domestic Abuse to Political Terror*. 1992. Basic Books, 2015.
Heuslein, Jeremy. "I Am and Am Not You." *Orphan Black and Philosophy: Grand Theft DNA*, edited by Richard Greene and Rachel Robison-Greene, Kindle ed., Open Court, 2016, pp. 75–84.
Hidden Figures. Directed by Theodore Melfi. Performances by Taraji P. Henson, Octavia Spencer, Janelle Monae, Kevin Costner, Kirsten Dunst, and Jim Parsons. 20th Century–Fox, 2016.
hooks, bell. "The Oppositional Gaze: Black Female Spectators." *Black Looks: Race and Representation*. South End P, 1992, pp. 115–131.
Hunt, Nigel C. *Memory, War and Trauma*. Cambridge, 2010.
"Infertility." *Office of Women's Health, U.S. Department of Health and Human Services*, 22 May 2018, www.womenshealth.gov/a-z-topics/infertility.
"Inside *Orphan Black*: The Collapse of Nature." *Orphan Black*, created by Graeme Manson and John Fawcett, performance by Tatiana Maslany, Season 4, episode 105, Temple Street Productions, BBC America, and Bell's Media Space, 2016.
"Inside *Orphan Black*: Ease for Idle Millionaires." *Orphan Black*, created by Graeme Manson and John Fawcett, performance by Tatiana Maslany, Season 5, episode 0, Temple Street Productions, BBC America, and Bell's Media Space, 2017.
"Inside *Orphan Black*: Gag or Throttle." *Orphan Black*, created by Graeme Manson and John Fawcett, performance by Tatiana Maslany, Season 5, episode 0, Temple Street Productions, BBC America, and Bell's Media Space, 2017.
"Inside *Orphan Black*: Transgressive Border Crossings." *Orphan Black*, created by Graeme Manson and John Fawcett, performance by Tatiana Maslany, Season 4, episode 106, Temple Street Productions, BBC America, and Bell's Media Space, 2016.
"Instinct." Writ. Graeme Manson. Dir. John Fawcett. *Orphan Black*. Season 1, episode 2. First aired 6 Apr. 2013.
Kelley, Sonaiya. "Hillary Clinton's First Recorded Comments After the Women's March: The Future Is Female.'" *Los Angeles Times*, 7 Feb 2017. www.latimes.com/entertainment/la-et-entertainment-news-updates-hillary-clinton-s-first-recorded-1486503583-htmlstory.html.
Lacan, Jacques. "The Mirror Stage." 1949. *Social Theory: The Multicultural Readings*. Edited by C. Lemert. Westview P, 2010.
LaCapra, Dominic. *Writing History, Writing Trauma*. 2001. Kindle ed., Johns Hopkins UP, 2014.
"Let the Children and Childbearers Toil." Writ. Greg Nelson. Dir. David Wellington. *Orphan Black*. Season 5, episode 4. First aired 1 July 2017.
"Manacled Slim Wrists." Writ. David Bezmozgis. Dir. Grant Harvey. *Orphan Black*. Season 5, episode 6. First aired 15 July 2017.
Manson, Graeme, et al. *Orphan Black*. IDW Publishing, 2015. *Orphan Black*, vol. 1.
Martin, Nina, and Renee Montagne. "Black Mothers Keep Dying After Giving Birth. Shalon

Irving's Story Explains Why." *NPR: All Things Considered,* 7 Dec. 2017, www.npr.org/ 2017/12/07/568948782/black-mothers-keep-dying-after-giving-birth-shalon-irvings-story-explains-why.
_____. "Many Nurses Lack Knowledge of Health Risks to Mothers After Childbirth." *NPR: Morning Edition,* 17 Aug. 2017, www.npr.org/sections/health-shots/2017/08/17/54392 4405/many-nurses-lack-knowledge-of-health-risks-for-mothers-after-childbirth.
_____. "U.S. Hospitals Struggle to Protect Mothers When Childbirth Turns Deadly." *NPR: All Things Considered,* 5 July 2017, www.npr.org/2017/07/05/535660628/u-s-hospitals-struggle-to-protect-mothers-when-childbirth-turns-deadly.
McLaughlin, Eliott C. "We're Not Seeing More Police Shootings, Just More News Coverage." *CNN,* 21 Apr. 2015, www.cnn.com/2015/04/20/us/police-brutality-video-social-media-attitudes/index.html.
Mettler, Katie. "Hillary Clinton Just Said It, but 'the Future Is Female' Began as a 1970s Lesbian Separatist Slogan." *The Washington Post,* 8 Feb 2017. www.washingtonpost.com/news/morning-mix/wp/2017/02/08/hillary-clinton-just-said-it-but-the-future-is-female-began-as-a-1970s-lesbian-separatist-slogan/?noredirect=on&utm_term=.2f3a39b95 66e.
Moers, Ellen. *Literary Women: The Great Writers.* Doubleday, 1976, pp. 90–98.
Morrison, Toni. "Unspeakable Things Unspoken: The Afro American Presence in American Literature." the Tanner Lectures on Human Values, University of Michigan, 7 Oct. 1988. tannerlectures.utah.edu/_documents/a-to-z/m/morrison90.pdf. Also available in *Michigan Quarterly,* vol. 28, no. 1, 1989, pp. 1–34.
Mulvey, Laura. "Visual Pleasure and Narrative Cinema." *Screen,* vol. 16, no. 3, 1975, pp. 6–18.
"Natural Selection." Writ. Graeme Manson. Dir. John Fawcett. *Orphan Black.* Season 1, episode 1. First aired 30 Mar. 2013.
"One Fettered Slave." Writ. Alex Levine. Dir. David Frazee. *Orphan Black.* Season 5, episode 9. First aired 5 Aug 2017.
Organization for Economic Cooperation and Development. *States of Fragility 2016: Understanding Violence.* Organization for Economic Cooperation and Development, 2016.
Pence, Gregory. *What We Talk About When We Talk About Clone Club: Bioethics and Philosophy in Orphan Black.* Kindle ed., BenBella Books, 2016.
Pinker, Steven. *The Better Angels of Our Nature.* Viking, 2011.
Plantinga, Carl. "Trauma, Pleasure, and Emotion in the Viewing of *Titanic*: A Cognitive Approach." *Film Theory and Contemporary Hollywood Movies.* Edited by Warren Buckland, 2009, pp. 237–256.
Salam, Maya. "For Serena Williams, Childbirth Was a Harrowing Ordeal. She's Not Alone." *The New York Times,* 11 Jan. 2018, www.nytimes.com/2018/01/11/sports/tennis/serena-williams-baby-vogue.html.
"The Scandal of Altruism." Writ. Chris Roberts. Dir. Grant Harvey. *Orphan Black.* Season 4, episode 6. First aired 19 May 2016.
Scarlet, Janina. "Psychology of Harry Potter." *Superhero Therapy Podcast.* 14 Oct. 2017. www.superhero-therapy.com/podcast-2/.
Sedgwick, Eve Kosofsky. "The Character in the Veil: Imagery of the Surface in the Gothic Novel." *PMLA,* vol. 96, no. 2, 1981, pp. 255–270.
"Things Which Have Never Yet Been Done." Writ. Alex Levine. Dir. TJ Scott. *Orphan Black.* Season 2, episode 9. First aired 14 June 2014.
"To Right the Wrongs of Many." Writ. Renée St. Cyr and Graeme Manson. Dir. John Fawcett. *Orphan Black.* Season 5, episode 10. First aired 12 Aug 2017.
Van der Kolk, Bessel A. "Foreword." *Trauma and Memory: Brain and Body in the Search for a Living Past.* by Peter Levine. North Atlantic Books, 2015.
"Variable and Full of Perturbation." Writ. Karen Walton. Dir. John Fawcett. *Orphan Black.* Season 2, episode 8. First aired 7 June 2014.
Walker, Alice. "In Search of Our Mother's Gardens: The Creativity of Black Women in the South." 1974. *Ms. Magazine,* 2002, www.msmagazine.com/spring2002/walker.asp.
"The Weight of This Combination." Writ. Graeme Manson. Dir. David Frazee. *Orphan Black.* Season 3, episode 1. First aired 18 Apr. 2015.

Wilson, Barbara J. "Media and Children's Aggression, Fear, and Altruism." *The Future of Children*, vol. 18, no. 1, 2008, pp. 87–118.
Wolff, Cynthia. "The Radcliffean Gothic Model." *The Female Gothic*. Eden P, 1983, pp. 207–223.

Performing Bodies
Multiplying Cyborg-Clones, CGI and the Invisible Special Effect

BRONWEN CALVERT

In September 2016, Tatiana Maslany was awarded an Emmy for Outstanding Lead Actress in a Drama Series for her work on *Orphan Black* Season 4. This achievement was celebrated on social media (where previously her lack of nominations had given rise to the hashtag #EmmyForMaslany) with accompanying tongue-in-cheek comments wondering which role had won Maslany the award and suggestions she be given multiple statuettes (@jdeuberry, @TeeEssMacWall, @vchen24). Maslany's multi-character performance saw her "credited for more roles in her nomination [7] than the rest of the lead drama actress nominees combined" (Brown).[1] Maslany's rightly lauded performance as all of the Leda clone sisters is the *tour de force* on which the entire series rests. So convincing are her physical manifestations of each clone that it is easy to forget that we are not watching several identical actors on the screen. However, this performance would not be possible—or believable—without the use of particular special effects. This combination of special effects so "invisible" that we take them for granted as we watch, highly complex technological filming processes, and embodied performance is the paradox of *Orphan Black*'s production.

In recent science fiction film and television, bodies and technology take on particular—and potentially cyborg—connotations as the bodies of actors combine with special effects technologies (Calvert 211). Cyborg embodiment, in which an organic body is augmented with technology, might take the form of physical additions or of virtual ones, and the resulting hybridity can be observed in fiction and fact. In film and television production, as Stacey Abbott notes, "actor and computer technology are increasingly being merged into a new form of digital/human hybrid" (91). Indeed, the use of these technologies "has gradually transformed other genres into a curious hybrid of the sf film," as Abbott notes of the computer-generated effects (CGI) used in martial-arts films that allow actors to "transcend the limitations of the performing body and do the impossible" (101).[2] This kind of hybridity is in evidence in the narrative and in the production of *Orphan Black*. As Lorna Jowett notes, the series blends science fiction, action-adventure and thriller, and "thoroughly enjoys its outrageous premise and its melodrama" ("The New Black"). Its subject matter—the creation of a female and a male set of clones, many of whom are unaware they are clones—falls into the domain of science fiction; the connection with the genre is further underlined through the presentation of some of these clone characters as technologically augmented cyborgs.[3] The concept of the "digital/human hybrid" is reinforced within the show itself, as the Neolutionists' aims are to use genetic modification to create improvements in human evolution, effectively making future human beings into versions of technologically manipulated cyborg-clones.[4]

We might contrast the presentation of clone characters in *Orphan Black* with that of the duplicated Cylons in *Battlestar Galactica* (2004–2009). In *Battlestar*, the same, numbered Cylon model ("a Six," "An Eight") can be duplicated and reduplicated, so that it is (theoretically) possible to create infinite copies. Scenes that depict multiple versions of the same Cylon model are generally framed in such a way as to accentuate feelings of distaste and horror around the replication process, and the appearance of many identical versions collected in one place is typically presented as monstrous. In, for example, "Kobol's Last Gleaming, Part II" (1.13), the character Boomer (Grace Park), who was created as a "sleeper" Cylon and was initially unaware of her origins, encounters a large group of her Cylon "sisters" (0:28:01). Boomer's encounter, as she is confronted by a seemingly endless procession of humanoid females that look exactly alike, and exactly like her, is framed as a horrifying experience. The sequence's lighting, pacing, and soundtrack reflect her fearful and panicked reactions, with low and indistinct lighting, fast percussive beats followed by string motifs, and shots that pan across a series of identical faces. This scene is a shocking moment of unpleasant revelation for this character who has discovered she is not a unique human, but one in a series of humanoid, vat-grown Cylons.

Orphan Black takes a different approach. The encounters between the individual clone characters are utilized to create surprise, mystery and suspense, not to generate reactions of horror in characters or audience. At the opening of the series, the central clone character, Sarah, looks at her clone sister, Beth, with puzzlement and confusion. Her expression turns to horror, but this is because she has witnessed a suicide, not because she has been confronted with a woman who looks like her. (Indeed, she makes use of their physical similarity for financial gain.) In other respects, the series is grounded through realism. Its action takes place in a recognizable urban location,[5] and Sarah, daughter Kira (Skyler Wexler), adopted brother Felix (Jordan Gavaris) and adoptive mother Siobhan Sadler (known as Mrs. S) (Maria Doyle Kennedy) are consistently portrayed as a realistic family group; Sarah's relationships with her sister-clones, especially Cosima, Helena and Alison, are similarly portrayed. Although the clones' existence brings science fiction elements to the narrative, the characters themselves pose no threat to humanity; rather, threat comes from the corporations and organizations like Dyad and Neolution that have created the clones and related technologies. The clone characters are represented through different forms of technological duplication, and Maslany can be viewed as a "digital-human hybrid" performer in this respect, yet the series' emphasis is on the individuality and difference of each clone character and on the interaction of these characters. This approach is reflected in commentary from the visual effects company Intelligent Creatures, which produced all the effects in the series:

> The truest testament to our skill is how little the audience notices it. If people can immerse themselves within the plot enough to forget that this shot was done with VFX, then our jobs are done. We used visual effects to help do what the show's creators intended to do: tell a story. The rest might as well be magic [Intelligent Creatures, quoted in Edwards].

Orphan Black's production tends to downplay overt technological elements of representation, even though it depends on the use of state-of-the art visual effects technologies to represent its clone characters in a convincing manner. Elsewhere in television and film, the visual effect is often used as an impressive set-piece in its own right, frequently pausing the narrative to give the viewer the fullest opportunity to revel in amazing and impossible visual excesses. In this series, with the exception of a few specific scenes, the main focus is on the everyday circumstances of the clones and on making special effects that are, in a sense, invisible to the viewer. In *Orphan Black*, technological aspects of filmmaking, especially digital manipulation, combine with embodied performance to create distinct and authentic individual characters through its five seasons.

Orphan Black's production includes such special-effect techniques as green screens and the use of tennis balls and tape markers to identify correct positioning so that additional actors (or in this case, additional instances of the same actor) can be digitally inserted into scenes in post-production. There are some connections between the special-effect processes in *Orphan Black* and those cinematic/televisual works that utilize digital actors or motion-capture technologies (with, for example, the completely digital characters/actors in *Final Fantasy* [2001], or the motion-capture acting work of

Andy Serkis in *The Lord of the Rings* trilogy [2001–2003], *King Kong* [2005] and others). A positive view of the use of motion-capture technology might see the "synthespian" (the actor re-imagined on screen as a digital body) "re-imagined as a transformative digital character that purports to empower and extend the abilities of its human operator" (Aldred 1). However, critical analysis of such "virtual actors" tends to focus on aspects such as the "uncanniness of the image" (Ayers 214), the way in which "moving human figures that are reaching for a photo-realistic aesthetic [...] call forth a disquieting uncertainty" (Bode 175). The digital/human hybrid of *Orphan Black*, however, in the form of Tatiana Maslany as all of the female clone characters, might allow us more readily to accept transformative technological possibilities. Maslany is not "motion-captured" as such, but digital and motion-control camera technologies combine with her embodied performances to create the illusion of multiple clones on the screen at the same time. *Orphan Black*'s visual effects team used a new device, the "TechnoDolly," which "can be programmed to repeat the same complex camera movements over and over again, allowing for complete consistency between takes" (Prudom). "It allowed us to create movements of unlimited length and complexity, and more importantly, repeat those moves with incredible precision" (Intelligent Creatures, quoted in Edwards). In this way, the team creates many visually and narratively pleasing moments in which different clone characters interact closely with one another.

Just as virtual actors are not completely separated from embodiment, but "rely on a multiplicity of human bodies, faces, and voices in order to be brought to life" (Aldred 4), the human actors of *Orphan Black*, especially Maslany, rely on the same things. The clone characters' presentation is facilitated through props, costume, and hair and makeup (Stutsman 88) as well as "input from other creative personnel" (Pearson 182), all of which emphasizes the "collaborative nature of [Maslany's] performance" (Stutsman 87). Critics and viewers often note the importance of costuming for Maslany's characters, including its importance for those scenes in which Maslany plays one clone masquerading as another (Fraser). The embodiment of the clone characters is rooted, too, in vocal register and movement (Stutsman 88), and these factors demonstrate the means by which "characterizations are crafted through the specific spatial design of movements and gestures" (Baron and Carnicke 207).

It is evident that Maslany creates strikingly different speech patterns and tones for each clone character[6]; in addition, she has spoken about other factors that are important for her process in developing character. While co-creator Graeme Manson makes the revealing comment that the method of creating the clones on screen is "not conducive to organic acting" ("*Orphan Black* Insider"), the processes Maslany discusses employ various embodied techniques that are arguably very organic indeed to capture the different clone characters. She speaks of her method of developing the different characters as a very physical, almost choreographed process: "It was about physicalizing and embodying that, putting it my body, walking differently depending on how I look at the world" (Ostime). Maslany has discussed the music playlists she uses to help her to distinguish and experience the clone characters: "I have different playlists for each that I feel is the rhythm of that character, whether that's how they walk or would dance, or the internal chaos going on inside them, or the melody of their voice" (Snierson). The music playlists are very individual and distinctive: "gritty" dance music for Sarah, American musicals for Alison, "ambient" music for Cosima (Kelly).[7] As with the forms of music she identifies, specific dance forms connect with specific characters: for example, flamenco dancing for Alison ("It had to be something very rigid, everything held tight"), club dancing for Sarah, rave for Cosima (Martin). Using the techniques of music cues and dance choreography, Maslany ensures that the movement of each character is significantly personalized, and these aspects of movement contribute to the sense that these characters are not copies but fully individual people. While scenes like the popular "clone club" dance party of Season 2's finale episode bring Maslany's personal movement cues into the wider narrative of the series, dance informs the show at the level of performance and development of character.

The very fact that multiple "copies" of Maslany can appear in the same screen space at the same time and can interact, speak, move, and touch each other, creates a definite uncanniness of duplication. But, crucially, this duplication depends in large part on embodied acting: that of Maslany as well as the co-acting of stand-ins. In particular, much of *Orphan Black*'s on-screen duplication relies on the participation of Maslany's "clone double," Kathryn Alexandre, who plays against Maslany in scenes involving two or more clones. Alexandre, like Maslany, is fully costumed and made up as the particular clone and acts the part(s) opposite Maslany. For example, in one BBC America special feature, Alexandre is costumed as Rachel, and can be heard speaking with an English accent in a key scene ("Inside *Orphan Black*"). Alexandre's invisible[8] co-acting thus creates another kind of doubling, that of diegetic and non-diegetic spaces. To illustrate this, we might consider the sequence when Sarah and Cosima are lying in bed together, holding hands, at the end of Season 2 ("By Means Which Have Never Yet Been Tried," 2.10). This short scene carries significant emotional weight, since, at this point in the narrative, Cosima is terminally ill, and Sarah fears losing her sister. Cosima takes Sarah's hand and strokes it and her arm while they talk. In a purely diegetic sense, this scene emphasizes the physical closeness of the clone sisters, and their intimacy, and these aspects are further accentuated by the low lighting, the deep reds of the pillows and bedcovers, and the quiet speech of both clones.

At the level of special effect, this scene emphasizes the skill employed in creating the illusion of two clones in a single frame; online special features stress the key participation of Alexandre, whose hand remains in the finished shot ("*Orphan Black* Double"). The "doubling" we see on screen, and that is part of the story of a family of clone-sisters, is replicated off screen in the co-acting of the "clone double."

Another kind of doubling and multiplicity is much in evidence in the frequent "clone swaps" that take place over the course of the series, in which one clone takes the place of another clone for various narrative purposes. These swaps are a further feature of the series that have a strong appeal for viewers, who often comment on their enjoyment in seeing Maslany act one clone who is playing another. The performances are doubled, like the doubling of Maslany and Alexandre in certain scenes that then show both diegetic and non-diegetic multiplicity (more than one clone in a frame; Maslany acting with her "clone double"). When the clone characters dress and perform as each other, in narrative terms "[a]s the other women learn how to perform the personas of their sisters, they call attention to the performative nature of their respective roles as they [...] learn to take up and enact the mannerisms and props that define their sisters' different types of femininity" (Stutsman 97).[9] Such examples often resonate against the behaviors that viewers associate with the "real" clones, deliberately foregrounding inauthenticity in a performance that is "not quite right" in certain ways, in order to demonstrate that one clone is acting as another. Beyond the narrative, these sequences also call attention to the very nature of performance, especially as it relates to Maslany's portrayal of multiple clone characters with clearly defined personalities. As Stutsman notes, these swaps "call attention to the labor of performance" (96) as they accentuate and reveal acting techniques that are usually meant to be subsumed into a character and therefore invisible.

In a few instances, the viewer is permitted to see the individual clone getting ready for her performance. Notably, on occasion, the narrative underlines the difficulty of the task and the possibility—or likelihood—that the clone will fail in her impersonation, thus creating additional tension when the performance takes place. When Felix (Jordan Gavaris) helps Alison to dress and speak as Sarah, so that she can pose as Sarah on a supervised visit to her daughter ("Effects of External Conditions," 1.4), their dialogue underlines how unlikely it is that Alison can succeed. Felix is unconvinced by Alison's community theater acting credentials. While she insists, "Well, I did just play Annelle in *Steel Magnolias* [...]," he retorts, "it's terrible casting," and the viewer is invited to agree that playing Sarah is similarly "terrible casting." Alison's first efforts at reproducing Sarah's accent are hopeless; instead of a London punk, she sounds so like Eliza Dolittle that a horrified Felix groans, "we need to pull a full reverse *Pygmalion* here." Alison's "worst clothes" are still too new and tidy (and too pink) to look like Sarah's, and Felix attacks them with scissors to produce a more authentic, worn look. Yet, once in costume and in character, Alison makes good her claim that "Sarah's no stretch." She does manage to impersonate Sarah convincingly enough, with Felix's help, that her adoptive mother is fooled (even though Kira is not). Indeed, Alison appears to take on Sarah's character so well that at the end of the visit she intervenes to argue that Sarah should have more visiting time with Kira.

Another scene in which one clone prepares to act as another occurs in the opening episode of Season 3 ("The Weight of this Combination," 3.1). Once again the viewer is able to see the preparation process and note the likely difficulties involved in the impersonation. In this episode, Sarah plays Rachel in a meeting with her business associate (and, as she discovers, former lover) Ferdinand. In a reversal of Alison's assertion that she could play Sarah, Felix insists "Rachel's a stretch for [Sarah]" and, when Sarah tries out a version of Rachel's voice, Felix responds, "That was terrible." As with Alison, Felix takes charge of costuming Sarah appropriately: "you need to wear white. Okay? White dazzles [...] God knows you'll need a distraction." Stutsman notes some aspects of the preparation process: "Sarah practices a few Rachel phrases in her RP accent and tilts her chin up. Maslany has her slightly square her shoulders and speak slowly, deliberately forming her lips around her words" (99). However, that analysis does not take account of the emphasis on Sarah's inability to succeed, which is provided through Felix's commentary. Far from inhabiting Rachel's character seamlessly, Sarah's portrayal reveals moments when her own personality appears, notably in her swift sideways glances as she tries to assess new information and to decide how best to respond as Rachel. The first shot of Sarah playing Rachel shows her walking awkwardly into Dyad's offices, wearing a fitted white dress, looking uncomfortable and unsteady in high heels. The longer she remains in character as Rachel, however, the more convincing her portrayal becomes. Sarah grows in confidence in her dealings with Ferdinand (James Frain), bargaining with him and agreeing to meet him privately; she even challenges him with a knowing, "You don't recognize me, Ferdinand?" that resonates with the viewers of this episode. Throughout this particular clone swap, there is the doubling effect of the two clones' characters as Rachel's character is interpreted and performed by Sarah. Having established the Sarah-as-Rachel swap, this episode then doubles the duplication, as we discover Alison has been drafted to play Sarah while Sarah continues to play Rachel, in order to maintain the illusion that both Sarah and Rachel are under the control of Delphine Cormier (Évelyne Brochu). Alison manages to remain convincing in front of Ferdinand, but her "darting eyes" (Stutsman 96) and trembling mouth show how close she is to losing her control. Such a sequence strongly reminds the viewer of the "labor of performance" (Stutsman 96) as we clearly see Maslany as Sarah and as Sarah-as-Rachel, as Alison and as Alison-as-Sarah, and the two performances together in a single scene.

My final clone swap example occurs during the Season 4 finale episode ("From Dancing Mice to Psychopaths," 4.10). The first part of the scene was BBC America's trailer for that episode ("*Orphan Black* Season 4"). The trailer shows a group of journalists questioning Brightborn representative Dr. Van Lier (Scott Wentworth). Krystal Goderitch joins them, airily asserts that she's with "TMZ" and proceeds to fire questions at Van Lier. The preview clip ends here with no further clues, yet YouTube commentators immediately noted their hunches that the clone in the scene was not Krystal, but Sarah. In the complete scene, the clone, dressed in a fake-fur jacket, high-heeled boots and huge sunglasses, with Krystal's blonde curls and frosted pink lipstick, follows Van Lier and asks, "Do you recognize me now?" "Of course, Krystal," he replies. But, as the viewers immediately suspected, this clone is not Krystal; Sarah has adopted her identity in order to get hold of Van Lier, and, as soon as she spits, "Cut the shit, all right?" he knows who she really is—and the viewers know they have guessed correctly. That Sarah-as-Krystal can be so readily identified (by viewers, if not by Van Lier) from a brief, out-of-context preview clip suggests that the aspects of Maslany's performance that capture Krystal's character have been exaggerated just enough as to make Sarah's impersonation obvious. It is particularly striking that this character swap is one in which Sarah performs an individual with distinct, almost parodic markers of femininity (the blonde wavy hair, manicured nails, big necklaces and form-fitting, glittery clothing). We might expect that those markers would make a duplication of character—at least, one that is good enough to "dazzle"—fairly easy to perform. Yet, instead, Sarah performs Krystal in a heightened, extravagant fashion that takes the identifying markers of this character over the edge of believability.

As *Orphan Black* moves through successive episodes and then through seasons, the clone characters are presented in ways that deliberately challenge the show's creative team. Each season sees new and arresting examples of multiple clones in a single frame, as in the first meeting of Sarah, Alison and Cosima ("Variation Under Nature," 1.3), where the three sit and talk together in Alison's house, a scene that is broken down into its technical components in BBC America's accompanying video ("*Orphan Black* Insider"). Such scenes culminate in the season finale set-pieces like the family dinner ("History Yet to Be Written," 3.10), the baby shower barbecue ("To Right the Wrongs of Many," 5.10) and, possibly most famously, the "clone club" dance party ("By Means Which Have Never Yet Been Tried," 2.10). These scenes are interesting in narrative terms because they often represent a pause in the narrative trajectory and a chance for aspects of the clone characters' personalities to be developed in different ways. Moreover, they combine aspects of embodied performance (especially Maslany's and Alexandre's) with technological processes like the workings of the TechnoDolly, CGI and other digital effects. In all these examples, aspects of duplication, technology and performance intersect with key themes of the show as a whole and come together to create a believable televisual experience, one that has the "digital/human hybrid" at its center.

In diegetic terms, these scenes show individuals (who happen to be clones and so look identical in their general appearance), together with their family and friends, engaged in celebration or commemoration. These scenes bring many different clones together in one (often domestic) space, continually emphasizing their ordinary lives and family bonds, which are no different from a non-cloned human. Such scenes serve the long-form narrative in offering temporary closure at the end of a season, even though other aspects of the narrative may open up new avenues for exploration in subsequent seasons. In Season 2, for example, when it seems that Sarah has achieved a temporary victory over Rachel, the clones' immediate storyline remains in a form of stasis until Season 3. Other aspects are unresolved—it is unclear at this point whether Cosima can be cured, or whether she is really terminally ill—and some new storylines are introduced. For example, the twist at the end of Season 2's final episode is that the existence of a male clone line, codenamed "Castor," is revealed to the viewers, but is evidently already known to the characters Paul (Dylan Bruce) and Mrs. S (2.10). Season 3's finale provides a similar moment of consolidation and success for the clones as they gather to celebrate Alison's election as a school trustee, and the season concludes with another shocking revelation in the apparent assassination of Delphine Cormier (3.10). Thus, the season finales manage to include elements that both reward and surprise the viewer. The viewer can enjoy seeing the characters succeeding in some way, and watch them reaffirm their family and friendship bonds; at almost the same time, the viewer can enjoy the confirmation that there is more of the story to unfold in subsequent seasons.

The clone characters are, of course, key to the ongoing narrative of the series, as well as its continuation (had Maslany dropped out, it would have been impossible for the series to continue). The set-piece finale scenes including multiple clones are a visual reminder of their particular status and of their individuality, too. In the Season 3 celebration dinner, for example, each clone very clearly demonstrates individual traits. In their meal choices, for example, Sarah is drinking red wine, Cosima has a meat-free dinner plate, and Helena makes a toast through a mouthful of food. Sarah, Cosima, Helena, and Alison are each dressed in clothes that reflect their personalities as established through previous seasons: Sarah in a dark-colored slogan t-shirt; Cosima in a multicolored embroidered jacket; Helena in an incongruous assortment of garments, including a pink t-shirt and a baseball cap. Standing to make her toast, Alison is dressed impeccably, from her smooth hairstyle to her carefully chosen necklace. As Alison speaks, the camera pans around the table, showing all four clone characters sitting with their family members and friends: Felix, Mrs. S, Art (Kevin Hanchard), Donnie (Kristian Bruun), and Scott (Josh Vokey). This fairly standard televisual moment—a look around the room at a key moment to note the presence of particular characters—is heightened in *Orphan Black* by the duplication of Tatiana Maslany, present in four different places in the scene, and playing four different characters.

Maslany's technological duplication is both accentuated and celebrated throughout the series in paratexts like the official BBC America "A Closer Look" series, that reveal the processes by which a scene like the celebration dinner is created. Shooting the scene is only the starting point, as these behind-the-scenes videos show; since there are four clones present in the scene, for example, the scene itself must be reshot multiple times, with Maslany playing each clone in turn, supported by her clone double Alexandre and other doubles who stand in for the other clones ("A Closer Look"). The interviewees in the video clip stress the complexity of such a scene, and both Maslany and the editor Jay Prychidny note the amount of time it takes to film and the need for actors and crew to be "very technical, very precise" (Prychidny in "A Closer Look"). Yet this video also reveals quite different aspects of the scene, in particular the achievement of naturalness and "reality" as the characters, including the clones, appear to be "just riffing and having a good time" and "Tatiana is improving with herself" (Prychidny in "A Closer Look"). The "real," "natural" aspects of group conversation—people reaching across each other, moving around the table, standing and sitting down, gesturing with their hands, and talking at the same time as each other—are created in this scene through multiple takes and the duplication of one actor into many.

The Season 2 finale "dance party" sequence is the first complex multiple clone scene of the series, and it immediately captured viewers' imaginations, with comments, unofficial gifs and clips, and recreations of the scene proliferating on social media. BBC America responded with a "making of" video that cuts together the different takes of the scene, revealing Maslany dancing on her own, dancing with Jordan Gavaris, and in character as one of the other clones ("Making of *Orphan Black*'s 4 Clone Dance Party"). Through its different versions, the video demonstrates how Maslany, Gavaris, and Skyler Wexler (Kira) worked together physically to choreograph the dancing, as well as the ways Maslany captured the characters of Cosima, Sarah, Alison, and Helena in their individual dance movements. In much the same way as the Season 3 finale's dinner, the dance party offers a respite from the relentless action and thrills of the narrative, and it gives the characters a chance to bond and celebrate their sisterhood and extended family (Felix and Kira) through dance. In the context of duplication and hybridity, it shows not simply the clone characters together, but demonstrates—indeed, celebrates—the technological special effects that enable this narrative to be told convincingly. In revealing something of how the scene was made, the BBC America video emphasizes the skill and competence of the *Orphan Black* visual effects team.[10] In addition, it appeals to and engages the viewers who appreciated the scene when it first aired and since. The "dance party" remains a touchstone for all these aspects: narrative enjoyment, appreciation of skills and effects, and acknowledgment by the studio of viewer engagement. Indeed, it is notable that one of the "farewell" videos released by BBC America at the end of the show was a "dance party" featuring Maslany as all of the clones and the supporting actors, including Alexandre, dancing; these shots are then intercut with clips from the series showing scenes when characters dance and with fan videos in which viewers recreate dance moments while costumed as particular clones ("*Orphan Black* Dance Party").[11] In this way, the show's creators validate the viewer/fan response to this particular sequence and celebrate the creation of the sequence by including a video like this among the show's key paratexts.

An amended version of the multiple-clone scene is present in the extended sequence of Felix's art show, which again emphasizes and plays with notions of duplication, identity and selfhood ("Guillotines Decide," 5.8). As at other points in the series narrative, the clones (Alison, Cosima, and Sarah) stage their entrances and exits extremely carefully; however, on this occasion they are not taking on each other's identities, but are maintaining the illusion that only one woman—introduced as Felix's sister Sarah—is present. The multiplicity in the set-pieces featuring several clones is reversed in this sequence, as each clone enters and exits the gallery space alone. Moreover, for the time each clone is within the gallery space, the emphasis is on her individuality as highlighted in Felix's paintings, which represent key aspects of each sister: Cosima is "Metis, goddess of wisdom and deep thought," Alison "Hestia, goddess of hearth and home," and Sarah "Athena, goddess of war." Those at the art show see a singular presentation: the same face in each artwork and (apparently) the same woman arriving and departing in different guises. The fact that this is a *performance* is clearly indicated as each clone passes through a velvet curtain as though moving onto a stage, and the dialogue plays with the clones' duplication; for example, Alison tells a group of art dealers, "I'm always different" while Felix asserts, "Identity is a social construct" (0:16:44–0:17:40). Thus, Felix's exhibition takes on the status of a complex performance-art piece that impresses those in attendance. For the television audience, the show has a different resonance. All the clones are present in the form of Felix's artworks; they are illuminated on the gallery walls for the gathering to view and admire. And, adding another layer to the viewing experience, the television audience sees the clone performances by Maslany, the paintings featuring each clone that have been especially designed for the episode, and the arrival and departure of each clone "backstage," which all contribute to the cumulative effect of the scene. At this moment of great importance for Felix, he uses his speech of thanks (00:32:35) to identify the importance of his adopted family and particularly addresses the women of his family. The sequence roots the presentation of each clone's distinctive qualities, represented as the individual goddess figures of Felix's paintings, within a celebration of family and family bonds.

This emphasis is reinstated in the unexpectedly quiet series finale (5.10), in which the focus is on the core group of clones, Sarah, Alison, Cosima, and Helena, sitting together in Alison's back yard after the baby shower for Helena's twins. The scene is low-lit and intimate, and the four women sit closely together and speak in low voices. The very unremarkable *mise-en-scène* is paradoxical, since once again this scene is the result of the work of highly precise technological special effects. As in many of the show's season finales, the Season 5 finale plays with ideas of pacing and narrative shape, dispatching the season's villains within the first fifteen minutes of the episode and thereafter focusing on the everyday lives of the clone sisters. The clones' duplication is present in the gathering of the sisters; indeed, their multiplication is strongly underlined when Felix obtains a complete list from Rachel, revealing two hundred and seventy-four other clones scattered over the globe. On the other hand, the technological, science-fiction aspects of their being is downplayed in favor of a concentration on their domestic lives and their futures which, it is implied, will be thoroughly ordinary.

Throughout *Orphan Black*, Maslany's key performance intersects with the performances of others (fellow actors and doubles) and with the performance of CGI and other visual effects, marking the central place of the "digital/human hybrid" (Abbott 91). The collaborative creation of the clone sisters and the demonstration of aspects of performance through narrative moments like the clone swap and the scenes of multiple clones together reveal different means by which this hybridization can be realized. This show serves as a heightened example of the "labor of performance" (Stutsman 96) that occurs in film and television production more generally. It presents the "digital/human hybrid" as both diegetic and non-diegetic: in a show about clones, the duplication of Maslany on screen is essential for the show's overall narrative, yet it is also a significant aspect of enjoyment for the viewers, reflected in and acknowledged by BBC America's video paratexts. That hybridization is central to the narrative itself, in the positioning of adversaries like Dyad, Brightborn, and Neolution that all aim to create hybrid versions of human beings. The show's refusal to position the clone sisters as anything other than ordinary individuals means that viewers see them as hybrid *and* as human, as marked not by patents or serial numbers but by their individuality and distinctiveness. All these features are made possible through the combinations created by Maslany's and others' embodied performances and by the visual effects manipulations that offer cutting-edge spectacle made invisible.

NOTES

1. Maslany's nomination listed Sarah, Alison, Cosima, Helena, Rachel, M.K., and Krystal as her roles. She also plays Katya, Beth, Jennifer, Tony, and Camilla over the five seasons of the show.
2. However, as Abbott also points out, the actors performing in these films are "specially trained in martial arts and perform all their own stunts"; the amazing feats are carried out by the actors and are then "technologically enhanced" (101). The combination of "real-world," embodied performance and virtual, technological enhancement is key to my analysis of *Orphan Black*'s effects.
3. I would include here such examples as the "bot" that Brightborn/Neolution experiment with (Season 4) and Rachel's artificial eye, which doubles as a surveillance camera (Seasons 4–5).
4. Neolution's aims sound very similar to those expressed by "transhumanists" who "seek the continuation and acceleration of the evolution of intelligent life beyond its currently human form and human limitations by means of science and technology" (More).
5. Toronto, which, like Vancouver, is often made to duplicate various U.S. cities in film and television, plays itself on screen.
6. Maslany carries out a demonstration of this at the 2016 San Diego Comic-Con, in a light-hearted "challenge" in which she is given a clone character and a scene to improvise ("*Orphan Black* Clone Improv"). It is possible to see Maslany transforming her face and body before speaking in the character of each clone.
7. Notably, Helena has her own musical cue on the show's soundtrack, an electronic burst of sound that preceded her appearance on screen.
8. Uncredited in Season 1, Alexandre appears in the end credits from Season 2 onwards.
9. The sisters' role-playing is explicitly referenced in an *Orphan Black* tie-in publication that includes "Alison Hendrix's Guide to Impersonating Sisters" (DeCandido 65). The list, designed to look like Alison's handwritten notes, includes tips such as "Shove out chin in defiance of authority" (for Sarah) and "Gesture a lot when you talk" (for Cosima).
10. The series' creative team is celebrated at the end of the video, when they join Maslany, Gavaris and others on set and create their own version of the dance party.
11. A mini-clone recreation of the dance party features Cynthia Galant, who plays the roles of Rachel as a child and the child clone Charlotte in the series ("*Orphan Black*—4 Mini Clone").

WORKS CITED

Abbott, Stacey. "Final Frontiers: Computer-Generated Imagery and the Science Fiction Film." *Science Fiction Studies*, vol. 33, no. 1, Mar. 2006, pp. 89–108.
Aldred, Jessica. "From Synthespian to Avatar: Re-Framing the Digital Human in *Final Fantasy* and *The Polar Express*." *Mediascape*, Winter 2011, www.tft.ucla.edu/mediascape/Winter2011_Avatar.html.
Ayers, Drew. "The Multilocal Self: Performance Capture, Remote Surgery, and Persistent Materiality." *Animation: An Interdisciplinary Journal*, vol. 9, no. 2, 2014, pp. 212–27.
Baron, Cynthia L., and Sharon Marie Carnicke. *Reframing Screen Performance*. U Michigan P, 2008.

Bode, Lisa. "From Shadow Citizens to Teflon Stars: Reception of the Transfiguring Effects of New Moving Image Technologies." *Animation: An Interdisciplinary Journal*, vol. 1, no. 2, 2006, pp. 173–89.
Brown, Tracy. "Tatiana Maslany Finally Wins an Emmy, Clone Club Celebrates." *LA Times*, 18 Sept. 2016, www.latimes.com/entertainment/herocomplex/la-et-hc-tatiana-maslany-emmy-reactions-20160918-snap-htmlstory.html.
"By Means Which Have Never Yet Been Tried." Writ. Graeme Manson. Dir. John Fawcett. *Orphan Black*. Season 2, episode 10. First aired 21 June 2014.
Calvert, Bronwen. *Being Bionic: The World of TV Cyborgs*. I.B. Tauris, 2016.
"A Closer Look at *Orphan Black* Season 3: The Four Clone Dinner Scene." *YouTube*, uploaded by BBC America, 25 June 2015, www.youtube.com/watch?v=MnccfiimE_I.
DeCandido, Keith R.A. *Orphan Black: Classified Clone Reports: Confidential*. Harper Design, an imprint of HarperCollinsPublishers, 2017.
Edwards, Graham. "Orphan Black and Twinning in the Movies." *Cinefex Blog*, 19 Apr. 2015, cinefex.com/blog/orphan-black/.
"Effects of External Conditions." Writ. Graeme Manson. Dir John Fawcett. *Orphan Black*. Season 1, episode 4. First aired 20 April 2013.
Fraser, Emma. "Clone Swap: How *Orphan Black* Uses Costume to Escape." Observerwww, June 2017, observer.com/2017/06/clone-swap-how-orphan-black-uses-costume-to-escape/.
"From Dancing Mice to Psychopaths." Writ. Graeme Manson. Dir. John Fawcett. *Orphan Black*. Season 4, episode 10. First aired 16 June 2016.
"Guillotines Decide." Writ. Aisha Porter-Christie and Graeme Manson. Dir. Aaron Morton. *Orphan Black*. Season 5, episode 8. First aired 5 August 2017.
"History Yet to Be Written." Writ. Graeme Manson. Dir. John Fawcett. *Orphan Black*. Season 3, episode 10. First aired 20 June 2015.
"Inside *Orphan Black*: Meet Tatiana's Clone Double." *YouTube*, uploaded by BBC America, 25 April 2014, www.youtube.com/watch?v=9fZLiRTL0-Y.
@jdeuberry. "@tatianamaslany Congratulations!!! So Well Deserved! Hope They Gave You a Statue for EACH Clone. #CloneClub #Emmys2016 #EmmyforMaslany." *Twitter*, 25 September 2016, 12:05pm. twitter.com/jdeuberry/status/777946636232364032.
Jowett, Lorna. "The New Black: Tatiana Maslany and TV Acting." *CST Online*, 11 July 2014, cstonline.net/the-new-black-tatiana-maslany-and-tv-acting-by-lorna-jowett/.
Kelly, Stephen. "Actor Tatiana Maslany Uses Music to Get Into (Clone) Character." *Wired UK*, 5 Feb. 2015, www.wired.co.uk/article/tv-clone.
"Kobol's Last Gleaming, Part II." Dir. Michael Rymer, Writ. Ronald D. Moore, and David Eick. *Battlestar Galactica*. Season 1, episode 13. First aired 1 April 2005.
"Making of *Orphan Black*'s 4 Clone Dance Party." *YouTube*, uploaded by BBC America, 21 June 2014, www.youtube.com/watch?v=XE2u_N8g6cs.
Martin, Denise. "Tatiana Maslany on Improv, Her Rick Moranis Crush, and *Orphan Black*'s Many Bare Behinds." *Vulture*, 24 July 2013, www.vulture.com/2013/07/tatiana-maslany-orphan-black-interview.html.
More, Max. "H+: True Transhumanism." *www.metanexus.net/h-true-transhumanism. 5 Feb. 2009*.
"*Orphan Black* Clone Improv—San Diego Comic-Con 2016." *YouTube*, uploaded by BBC America, 22 July 2016, www.youtube.com/watch?v=PSVBfUx8zc4.
"*Orphan Black* Dance Party." *YouTube*, uploaded by BBC America, 12 August 2017, www.youtube.com/watch?v=jMIGUDVB2Aw.
"*Orphan Black* Double Helps Tatiana Maslany Play So Many Clones." *YouTube*, uploaded by the Canadian Press, 1 May 2015, www.youtube.com/watch?v=pr3eb845R8M.
"*Orphan Black*—4 Mini Clone Dance Parody (Cynthia Galant)." *YouTube*, uploaded by Alexander Galant, 30 June 2014, www.youtube.com/watch?v+o_bHQq13jvE.
"*Orphan Black* Insider: Three Clones, One Frame." *YouTube*, uploaded by BBC America, 23 April 2013, www.youtube.com/watch?v=4rALHr8gV1E.
"*Orphan Black* Season 4—Finale Sneak Peek: Krystal Intervenes (Spoilers)." *YouTube*, uploaded by BBC America, 16 June 2016, www.youtube.com/watch?v=oSLwiG_SDXA.

Ostime, James. "Tatiana Maslany, Beside Herself." *Interview Magazine*, 31 May 2013, www.interviewmagazine.com/culture/tatiana-maslany-orphan-black.
Pearson, Roberta. "The Multiple Determinants of Television Acting." *Genre and Performance: Film and Television*, edited by Christine Cornea, Manchester University Press, 2010, pp. 166–83.
Prudom, Laura. "*Orphan Black* Has Changed the Game for TV Visual Effects, and Half of Them Are Invisible." *Mashable*, 9 June 2017, mashable.com/2017/06/09/orphan-black-season-5-visual-effects-clones-geoff-scott/#UaWdzUPrcmqh.
Snierson, Dan. "*Orphan Black*: How Does Tatiana Maslany Get Into Character(s)?" EWwww, 5 Aug. 2013, ew.com/article/2013/08/05/orphan-black-tatiana-maslany-new-hollywood/.
Stutsman, Staci. "The Unruly Clones: Tatiana Maslany's Melodramatic Masquerades in *Orphan Black*." *Journal of Film and Video*, vol. 68, no. 3/4, Fall/Winter 2016, pp. 83–103.
@TeeEssMacWall, "Which Character Did You Win For? Congrats to Our Goddess! ____CloneClub ____OrphanBlack ____EmmyForMaslany." *Twitter*, 20 September 2016 10:01pm. twitter.com/TeeEssMacWall/status/778459132017782784.
"To Right the Wrongs of Many." Writ. Renée St. Cyr and Graeme Manson. Dir. John Fawcett. *Orphan Black*. Season 5, episode 10. First aired 12 August 2017.
"Variation Under Nature." Writ. Graeme Manson. Dir. David Frazee. *Orphan Black*. Season 1, episode 3. First aired 13 April 2013.
@vchen24. "FINALLY an ____EmmyforMaslany! the Hardest-working Actress on TV Just Won an Emmy After Playing Eight Roles This Season." *Twitter*, 19 September 2016, 10:06am. twitter.com/vchen24/status/777916880816214016.
"The Weight of This Combination." Writ. Graeme Manson. Dir. David Frazee. *Orphan Black*. Season 3, episode 1. First aired 18 April 2015.

Sheeply Empowerment
An Analysis of M.K.'s Reappropriation
in Orphan Black

Jennifer DeRoss

Orphan Black is a deeply complex television show, tackling issues surrounding bodily autonomy and agency within the context of human cloning. While the study of the show is still relatively new, much of the work already done has focused on the core group of clones, otherwise known as Clone Club, including Sarah, Alison, Cosima, Helena, and Rachel (all clones played by Tatiana Maslany). This makes work on the clones outside of this group a key gap in the literature, and M.K. is particularly important to consider. Primarily, she is important because of the way in which she uniquely understands her role as a clone and what that means, but also because of the way her story is singularly told in both *Orphan Black* the television show and the comic of the same name, as well as the comic *Orphan Black: Helsinki*. This multiplatform storytelling requires fans to put together her full story through the seeking out of each piece of media in order to discover the co-constituting layers. As the combination of her life experiences in the books and her actions in the television series suggests, M.K. has had to develop and apply multiple strategies just to survive. One such strategy is to re-appropriate the symbology of a sheep by wearing a mask of the animal whilst undermining the system insisting that that is all she is, thus communicating her indomitable spirit. This visual indication of reclamation also signals a trickster-like, multifaceted self-awareness, which is significant within the *Orphan Black* universe because that is the basis of all resistance within the show. M.K.'s awareness-based strategies are essential to our understanding of the story as a whole.

This essay uses comic-based icon theory to explain the way that the sheep mask, M.K.'s most defining feature, functions as a means of re-appropriative communication. The fact that it is a sheep mask brings in a lot to be explored. While understanding the array of symbolism behind the mask is important, the identity of the viewer of the mask also informs their understanding of it; the sheep mask can only be re-appropriated if self-awareness is established. The way that clonehood becomes incorporated into each clone's individual and collective identities once they become aware varies greatly, and this variance impacts each of the characters' choices. After becoming the sole survivor of a cleaning operation where she and her fellow clones were herded and exterminated like sheep, she reclaims the symbol of the sheep in order to re-appropriate the slur much in the way that others have done with the word "queer." This reclaimed slur is apt as the clones all interact with the mask differently, with Cosima being the only character who seems to understand this methodological approach. All of this is crucial to understanding the levels at work in the producer's emplotment of M.K.'s death scene, ending with Ferdinand (James Frain) placing the sheep mask over the area of her chest he had stomped upon. This death is not simply seen as tragic, though, as she was already dying and willingly sacrificed herself to give Kira (Skyler Wexler) and her sisters more time to escape, thus giving her death more meaning. Instead of simply dying from the same sickness as her sisters, her death can be seen as a tribute to her claimed agency. More than any other moment in the show, this highlights the way that the producers, through M.K. in particular, re-appropriate the broader social imagery and show it as a marker of agency for both the characters within *Orphan Black* as well as its readers and viewers. By wearing a sheep mask, a symbol of the oppressive treatment clones experience, while subverting the system supporting that treatment and choosing her own manner of death rather than succumbing Dyad's intentions, she re-appropriates it into a symbol of empowerment, thereby showing those who seek to control the clones that she will not be the sheep they want her to be and neither will her sisters.

Readers and viewers learn about M.K. though multi-platform storytelling, which provides a wider range of narrative possibilities. This type of storytelling has become increasingly popular and *Orphan Black* provides yet another example of it with the producers of the television show extending the narrative into multiple games and comics that are canonical. Most importantly, each additional medium uniquely influences the way in which the larger piece is understood. While both mediums outside the television show function in a way that extends the narrative, they do so differently: the games allow a fan to put themselves into the world of *Orphan Black,* thus creating another way of exploring it, whereas the inclusion of the comics into this form of storytelling allows the reader to ponder what might have happened if a moment in the show changed or supplements the story already told. *Orphan Black: Helsinki* and the first comic release, also titled *Orphan Black,* functions as the latter. Television can be restrictive as far as individual character exploration. This is especially true when introducing a new character as it can break up the pacing, slow down the narrative flow, and cause a viewer to lose interest. The same can be said when it comes to the inclusion of character's backstories. Because of these considerations, the creators of *Orphan Black* turned to comics in order to tell the story of what happened in Helsinki and provide the background for their new Finnish character. The comics also provide an opportunity for us to get a glimpse at M.K.'s interior psychology. Because M.K. remains a mysterious and secretive character in the show, the comics serve as an extrapolation point, allowing those who read them to better understand her actions through the telling of her personal history as well as the thoughts we are privy to in this written form. The way the world itself is depicted does not change in the comic and some of the characters in the show are main characters in the comic, with Rachel and Ferdinand in particular getting spotlighted, but it also introduces us to six new clones as well as Veera Suominen, who is later known mostly as M.K. and functions as the main character of the comic series. It is noteworthy that the shared faces of the clones function as the cross-platform *mise-en-scène*, indicating that this is indeed a part of the larger narrative more than any other visual cue. In other words, the sight of Tatiana Maslany's many faces in the television show cue the viewer that they are watching an episode of *Orphan Black* and the comics have replicated this cue in the depiction of her likeness as a form of world building. That said, there are differences between the two. In the *Orphan Black: Helsinki* comic series, we know that Ferdinand killed six clones and thirty-two civilians during his time in Helsinki, culminating in the burning down of a high school. This done not quite match the explanation given in the episode titled "From Instinct to Rational Control" (4.4), where we are told he gassed Niki's family and burnt her alive. In the comic, that is just hinted at and Ferdinand only feeds the gas-caused fire that M.K.'s uncle set as a diversion. His other acts were much worse. These changes were needed in order to streamline the narrative. Another example of this streamlining is how M.K. states that Niki just met her boyfriend and had her whole life ahead of her instead of her having an established boyfriend, but wanting to explore her homosexual desires, implying she is at least bisexual. Despite these disjunctions, this episode explains her back story to the viewers of the show. Most of this is done through newspaper clippings and photographs referencing the events of the incident, much like those found in *The Cormier Files*.[1] This expository episode containing these multiple types of texts also provides an example of how multi-platform storytelling can function.

Multi-platform storytelling allows for the cross-application of medium-specific reading methods, and these are crucial to fully understanding the character of M.K. Intertextuality is an important part of the series, and we can see examples of it in both the show and in the comic. In the previously mentioned episode, Sarah is placed in a position where she must construct a narrative using individual items. As she digs through M.K.'s trailer looking for evidence of what she knows, Sarah comes across newspaper clippings depicting the "accidents" we know were a part of the purge as well was photographs of M.K. and Niki together. Meanwhile, M.K. is narrating the same information to a restrained Ferdinand as the words of the article about the supposed car wreck are projected onto her burn marks, firmly establishing herself as the embodiment of this narrative. Shortly after, Sarah, too, finds the through line in the narrative, and her reading methods function almost as if she is flipping through the pages of a comic, making meaning out of the combinations of image and textual clues (4.4). Without having read the comics, the items Sarah flips through would not resonate in the same way. There are several other items that can be seen as similarly intertextual because of the way they allow for a deeper meaning for those who know the larger context, with the most notable of them being the sheep mask. While it may have made its earliest appearance in the show, air date 14 April 2016, the mask was likely planned to be in the comic before then as M.K. makes her initial appearance in the *Orphan Black* issue titled "Rachel," released on 12 August 2015, and the motif of the sheep is already present at that point.

M.K.'s use of the sheep mask immediately makes her stand out from the other characters, and this makes it into her main form of identification. In M.K.'s introductory appearance on the television show in the first episode of Season 4, titled "The Collapse of Nature," air date 14 April 2016, her hair obscures the burns on her face every time she takes her sheep mask off, thus preventing readers of the comic from immediately identifying her as Veera Suominen; however, clever fans may have connected her newly chosen name of M.K. to her genetic code marker, 3MK29A. The next month provided confirmation that M.K. and Suominen are the same character when we see her mask on for what is chronologically the first time in the concluding issue of *Helsinki* titled "Kill Switch," released on 25 May 2016. This delay functions like a big reveal in the comics in addition to making Beth's anonymous tipper a fully formed character in the show. In this context, the mask functions primarily as a means of identification for the reader. As an icon, it functions as much more.

The use of the sheep mask can be read as a form of iconization thanks to multi-platform storytelling strategies. Iconization is a tool comic artists use to encourage identification and as a visual shorthand that can convey additional meanings to readers aware of the reference points. Alan D. Manning, in "Scott McCloud: *Understanding Comics: The Invisible Art*," explores the comic-book based semiotics McCloud uses when discussing how to read comics as an information designer in relation to the decision to use photographs or line sketches to convey an idea. Manning explains C.S. Pierce's development of icon theory in semiotics as being broken into three basic types, including *iconic qualisigns, iconic sinsigns,* and *iconic legisigns.* The most relevant categorization for this essay is *iconic legisigns,* which are described as "diagrams or cartoons—abstracted from real appearances, but still perceived as resembling some real thing" (66). In this case, the sheep mask abstracts M.K.'s individually detailed face and makes the reader/viewer contend with the meaning of the sheep as the primary meaning maker. It is the way this process conveys only the most needed information that causes Manning to make the case that information designers should continue using these simplified icons because "Cartoons and cartoon-like sketches provide an ideal medium for new ideas, new ways of seeing" (67). The same strategies are utilized by comic artists. With these stripped-down illustrations, artists are more able to easily simplify large ideas and highlight their most important aspects, thereby encouraging additional perspectives and a wider application. For M.K., her face no longer matches that of her sisters, but they share similar experiences and views of the world. Their experiences are represented by the mask, and this makes it an identification point for her fellow clones to recognize her as a clone. More than a passive symbol, the image of the sheep provides a point of self-chosen iconic identification, and it also makes it easier for the reader/viewer to insert themselves into the storyline because the mask removes identifiable facial features, thus providing a heightened sense of emotional response and an invitation to consider how living as owned property might impact one's life. Of course, the matter of the mask being that of a sheep is also significant.

When most people think of cloning, the sheep named Dolly quickly comes to mind, and *Orphan Black* makes use of this connection to invoke the same kinds of reactions Dolly invoked as well as using her as a biological touchstone. Indeed, the show's producers have stated that the mask is a direct reference to Dolly (Manson and Fawcett). As most people know, Dolly is the first mammal to be cloned from an adult cell and constituted a huge scientific breakthrough. When news broke about Dolly, many believed that humans would be next, and popular media exhibited a range of responses to this event. As excited as some people were, there was also a lot of fear. In fact, regulations and laws prohibiting cloning were under heavy discussion shortly afterward as people realized there were no established precedents. These types of concerns and legal grey areas make up a principal backdrop for the series.[2] *Orphan Black* came out several years after Dolly had been put down, but these parallels remain clear, and this includes what physically happened to Dolly as well. Unlike Dolly, whose issues were unintentional, the Leda clones are created so that they were not fully functional. Still, the lack of functionality mirrors Dolly's problems. She had arthritis in a hind leg as well as lung tumors. This is replicated in *Orphan Black* in the way Charlotte (Cynthia Gallant) is disabled in one leg as well as the tumors that the female clones developed as a byproduct of their designed infertility. That said, Dolly was able to reproduce, which all but the twins, Sarah and Helena, were unable to do. While Manson and Fawcett were clear on their purpose in choosing Dolly as the reference point, they still spent a lot of time picking the specific mask they did. The interview ends with them describing this process with Fawcett stating, "We wanted it to be spooky but kind of childlike at the same time" (Manson and Fawcett). This duality is very much a part what makes M.K. distinctive: her social skills are lacking for many reasons while, at the same time, she is brilliant and capable of considering things other clones would not because of what she went through in Helsinki. Additionally, the very fact that they went through 5,000 different masks before settling on the right one and worked to include references to sheep throughout the entire show proves that there is more at work than just the invocation of Dolly.

There are many additional meanings attributed to sheep in our culture, and each of these contexts bring to light other potential meanings for each of the other appearances of the sheep motif within the *Orphan Black* universe. One of the most pertinent early appearances is in the episode titled "Parts Developed in an Unusual Manner" (1.7). In it, when trying to ascertain the names of the other known clones from Sarah, Helena states: "That's not the name of a sheep" (1.7). She even baas at her when Sarah asks for clarification, as if Sarah was incapable of understanding English as a sheeply clone. She saw herself as needing to cull the herd, thus placing herself outside of it despite the reality that they share a genetic template. One major reason she feels superior is that she believes she knows more than her fellow clones. This knowledge-based positioning very much brings to mind the concept of "sheeple," referring to people who are unaware of the ways in which controlling agencies are keeping them docile and compliant. That is also strongly mirrored in the show as that is the reason there are so many "shepherds" and monitors. As each clone becomes more and more aware of everything going on around them, she is no longer able to be easily controlled or culled. It is this awareness that prevents the clones from being perceived as just sheep by those in control within *Orphan Black* and the viewers/ readers of it as well. It also permits the re-appropriation M.K. takes on. Of course, M.K. is not the only clone who has been self-aware for much of her life.

Rachel and M.K. were both raised for much of their early lives in a Dyad testing facility, and the parallels between the way the two characters understand their role forms an important framework for the show as a whole. In "I Am and Am Not You," Jeremy Heuslein applies Husserlian phenomenology to *Orphan Black* in order to discuss the shift in perception Sarah undergoes when she sees Beth at the train station. According to Heuslein, Husserl describes the body as being understood in two facets: the body as a physical thing and the body as a lived-in experience. That is, he draws out the relationship between the location of being within the body and the perceptions felt within the body. It is through this relationship that individual identity is formed. Tying it to *Orphan Black*, Heuslein asserts that seeing another body like her own causes Sarah's identity to unravel as she must find a way to generate a new self that reflects the changed knowledge of her physicality. The fact that the members of Clone Club have all gone through this process of unraveling is one of the most vital means of bonding between them. Heuslein states that this is one of the reasons Rachel can never be a member (79); however, she did have this moment of unraveling. It just happened at a much younger age. In the *Orphan Black* comic "Rachel" (part 5), we see when Rachel and M.K. meet as little girls. Rachel asks her why she has her face, and M.K. shows fear that she will be caught interacting while Rachel tells her to "go away." This makes all the times Rachel is shown watching videos of her youth into moments where she is reminiscing about her time before she was aware rather than simply looking back on happier years. This small window of time is the only point where her life was like that of the other unaware, seemingly freer, clones, and this is one source of her jealousy. Because M.K. had no reaction to seeing another girl with her face, we know that she was, on some level, already aware. Although we are not privy to when she had her primary unraveling, this knowledgeable status is one of the things that is stressed repeatedly in the show. Just like Rachel, she carries the weight of being increasingly aware and tries to keep her other sisters from having to carry it, too. Before Rachel and M.K. are able to bond through the same means as those in Clone Club, they were separated because of the fire that Rachel believed killed her parents and which left M.K's face badly scarred.

Haunted by dreams of the fire and Rachel's face, M.K. continued to grow up in a controlled environment where she received very little real-life interaction with anyone outside of her uncle/monitor. Once she realizes what is going on, she begins to recognize that the dreams are memories, whereas Rachel remains within the institute and feels jealousy towards the unaware clones who have been able to have more fulfilling lives. Being the only clone raised by her creators, it is rather telling that they named her Rachel. It could be an intertextual reference to the self-aware android named Rachael Rosen from Philip K. Dick's *Do Androids Dream of Electric Sheep*. Rachael Rosen is an android who was designed to believe she is human through the implantation of false childhood memories. This could imply that her so-called parents did not want her to be self-aware as is discussed in "Rachel." Nevertheless, her name might also be in relation to the fact that it means "ewe" in Hebrew, which would suggest that they always saw her as a sheep, regardless of their feelings towards her. It could be a reference to both or neither, but it could indicate the conflicted nature of the project right from the beginning, revealing how the sheep motif was at play even then. Both Rachel and M.K. are aware of their clone status, yet respond very differently to it. Spending their lives, either explicitly or implicitly, aware of how they are being controlled prevents them from being able to create strong bonds with the people around them because of an inability to trust anyone; it also causes them both to seek any means necessary to achieve some kind of agency, with Rachel refusing to be a sheep from within the system and M.K. refusing to be a sheep outside of it. They both know that the secret to continued existence is gathering more knowledge. In the end, they both find ways to empower themselves using whatever means available to them. The main group of clones that the show follows would not have been able to succeed in the end without the help that each of them provided. This help consistently comes in the form of sharing their hard-earned knowledge, thus making their self-awareness and uniquely positioned identities into a very specific form of resistance. This resistance is, of course, seen as a threat to those who seek to control them, making suppression a fundamental means of keeping their positions of power for those in charge.

One form of suppression is the use of derogatory terms in order to subordinate individuals, or groups of individuals, for their membership within a specific group in a way that reflects an outside desire to keep them oppressed; however, the re-appropriation of those terms provides a means to reject negative meanings and recodify them. In *Orphan Black*, "sheep" is seen as derogatory as it codes the clones as less than fully human; because they are only seen as property to be controlled, their individual agency and identity is suppressed. This also permits and even sanctions their treatment throughout the series. The treatment we witness includes the clones being constantly monitored, experimented upon, forcibly impregnated and operated upon, and even killed. In "Precarious Projects: The Performative Structure of Reclamation," Cassie Herbert explores the role that derogatory terms play in our society and the way that re-appropriating them changes the way they function. She claims that, "Slurs are emblematic of these broader social systems and use of a slur is itself an instance of subjugation. Reclaiming a particular slur, then, serves as a way to take away a tool that is used to demean and marginalize the targeted group" (132). An example of this kind of project is the once pejorative word "queer." The word was used to separate and dehumanize people outside of heteronormative culture, resulting in much of the same treatment the clones experience in *Orphan Black*. After years of re-appropriation, the term "queer" has been mostly re-codified to represent an individual whose sexual, or gender, based identity doesn't fit into the traditionally understood binary and has become something that a self-identified queer person can be proud to identify as. Self-identification is key. As a clone, M.K.'s use of the sheep mask allows her to take control of the way in which that part of her identity is understood.

Through Cosima, we can see how the overlap between these two forms of re-appropriation functions. Cosima hears of M.K. for the first time in "Transgressive Border Crossing" (4.2); she asks, "[…] a clone in a mask; what's up with that?" Sarah explains, "Art just said she wore a sheep mask," and Cosima replies, laughing, "Oh, right. Uh, Dolly the sheep" (4.2). Cosima is represented as part of the community that has worked at re-appropriating the term "queer" and seems to understand this methodological approach as well as the context. There are eight named characters[3] in the series that fit under the category of LGBTQIA+, but Cosima is the only one of the core group that is in an openly queer relationship. Because of her job working at Dyad, she is also more openly a clone as compared to most of her sisters. This makes her particularly aware of the inherent risks she takes by living as both a clone and a queer woman. As such, she has a notable perspective that is highlighted in the way that the presumably bisexual Sarah only found it amusing after the scientific reference was explained and Alison, a clone who has shown no evidence of queerness nor scientific knowledge, did not think it was funny. Cosima understands what the mask means and does not make her take it off when she finally sees M.K. in the episode titled "The Redesign of Natural Objects" (4.8). The correlation between these two groups—those who are queer and/or those who are clones—makes sense as the individuals in each group are seen by some as abominations against the Christian God, may not be able to reproduce, and are targets for those who believe that killing them is acceptable. Derogatory terms support and continue these modes of thought, making re-appropriation a literal means of survival.

While the television show only hints at the re-appropriation at work, both comics showing M.K. fleeing Helsinki contain explicit references to it both in context and in words. She was fleeing the Finnish capital because she was part of a group of clones who had become self-aware and discovered terrible experiments being performed on them. Consequently, they became harder to control. This prompted drastic measures. The Topside cleaner Ferdinand was sent in to eliminate the threats, and M.K. was the only survivor. She was there to bear witness to the way they treated her and her sisters like sheep. The first time we get a chance to behold the events of the incident is in the chapter of *Orphan Black* titled "Rachel." At the end, the radicalized context for the sheep mask is made clear albeit before she dons the mask. Purple narration boxes, denoting M.K.'s storyline, state:

> They think we'll lie down and accept it. Sheep for the slaughter. Nothing more than property. Now they will also think Veera Suominen is dead. But they'll learn just how wrong they are on both counts—I'm alive, and we belong to no one [*Orphan Black*, part 5].

Because she had already gone through the process of unraveling twice over now, she differentiates between the experiences of her body being treated like property and her selfhood being relegated to that status. She knows they see her as both a generalized sheep that needs to be slaughtered and a specific individual that they want to kill. This is another example of the separation between being in what is perceived as an owned body and knowing that she, as an individual, cannot be owned. Both facets of her are currently under threat for slightly different reasons. Rachel knows Veera Suominen and wants her dead specifically because she survived the fire that Rachel believed killed her parents. Veera has also proven herself specifically uncontrollable multiple times, starting from when she ran away from her uncle. A similar statement is at the end of *Helsinki* where the same purple narrative boxes state:

> 3MK29A and 836XK9. Bound together. Twisted together. You have never left me, Niki. I have never been alone. And I will remind them that you are still alive. That we do not simply fade away, like ghosts. Or allow ourselves to be tagged, herded, and slaughtered like sheep…. Buried away and hidden, we will dig deeper for the truth. And for justice… [*Helsinki*, part 5].

Instead of focusing on being alive herself, she is now focused on proving Niki is still alive through her. There is still a rejection of ownership with the invocation of being "tagged," but now there is an inclusion of "herded," too, bringing in the specific way in which the clones are monitored and treated like sheep based on this perceived ownership. The use of the word "sheep" here draws attention to how derogatory terms like these are used to endorse this kind of malicious behavior. This is where the re-appropriation aspect becomes fully elucidated. With this more completed storyline, including the death of Niki, we can now understand where her sense of protest and drive for justice comes from. She takes on the mantle of the sheep in order to fight for her sisters instead of only fighting against those who seek to harm them. That is, she refuses to act like a sheep or allow herself to be treated like one, and this refusal is highlighted by her wearing of the sheep mask that represents both herself and all her sisters. This is what we see in the television show where this storyline is continued.

In the episode titled "From Instinct to Rational Control" (4.4), the *Helsinki* storyline is brought into the show, elucidating the way Ferdinand himself sees the clones in a derogatorily sheep-like manner. When Ferdinand sees the mask the first time, he comments, "How apropos: Sarah's deep throat is a sheep" (4.4). He says this before he knows she is Veera Suominen, so he could only make this assessment using the evidence that Sarah is a clone, and the person he is talking to is hiding behind both the mask and the computer. This invokes two separate derogatory contexts as he deems her as sheeply for hiding and because of her connection to her fellow clone Sarah. He also describes the Helsinki incident as a purge, revealing how he sees the rebellious clones as impure or imperfect, bringing in yet another derogatory context. The viewer can more easily sympathize with M.K. (as she attempts to bring her revenge fantasy to life) under these circumstances. Ferdinand certainly is a danger to her and her sisters. In an attempt to save his own life, he asserts that he can help them with his money. She steals this figurative lifeline from him and uses it to do just that later, explaining that it is "well invested" and thereby implying that this is how she was able to continue helping her sisters. We do see evidence of this as she continues to dig and provide information to help them (4.8). Even though his survival means that he is present later to inadvertently help the clones get the information needed to expose Neolution, it also leads to the unfortunate deaths of both Mrs. S (Maria Doyle Kennedy) and herself.

While hard to watch, there are many layers at work in the brutal murder of M.K., and each layer connects to the deeper meanings in the show. The most obvious is the resolution of the hunted-turned-hunter-turned-hunted again storyline that represents the complicated relationship M.K. and Ferdinand have. His completion of Helsinki couples with his fulfilled revenge for the theft of his money, making this a personal vendetta. Veera Suominen was no longer just another sheep in his eyes. This is further complicated by the context of the scene. Previously, Sarah had dressed as Rachel to pick up her daughter from school and escape Neolution. Ferdinand followed her back to Felix's (Jordan Gavaris) flat where she was going to pick up M.K. Seeing that Sarah was followed, M.K. swapped clothes with her so she could escape. Her clothing is coded as Rachel's and the unstable Ferdinand begins to call her by that name. Once he realizes that it is Veera and not Sarah, he states, "This is like two revenge fantasies in one" meaning that he is taking his anger and sexual frustration regarding Rachel out on M.K. at the same time ("Clutch of Greed," 5.2). This explains why he climbs on top of her and pins her arms as well as the way he tells her to turn around slowly when he believed she was Sarah because that is who he was chasing down, and M.K. was acting like her to buy Kira more time. This amalgamous perception of identity is one of the desired purposes of the mask as she represents and fights for all her sisters. Interestingly, this is replicated in the way that he consistently recognizes her by her scars. Her scars are not just a result of the burns, but also the skin grafts she received at a Dyad facility where they had "ample source," making both her face and her mask representative of not just herself in a more tangible way than with the other clones (*Orphan Black*, part 5). This makes his emotionally charged switching between names more telling as he is able to see this represented in her. This is also one of the reasons why she is able to say that he can't hurt her anymore. She is tired of running and is now dying. She knows she will still be a part of her fellow clones, much like

Niki is a part of her, and she knows that her death will help her sisters through buying time for Kira. She is a willing victim. Ferdinand is too emotionally caught up to see this, though, as he violently stomps on her chest, screaming about her hurting him. Which clone he is specifically thinking of as he screams this doesn't matter as much as the fact that he feels hurt. As his emotions fade after crushing her ribs, he places the sheep mask over her chest in a morbid salute, and the music becomes sad and almost tender. It is hard to read what Ferdinand is thinking in this moment, but it does not matter. A derogatory term is only derogatory if that is what the hearer (and the speaker) understands it to mean, and the same concept is at play for the sheep mask. We, the viewers, have an understanding of the mask that Ferdinand does not. This perspective is supported by the way that, after he places the mask on her chest, he walks away and is not in the frame during the lingering zoom out ("Clutch of Greed," 5.2, 00:43:33). At this point, she has fully re-appropriated the negative connotations of the sheep and made it into a sign of her agency as an individual identity and as a clone with a genetically shared template despite the constant attempts to undermine her ability to do so.

As much as M.K.'s death can be read as tragic, it is also fulfilling in that the creators have shown how the character has proven she is not a sheep; consequently, she has become an empowering character for the readers and viewers as well as making the meaning behind the sheep mask a symbol to rally behind. In a patriarchal society, within which too many men don't see women as having the same level of bodily agency or selfhood, the simple sentiment that they don't belong to anyone is powerful. This is what we see over and over again in M.K. Re-appropriation is based on accepted community use and, in this case, the community includes the readers and viewers of the show in addition to the characters in it. As already stated, the show designates the core group of clones through their induction into Clone Club. Using this concept, the readers and viewers identify themselves as a part of the fandom through the use of #CloneClub. They remain an active community who identify with and organize around themes of female empowerment and agency. Knowing this, BBC America embraced them and even provided printable sheep masks as a promotion for Season 4. The page where fans can print masks off is titled "Go behind the sheep mask—literally. Print it. Cut it. Wear it. Share it! #OrphanBlack #CloneClub." This emphasizes the way that the mask allows viewers to insert themselves into the show much in the way that iconization in comics encourages reader identification.

Inclusiveness is another reason fans gravitate to the show. The clones have diverse. identities, and yet they all embrace and support each other; the connection shared between members of clone club is another key theme that is represented through the sheep mask. At the moment of M.K.'s death, she embodies multiple Leda clones at once, and, when the mask is placed on her chest, it can be seen as representing her ability to embody all of them as well as herself as she finally gets her freedom from a life that has not been kind to her. This kind of connection between the clones is well established. Helena felt the connection between her and Sarah as far back as the first season. It is referenced again in the final panel of *Helsinki*, where it is shown that M.K. believes that Niki stayed with her because they are bound together. And, lastly, it is seen in the finale where Helena describes her story as the story of her *sestras*. The concluding moments show her reading from her memoir, "My story is an embroidery with many beginnings and no end. But I will start with the thread of my *sestra* Sarah who stepped off a train one day and met herself" ("To Right the Wrongs of Many," 5.10). These final words of the series perfectly capture everything that M.K. represents with her mask. They are all a part of a single picture, bound together, but each individual in their own way. This makes it clear that none of them were ever alone. By printing or wearing the sheep mask, fans are able to connect in the same way and vicariously earn their own physical and identity-based freedom as well.

Science fiction creators have long used the motif of the sheep to question deep concepts such as sentience, agency, and humane treatment. *Orphan Black* takes this and, through multi-platform storytelling, turns a clone who is treated like a sheep into an empowering figure who is capable of representing all those like her. This multi-platform storytelling allows for the use of comic shorthand in the television show as we can read the mask as representing the treatment of the clones, thereby better enabling the communication of the re-appropriative work M.K. is doing by wearing it to the readers/viewers. The reason that M.K. is the character most capable of this work is that she went through two unravelings, making her particularly aware of the way in which she may be within a body that shares a genetic template; however, the feelings she perceives as an individual are more important. This allows her to form an identity that can represent both of these concepts. The identity that she constructs, even changing her name to do so, also allows her to iconize the symbol of her oppression and re-appropriate it. This is crucial for the clones' survival as, much like people who identify as queer, the clones are looked down upon simply for being clones. They may even be killed if they are seen as a danger to the hierarchical structure that has been established, making something as simple as self-awareness and self-acceptance radical. Treated as less than human, each clone found ways to fight back against those that wanted to control them because they wanted to gain the agency taken from them since before they were born. This is particularly resonating for female and minority fans of the show who are able to recognize the struggle to have their personal agency respected. By re-appropriating the symbol of the sheep, M.K. models resistance against those who seek to harm her sisters while, at the same time, allowing herself to assert an identity that is inclusive of them and the freedom they fight for. More than that, M.K. shows fans of *Orphan Black* that it is possible for us all to "go behind the sheep mask" and fight for our own rights as agency-filled individuals. We do not have to be docile and compliant. If we work together with all our individual strengths, we, too, can claim our own form of freedom.

NOTES

1. A book designed to resemble Delphine Cormier's classified files and personal journal entries along with several newspaper clippings, and other forms of ephemera. The structure of the book invites readers to do the same kind of constructive reading shown in "From Instinct to Rational Control." While not confirming Ferdinand's fiery actions, it does provide clippings that bridge the two mediums as we learn about a supposed oil line rupture that resulted in explosions both in the chemistry laboratory at the school and in the private residence of the Lintula family (DiCandido 104–105).
2. See Jessica Lee Mathiason's essay in this volume for more on the legal issues involved in cloning.
3. Sarah Manning, Cosima Niehaus, Delphine Cormier, Felix Dawkins, Tony Sawicki, Shay Davydov, Colin, Niki Lintula.

WORKS CITED

"Clutch of Greed." Writ. Jeremy Boxson. Dir. John Fawcett. *Orphan Black*. Season 5, episode 2. First aired 17 June 2017.
DeCandido, Keith R.A. *Orphan Black: Classified Clone Reports: Confidential*. Harper Design, an imprint of HarperCollinsPublishers, 2017.
Fawcett, John, et al. *Orphan Black: Helsinki*. Temple Street Productions, 2016.
"From Instinct to Rational Control." Writ. Alex Levine. Dir. Peter Stebbings. *Orphan Black*. Season 4, episode 4. First aired 5 May 2016.
"Go Behind the Sheep Mask—literally. Print It. Cut It. Wear It. Share It! #OrphanBlack #CloneClub" *BBC America*, www.bbcamerica.com/shows/orphan-black/download-orphan-black-sheep-mask. Accessed 27 March 2018.
Herbert, Cassie. "Precarious Projects: The Performative Structure of Reclamation" *Language Sciences*, vol. 52, 2015, pp. 131–138.
Heuslein, Jeremy. "I Am and Am Not You." *Orphan Black and Philosophy: Grand Theft DNA*, edited by Richard Greene and Rachel Robinson-Greene. Open Court, 2016, pp. 75–84.
Manning, Alan D. "Scott McCloud: *Understanding Comics: The Invisible Art*." *IEEE Transactions on Professional Communication*, vol. 41, no. 1, 1998, pp. 66–69.
Manson, Graeme, et al. *Orphan Black: Volume One*. Temple Street Productions, 2015.
_____, and John Fawcett. Interview with Dalton Ross. "*Orphan Black* Season 4: Tatiana Maslany Stars as the Newest Clone in First-look Photos" *Entertainment Weekly*, 28 Dec. 2015, ew.com/article/2015/12/28/orphan-black-tatiana-maslany-season-4-new-clone/. Accessed 27 March 2018.
"Parts Developed in an Unusual Manner." Writ. Tony Elliott. Dir. Brett Sullivan. *Orphan Black*. Season 1, episode 7. First aired 11 May 2013.
"The Redesign of Natural Objects." Writ. Peter Mohan. Dir. Aaron Morton. *Orphan Black*. Season 4, episode 8. First aired 2 June 2016.
"Transgressive Border Crossing." Writ. Russ Cochrane. Dir. John Fawcett. *Orphan Black*. Season 4, episode 2. First aired 21 April 2016.

cDNA/©DNA in *Orphan Black*
Eugenics, Surplus Life and the Castor Virus

JESSICA LEE MATHIASON

Dr. Aldous Leekie: "You're a eugenicist, Dr. Cormier. Is that a dirty word for you as a scientist?"

Dr. Delphine Cormier: "No."—"Nature Under Constraint and Vexed," 2.1

Biopunk thriller *Orphan Black*, a TV show about a mysterious human cloning project, kicks off its Season 2 premiere with the evocative prospect of reclaiming the word "eugenics." It introduces this pernicious ideology through the charming personage of Dr. Delphine Cormier (Évelyne Brochu), the lesbian girlfriend and monitor of epigenetics Ph.D. student and science nerd clone Cosima (Tatiana Maslany). Lilting the edges of her vowels as she speaks, Dr. Cormier's unfettered sexual attitude, feminist *jouissance*, and impeccable scientific reputation make her a more palatable incarnation of new eugenics or, as she refers to her own philosophy, "Neotopian, maybe" (1.6). As they stand kitty-corner to one another in an upstairs laboratory, Dr. Cormier's ashen blonde curls and street clothes contrast sharply with the aging Dr. Leekie's (Matt Frewer) white hair and signature lab coat, emblazoned with Dyad's corporate logo. Through his first name, Aldous, he is an old-world embodiment of the dystopian future presaged in Huxley's *Brave New World* and, through his last name, bears a trace of Louis Leakey, who introduced the "Out of Africa" hypothesis. Though they are both eugenicists, Dr. Cormier is everything Dr. Leekie is not: she is young, queer, inquisitive, and emotionally invested in her subjects. This juxtaposition gives us our first glimpse into the complex web of eugenic ideology in the *Orphan Black* universe as well as our own: there is not *one* eugenics, but several.

In their book *Flesh Machine*, the cultural critics known as the Critical Art Ensemble[1] argue eugenics "never died after its failed implementation during the early portion of the 20th century. It has merely been lying dormant until the social conditions for its deployment were more hospitable" (119). The contemporary re-emergence of eugenics is due largely to a change in how it is being framed and put in the service of different forces. Whereas eugenic science was once articulated by the state and enacted through public policy reforms, it is now administered by the corporation and subject to the individual profit motive. With eugenic consciousness spreading rapidly, we are at a precipice: it is up to us, as a society, to determine philosophically, scientifically, and legally which brand(s) of eugenics we will implement and how. It is in this way *Orphan Black* provides a valuable template as it examines the different branches of power—corporate, legislative, military, and religious—interested in owning and deploying human genetic substance.

We enter the *Orphan Black* universe in 2013, when the clones have reached young adulthood and are just beginning to uncover their origins. We learn, along with them, that they have been created by the fictional biotechnology company Dyad, steered by the secretive, multi-national cabal Neolution, whose tentacles also extend to the upper echelons of *Orphan Black*'s military and governmental factions. Through a combination of cloning via somatic cell nuclear transfer and gene editing using cDNA, now practiced on lower organisms, *Orphan Black*'s covert cloning operation includes two distinct lines: the female Ledas (played by Tatiana Maslany) and the male Castors (played by Ari Millen). They have both been generated from a single source: a human chimera,[2] Kendall Malone (Alison Steadman), who absorbed a male twin in the womb and thus carries two distinct sets of genes. The brothers and sisters, or *sestras* as Ukranian-raised feral assassin clone Helena calls them, were born via *in vitro* fertilization in 1984, one of the series' many allusions to Orwell's dystopian novel of the same name. Significantly, the early 1980s also marks the beginning of the neoliberal era in North America and Western Europe. Neoliberal ideology—privatization, perpetual crisis, future speculation, and a desire to capitalize on the life of the nation—is helically woven into the show's textured fabric.

Orphan Black's animating eugenic mythos is a byproduct of how the modern life sciences and the political economy have developed in tandem. It is in *The Order of Things* that Foucault first theorizes how these two disciplines have continually informed one another as "the relation between visible structure and criteria of identity" in living organisms, observed by biologists Lamarck and Candolle, is "modified in just the same way as Adam Smith modified the relations of price. [...] This principle (which corresponds to labour in the economic sphere) is *organic structure*" (245-6).

This ideological convergence between the life sciences and political economy has only deepened since the 1980s, due to the formation of a strategic alliance among state-funded biomedical research, financial capital, and the market in new technologies. At first, the new life sciences may appear radical but, on closer inspection, it is clear they owe much of their ideological foundation and practical support to neoliberal economic policy. Examining the growth of neoliberalism and the life sciences together in *Life as Surplus*, Melinda Cooper argues that the boundaries between the spheres of production (labor) and reproduction (life) have become deliberately blurred, making reproduction—once thought to exist outside the market—suddenly available for commodification. Neoliberalism capitalizes on "the life of the nation" as it projects its strategies for accumulation into a speculative future where fluctuation is located at the center of production (9), unlike the earlier welfare state that maintained a foundational value. With neoliberal theories of economic growth, crisis, and speculation infiltrating the life sciences, a new relationship emerges between debt and life. We are isolating stem cell lines, creating transgenic organisms, and buying stock based on the promise of future life in the form of cures for diseases, the regeneration of tissues, and, in the sci-fi world of *Orphan Black*, the infinite replication of ourselves through human cloning. In so doing, life is incorporated into the "non-measurable, achronological temporality of financial capital accumulation" (10). Neoliberalism and the life sciences both seek to overcome the ecological and economic limits to growth associated with a Fordist system of production via a speculative investment in—or invention of—the future.

While *Orphan Black* presents several eugenic projects at once, the clones—and their cDNA—are the most suggestive for demonstrating how the infusion of neoliberal ideology into the new life sciences is shaping our deployment of genetic technologies in the 21st century. The synthetic DNA[3] of the Leda and Castor clones works on three levels: as the object of an intellectual property patent, as a mechanism of both surplus life and sterility, and as a sexually transmitted virus or bioweapon. The increasing shift towards privatization entails a reframing of the question of private property. While the modern legal subject had ownership over its body, the meeting of eugenic science and intellectual property law today begs the question: to whom does the body and its self-reproducing parts belong? In a departure from the distinction Cooper draws in 2008 between the stem cell line (not equivalent to a human and therefore patentable) and the germ cell line (equivalent to a human and therefore not patentable), I examine the new wave of biotechnology litigation which centers on patenting isolated genes and synthetic DNA sequences. The same forces that enable Neolution to proceed with its "next tranche of patent claims" (2.1) also corner several real high courts into leaving the door open to patenting life itself though a series of structural loopholes, like that created by the U.S. Supreme Court in *Association for Molecular Pathology v. Myriad Genetics, Inc.* (2013). *Orphan Black* thus provides an explanatory tool for how the modern legal system is structured by corporate pressures and a mode of legal interpretation that privileges private property rights. The synthetic biology that makes the clones' DNA patentable also carries sex-linked differences. Despite the insistence of Dr. Coady (Kyra Harper) (the leader of the military faction) that "Castor and Leda have the same disorder" (3.6), the fact that it manifests as a reproductive condition with auto-immune effects in the women and a neurological, sexually transmitted virus in the men means it carries different consequences for the sexes which are, presumably, different by design. The women are, first and foremost, a biomedical experiment; the men, a military weapon. By investigating the disparities in how the Ledas and Castors are affected by—and affect others through—their cDNA, we gain insight into how our cultural understandings of gender are shaping scientific knowledge and experimentation. In its entirety, *Orphan Black* serves as a model for how the cultural projects of neoliberalism, capitalism, and advanced scientific technologies are molding the eugenic project as it re-emerges as 21st century genetic engineering.

Patenting the Human

The neoliberal era's ethos of individualism, underlying corporate profit motive, and drive to protect proprietary information has shaped the legal battle over eugenic legislation as it comes to center on the intellectual property patent over human genetic material. The new eugenic wave is informed by the fight to maximize life itself. Entrenched in what is often couched as a Christian, theological understanding of life that presupposes we have been put on Earth, by God, to fulfill a purpose, the quest to maximize life has long been touted as inherently valuable. But should life necessarily be maximized? When we are told to maximize life, that directive usually entails a specific objective: to increase the reproduction rate of the "fit," to supply the nation with more workers, and so on. This is nowhere more evident than in how the drive to maximize life has reemerged under late capitalism as the quest to maximize profit.

Our understanding of life itself is at the center of a Foucauldian notion of modern biopolitics, as well as postmodern bioethical concerns over genetic engineering and biological patent law. In *Society Must Be Defended*, Foucault argues that contemporary politics challenges the nature of life itself as the modern era brings with it "something that is no longer an anatomo-politics of the human body, but [...] a 'biopolitics' of the human race" in which the nation-state exercises power over "the ratio of births to deaths, the rate of reproduction, the fertility of a population" (243). When the goal is maximizing life itself, history has shown that extreme measures, including racial genocide, become thinkable. The transition to neoliberalism entails another shift: we are no longer dealing with "the life of the nation" or "bioregulation by the State" (250) but the life of the human race in a global context, in which control is exercised by a web of multinational power networks. Foucault's concept of race war here becomes a truly genealogical genocide, designed to erase deleterious genes while introducing artificial DNA enhancements. This mode of bio-engineering in the name of life itself materializes through the clones' synthetic genomes, patented by Dyad. In the series, the intellectual property patent emerges as the genetically imposed prison of the control society.

From the 17th century through the late 20th century, Foucauldian disciplinary societies maintained order by using surveillance and the threat of punishment to compel individuals to regulate themselves by adopting normalized behavior. With the technological revolution and the economic shift to capitalism of higher-order production, Deleuze argues in *Postscript on the Societies of Control*, forms of discipline moved beyond enclosed structures and outward, towards a more sophisticated network of diffuse and mobile systems (6). These newer societies of control are not governed by the factory, the guard, or panoptic systems of surveillance but by "a code: the code is a *password* [...]. The numerical language of control is made of codes that mark access to information or reject it. We no longer find ourselves dealing with the mass/individual pair. Individuals have become '*dividuals*,' and masses, samples, data, markets, or '*banks*'" (5). The dividual is a "physically embodied human subject that is endlessly divisible and reducible to data representations via the modern technologies of control, like computer-based systems" (Williams 1). *Orphan Black*'s clones are quintessential dividuals. Engineered in the image of computer and military codes, their invisible genetic sequences materialize onscreen through computer code and consist of three components: a message, a cipher, and a key. Although the clones are patented by Dyad, the corporation lost the key in a fire and can no longer create new clones. While Dyad's patent covers the clones and their genetic derivatives ad infinitum, its patent over their mechanism of generation is useless until they can find the key. *Orphan Black* thus revolves around the race between Clone Club and Neolution to obtain the key, decode the cipher, and control both the clones' genetic destinies and the future of human evolution.

Biological patenting emerges in *Orphan Black* through the juxtaposition between the public façade of Dyad, represented by Dr. Leekie and his stated project of patenting "a pluripotent stem cell line from human baby teeth"

(1.7), and the company's covert mission to steer evolution through human cloning. In the aptly titled episode "Nature Under Constraint and Vexed," we learn Dyad intends to expand its control by pursuing its "next tranche of patent claims" (2.1) which will further put human "nature under constraint." Entering the episode on Dyad's top floor, an elegant, open space lined with floor-to-ceiling windows, we find a moving mass of scientists and investors, mingling as they sip champagne. Taking his place at the podium, Dr. Leekie introduces himself and then begins: "It is my great pleasure to welcome you here on behalf of the entire Dyad Group of Companies. [...] Today, worldwide, the majority of biotech research is funded by private capital" (2.1). With the word "capital," the scene cuts to the outer recesses of Dyad's private offices, where a group of Korean businessmen are being led through a series of closed doors and, finally, into the executive suite of icy pro-clone Rachel, the Duncans' adopted daughter. Shooting from behind glass walls, the camera looks in from the outside as the men file into her office, crowding the tight space around her desk. As the transposition between the open, public space of the cocktail party and the cramped, private space of Rachel's office suggests, Dr. Leekie is Dyad's superficial figurehead while Rachel is its covert director.

While Dyad hosts an elegant fundraiser to generate money for its public projects, it is the businessmen in Rachel's office who provide the private capital for its covert projects. As Rachel explains: "The recent Supreme Court decision characterizing the legal status of natural versus synthetic DNA was the successful result of our lobbying strategies. We are proceeding with the next tranche of patent claims" (2.1). Airing on April 24, 2014, this is almost certainly a reference to the U.S. Supreme Court's landmark decision in *Myriad* nine months earlier, which upheld the patentability of synthetic DNA and will likely set the tone for biological patent cases in other countries, including Canada, the home of the series. With billions of dollars of revenue riding on this decision, Myriad spent $550,000 in lobbying efforts in 2013, up 131 percent from the year before.[4] Taking us into the private negotiations and political pressures that affect judicial interpretation, *Orphan Black* illustrates how our legal system is steered toward corporate privileges and private property rights. Together, the clones' patented DNA and the ambiguous "next tranche of patent claims" (2.1) allow us to imagine how this new structural loophole might enable biotech companies, like Myriad, to go even further in patenting human life itself.

To unpack the complex web of ideologies operating beneath *Orphan Black*'s genetic mythology, it is necessary to explore the heated ethical, economic, and legal debates surrounding intellectual property patents on human life. On January 25, 2016, the front page of the *St. Thomas Lawyer* boldly proclaimed: "Playing God? Moral Arguments on Patents on Life." Such controversial headlines have exploded in recent years, following the dramatic rise in biological patent claims. The idea of patenting human life has not only garnered widespread media attention, but spurred a proliferation of local, appellate, and Supreme Court cases. While the popular press is fixated on the ethical implications of "playing God," the court cases instead center on the economic fallout of granting biological patents to private companies. Patenting isolated DNA sequences creates a corporate monopoly and makes it difficult (and expensive) for patients, doctors, and researchers to access materials. Of course, the ramifications of patenting human life are not new. The first patent on an organic compound found in the human body—adrenaline—was granted to Parke-Davis (a Pfizer subsidiary) in 1911. Since then, thousands of isolated and altered organic compounds have been accorded patent protection. The mounting fear of opening the door to intellectual property claims on human life itself has prompted patent offices across the globe to voice their opposition. In 1987, Donald Quigg, the U.S. Commissioner of Patents and Trademarks, issued a memorandum declaring that "a claim directed to or including within its scope a human being will not be considered patentable" (quoted in Cooper 146). His statement raises a fundamental question: how do we define the human being, or human life itself?

In *Life as Surplus*, Cooper contends that patent law in the Anglophone world has responded to this question by drawing a distinction between the germ and stem cell lines. "Human embryonic stem cells defined as 'totipotent,'" she argues, cannot be patented since they have "the potential to develop into an entire human" while stem cells defined as pluripotent (capable of differentiating into defined subsets of body cells) are patentable because they are "'not equivalent' to the potential person in its powers of development" (146–7). This division garnered precedent in U.S. patent law on March 13, 2001, with the granting of patent 6,200,806, which declared James A. Thomson the inventor of a purified preparation of pluripotent human embryonic stem cells (USPTO). Discussing the patent's significance, Cooper argues that while "the potential person [defined by the germ cell line] will not be commodified [...] the surplus life of the immortalized human stem cell will enter into the circuits of patentable invention" (147). The effect of this division is that it:

> equates the self-regeneration of the ES cell with the accumulation of surplus value: as the cell line is subdivided, expanded, and circulated [...] its "intellectual value" accumulates and multiplies, returning to the patent holder in the form of interest. It is this property right that decides, through the force of law, that the self-regeneration of life will coincide with the self-valorization of value, that the future materializations of the stem cell will have been appropriated even before their birth [, culturing life in a] state of permanent embryogenesis [147, 149].

The value of life itself is thus projected into a speculative future where value lies not in the individual life form, but in all the new life forms it may spawn, which also belong to the patent holder.

While Cooper's application of Marx's theory of value to the life sciences is convincing in showing how the self-regeneration of life creates surplus value, it seems naïve to suggest the division between the germ and stem cell lines will prevent "the potential person" from being commodified. It fails to account for future evolutions in genetic science and patent law, the latter of which is becoming increasingly skewed toward government deregulation and private property rights. In fact, since the publication of *Life as Surplus* in 2008, another type of biological patent has made its way through the courts. This new class of litigation involves (1) individual genes as they are isolated and manipulated through techniques such as gene editing, and (2) DNA segments not found in native systems, like synthetic DNA created through artificial gene synthesis and cDNA which has been altered by the removal of its introns. In the courts' published decisions, the issue of whether these isolated genes and DNA sequences originate from material found in the germ or stem cell line is never mentioned.

On June 13, 2013, the U.S. Supreme Court's 9–0 decision in *Association for Molecular Pathology v. Myriad Genetics, Inc* hit the front page of the *New York Times*. For the justices, the central question was whether the DNA sequences in question are products of nature or human-made inventions eligible for patent protection. In their brief to the court, Myriad defends patenting synthetic DNA by insisting it is a product of human ingenuity: it is created by man, in the lab, and offers significant utility in disease treatment. Providing only a partial victory to Myriad, Justice Clarence Thomas writes in his majority opinion that isolated genes (including BRCA-1 & BRCA-2) cannot be patented because they are not new "compositions of matter" under § 101 of the Patent Act, but that "synthetic DNA created in the laboratory [...] known as complementary DNA (cDNA)" (6) should be patent protected because it is "unquestionably [...] something new" (17). cDNA is synthesized from a messenger RNA template and used to clone eukaryotic genes (which have a nucleus) in prokaryotes (which do not). In the process, the introns (non-coding sequences) are cut from the primary RNA leaving only the exons (coding sequences). The removal of the introns, Justice Thomas argues, makes cDNA "distinct from the DNA from which it was derived" (17). Assessing the impact of *Myriad* on the future of biological patenting, the law firm Foley Hoag contends: "The Court's reasoning almost certainly validates the patent-eligibility of highly engineered DNAs such as those coding for humanized or chimeric antibodies" ("So Now What?"). What the Court's decision leaves ambiguous, however, is the extent to which a human DNA sequence must be modified to be patentable. The U.S. is not the only country facing this kind of controversy. Cases in Australia and Europe have resulted in similar conclusions.[5] On November 3, 2014, the Children's Hospital of Eastern Ontario (CHEO) filed a case with the Supreme Court of Canada questioning the legality of five specific patents related to long QT syndrome, held by the biotechnology company Transgenomic. On March 9, 2016, CHEO reached an out-of-court settlement with Transgenomic: the company will continue to hold the patents but will provide CHEO and all other Canadian public-sector labs and hospitals the right to test for the conditions on a not-for-profit basis (Waubgeshig 1). While this may be good news for Canadians seeking access to these specific tests, it upholds the validity of Transgenomic's biological patents, thereby establishing precedent for other biotechnology companies seeking to patent human genetic material. Together, these multinational cases reveal that the primary issues concerning the patentability of genes and cDNA is whether they have been modified by human intervention, whether they can be traced back to a specific individual, and/or whether they have a clear, industrial application. In other words, genetic materials may be considered intellectual property if they have been invested with what Marx refers to in *Capital* as human labor-time and have value as commodities.

The real-life issue of gene patenting and its attendant biological and legal consequences come to a head in *Orphan Black* as the Ledas uncover the mysteries behind their DNA, patented by Dyad. While certainly fictional, Dyad's intellectual property patents are the result of the same systemic pressures that have cornered North American, European, and Australian patent law into creating structural loopholes that could lead to the patenting of life itself. In fact, *Orphan Black*'s clones meet the criteria for patentability above. Both clone lines differ from naturally occurring genetic material in two ways. First, because they are the product of a human chimera, they are not exact copies of a living person. They are each half of Kendall Malone, much like naturally conceived children receive half their DNA from each parent. Second, because of the insertion of their sterilization sequence and ID tags, the Castors and Ledas have been categorically altered and are not exact copies of either Malone's male or female cell line.

Through *Orphan Black*'s use of *mise-en-scène* and narrative, the clones' synthetic DNA sequences look and operate like both computer and military codes. Onscreen they become a visual manifestation of bioinformatics, which uses computer science to represent and analyze genomic information. "Modern encryption systems involve three basic elements: a message text (or plaintext), a method of encrypting the plaintext (cipher), and a means of decrypting the ciphertext (the key). Might it be possible," Eugene Thacker asks in *The Global Genome*, "to encrypt a message into an actual DNA sequence?" (246). This is precisely what the Duncans have done in *Orphan Black*; they have encrypted a message into the DNA of each Leda and Castor. Thinking of their DNA as computer code, the message (plaintext) is to make them sterile so their human creators can control their mechanism of reproduction. The non-repeating substitution cipher is the synthetic sterility sequence and ID tag embedded in their DNA. The key (or means of decrypting the ciphertext) is hidden in a copy of *The Island of Dr. Moreau*, written in yet another code: a language only the Duncans understand. This final code resembles the book ciphers used during the American Revolution,[6] and it is only fitting that *Orphan Black* replaces William Blackstone's *Commentaries on the Laws of England* with its own galvanizing text: *The Island of Dr. Moreau*.

In the last scene of "Endless Forms Most Beautiful" (1.10), Cosima meets Delphine at Clone Club's makeshift headquarters to research her genetic sequence. Gesturing at the disc drive plugged into Cosima's laptop, Delphine explains that the genome it contains—Cosima's genome—is incomplete. Dr. Leekie scrubbed the synthetic sequence, or ID tag, which differentiates her from her sisters. Not only is it a marker of identity, Cosima realizes, but "the sequence is a message, like Dr. Craig Venter watermarked his synthetic DNA" (1.10, 28:35). As the Dyad logo on her disc drive suggests, their origins are not natural but man-made, corporatized, and patented. Venter, the real-life geneticist who worked on the Human Genome Project, created a self-replicating bacterial cell made entirely from synthetic DNA. In it, he encoded four watermarks to identify it as synthetic and enable the tracking of its descendants.[7] Applying the logic of Venter's sequence to her own genome, Cosima realizes that the synthetic portion of her DNA must also contain a message. "But how to decode it?" (1.10) she asks, highlighting the differentiated portion of her DNA with the cursor. The green, purple, and blue parabolas—which correspond to the row of nucleobases above (ATCG)—mimic the lines in the painting behind the couch Cosima and Delphine are sitting on. It is one of the many paintings rebel-punk clone Sarah's brother has drawn of the nearly identical Ledas. It is also these computerized images that constitute the ciphertext. As the computer screen fills the frame, Cosima's unique genomic information is complemented aurally by the chorus of The Belle Game's pop hit "Blame Fiction." With each repeated "I, I, I," in the song lyrics, we are forced to think about not only the Ledas' genetic substance, but also their subjectivity. Together, the paintings, the refrains of the pop song playing in the background, and the sisters' DNA sequences, all signify repetition with a difference. Visually and metaphorically, the squiggly lines on Cosima's screen represent her cDNA, which distinguishes her from her sisters. In a bioinformatic context, cDNA indicates an mRNA transcript's sequence expressed as DNA bases; the appropriately named messenger RNA delivers the genetic code through its sequence of exons, or coding regions. The project of *"connecting information to the biological body"*—here done through the analogy between DNA and computer code—is, in Thacker's view, *"the pri-*

mary challenge of 'life itself' in the age of bioinformatics" (79, emphasis in original). In *Orphan Black*, however, it is the decoding of life itself and the ensuing struggle over ownership that present the biggest challenge.

As the clones soon realize, being able to decode their biology will be insufficient if they do not own the intellectual property. Still, cracking the cipher is the first step. Sitting down next to Cosima, Delphine reveals: "I know your tag number.... If we know how that translates, then we can figure out the rest [...]. It's 324B21" (1.10). Cosima repeats: "I'm 324B21" (1.10). She—her personhood and her biology—has been reduced to information, to a six-digit alphanumeric tag. Learning the ID tags of other clones (3MK29A, 836XK9) reinforces the fact that they are bioinformatic code and not sequential numbers, allusions, or a form of nomenclature that identifies them with their producers. This departs from how, Marilyn Strathern argues, "the products of mental and intellectual labour" in Euro-American culture typically "carry the producer's [father's] name and the relationship between producer and product is one of identification" (20). Unlike the transmission of the father's name in patrilineal culture, the clones' numbers are unique, secretive, and do not identify them with either their human engineers (Susan and Ethan Duncan) or the source of their genetic material (Kendall Malone). Not only do the clones not carry their creators' name, they also do not bear their likeness.[8] In fact, upon meeting Malone, the first question Sarah asks is: "How come my original looks nothing like me?" (3.10, 4:35). Since Malone carries two distinct cell lines, she looks like neither in its isolated form (which is enhanced by the show's casting choices). In one of *Orphan Black*'s characteristic false positives, Clone Club translates a riddle scribbled in the margins of a copy of *The Island of Dr. Moreau* which gives them a similar six-digit number to help them track down their original. The translation reads: "In London town we all fell down and Castor woke from Slumber. Find the first, the beast, the curse; the original has a number: H46239" (3.8). While the number does lead to Malone, it turns out to be her prisoner ID and not a bioinformatic code like the ones inserted into the clones' DNA.

The similarity between prisoner numbers and bioinformatic codes in *Orphan Black* delivers a striking metaphor; the clones' patented DNA becomes their bioinformatic prison. The choice of six-digit ID tags bears an allusion to a specific, real world antecedent. In Nazi Germany during World War II, concentration camp prisoners were branded with alphanumeric tags of up to six digits so they could be identified and used for genetic experimentation. Unlike a tattoo on the forearm, however, the clones' ID tags are invisible. Cosima was never meant to know she is 324B21. Ciphers rather than numbers, their ID tags carry a message: a message that works by intervening in and directing their biology. It not only identifies them, but alters them. It also imprisons them without having to contain them within four walls. After all, the objective is not to regulate their behavior, but their biology. The only possible mechanism of escape is to find the key; in this case, not a physical key that unlocks a door, but an informatic key that decodes a cipher. It will allow them to alter their DNA, restoring their fertility and curing their auto-immune disorder. Remembering that the code was created in the late 1970s, when molecular encoding contained only two base-pairs (AT, GC). Cosima realizes she needs to use binary code, or ASCII, to translate her ID tag. She types in a series of 1s and 0s and presses "convert." On the black computer screen, a phrase writes itself across the monitor: "THIS ORGANISM AND ITS DERIVATIVE GENETIC MATERIAL IS INTELLECTUAL PROPERTY" (1.10). The prison in which the clones find themselves trapped is a specifically neoliberal one: the intellectual property patent. Picking up her cell phone, Cosima calls Sarah to report her findings. Through the use of selective sound, we hear her voice play over Sarah's image as the latter rides the elevator up to her apartment: "That synthetic sequence, the barcode I told you about, it's a patent [...]. We're property" (1.10). The horror of this discovery etches itself across Sarah's face as the camera cuts in. The frame is tight, with only the elevator's gleaming silver walls creeping into the shot. It is a fitting metaphor for the prison of the intellectual property patent.

While the idea of patenting the human may still be science fiction, the fact that the Ledas and Castors are patented property is grounded in real world patent law. The United States, like many countries, issues secret technology patents, protected under the Invention Secrecy Act of 1951. This act was passed by Congress to regulate the kinds of temporary orders generated by the Patent and Trademark Office during both world wars to classify defense-related patents. The act reads, in part: "Whenever publication [...] by the grant of a patent [...] might [...] be detrimental to national security, the Commissioner of Patents upon being so notified shall order that the invention be kept secret" (35 U.S. Code § 181). Human cloning is certainly the kind of patent that, if published, would be "detrimental to national security" and thus qualify as an invention to be kept secret.[9]

Returning to the sisters' phone call in the elevator, Cosima's voice details the patent's implications while the reaction takes shape on Sarah's face: "Our bodies, our biology, everything we are, everything we become, belongs to them. Sarah, they could claim Kira" (1.10). Kira (Skyler Wexler) is the "derivative genetic material" mentioned above: as Sarah's biological daughter, she has the same synthetic watermarks in her DNA that identify her as Dyad's property. This mode of eugenic control—of creating surplus life to generate a profit—harkens back to how, centuries earlier, plantation owners controlled their slaves' means of reproduction, often forcibly mating those with desirable attributes to breed new generations of enslaved workers to cultivate their land. In the age of post-mechanical reproduction, however, the objective is no longer to reproduce individuals, creating "the standardized Ford-T model in nature" but, in Cooper's words, "to generate and capture production itself, in all its emergent possibilities [...] what counts here is the variable code source from which innumerable life forms can be generated" (24). In *Orphan Black*, it is this idea of surplus life—of owning the clones' "principle of generation"—that is encapsulated in the episode's title. By virtue of its patent, Dyad owns all the "Endless Forms Most Beautiful" generated from Leda's source code. They own "production itself, in all its emergent possibilities," which, in this case, includes Kira, Helena's twins, and those children's children, ad infinitum.

Moreover, through its biological patents, Neolution and its subsidiary companies have protected themselves against many of the unforeseen consequences of their human experiments. In fact, it is their mistakes that may prove the most lucrative. Once the synthetic sequence is implanted into human bodies, epigenetic factors take over: the activation and de-activation of certain genes, responses to environmental stimuli, and interaction with other biological and synthetic agents. In the case of *Orphan Black*, some clones are susceptible to the sterility concept while others are immune. It failed to work on Sarah and Helena, and yet Dyad owns the unintended, human result. The Ledas' children have been patented before their birth and, as man-made *products*, patent law (presumably) supersedes the custodial rights of their biological parents. With the intertwining of biology and information, of genetic and informatic code, these human products possess "two types of value—medical and economic—based on effectively transforming something immaterial that is exchanged into something material that is consumed as its endpoint" (Thacker 79). Since, as Thacker reminds us, "*encoding is synonymous with production*," it is in "the process of encoding the biological that the biotech industry is able to accrue profits (as intellectual property)" (xx-xxi, original emphasis). In other words, by controlling the mechanism of generation—the ability to encode each clone with a cipher—Dyad stands to make a profit. Sarah's and Helena's immunity to Leda's disorder has incredible medical benefits: Helena's ability to heal herself after being stabbed in the stomach, Sarah's immunity to the Castor virus, and Kira's stem cells as treatment for disease. If isolated and harnessed, these biological components could be made into pharmaceuticals that would draw a hefty price on the market. They would also increase Neolution's biopolitical influence through its ability to maximize human life not only through cloning, but also by extending existing life through improving the immune system (and controlling who has access to this increased life and who does not). This is why the rush to decode Duncan's sequences, by Clone Club and Neolution, is so important. Finally, even though Dyad holds the patents over the Ledas and their "derivatives," it will need the lost key to resume production of new clones. The missing key is essential to bringing about Neolution's desired, eugenic future.

Sterilization, Self-Regeneration and the Castor Virus

Neolution's quest "to create a more perfect human being" (4.3) reimagines the early 20th century dialectic of progress and degeneration in the context of advanced, genetic technologies. The trope of degeneration takes on many forms in *Orphan Black*: the revival of vestigial structures like Olivier's tail, the simulation of asexual reproduction through cloning and the bifurcation of body parts (tongues, penises),[10] and the introduction of the sterility sequence. The very mechanism which creates the clones also carries a potentially deadly virus. Cloning itself, Baudrillard writes in *Simulacra and Simulation*, is a "monocellular utopia" that "allows complex beings to achieve the destiny of protozoas" (96). Its cancerous duplication of cells is not only a "hell of the same," but a "fatal strategy" powered by the death drive: it eliminates sexual reproduction which, he argues, is the guarantor of life (96). *Orphan Black* contests Baudrillard's admonishments against cloning as a degenerative return and offers a compelling alternative. While queer theorists like Jackie Stacey and Leo Bersani have offered varying ways of locating alterity in non-reproductive sexuality, *Orphan Black* takes us in a distinctly new direction by offering a mechanism of biological reproduction not rooted in heterosexual procreation. Cloning in *Orphan Black* is not, as Baudrillard imagines, a "reiteration of the same" (97) in which the copy "is nothing more than [the original's] scaled-down refraction" (23). If anything, the clones are a hyperreal improvement of Malone, a cranky murderess who smokes two packs a day. *Orphan Black*'s cloning technique also reverses the traditional process of parentage. Instead of being the composite of two donor parents, the clones are each half of a single parent. By isolating and cloning the Leda and Castor lines, Neolution uses scientific intervention to create male and female children who are not previously born as individuals because of Malone's chimerism—because of an intersexual mutation during sexual reproduction. Were the series to follow Baudrillard's insistence on heterosexual reproduction as the guarantor of humanness, Malone herself could, presumably, use her own cell lines (male and female) to conceive new children who would be the incestuous product of a single parent. Instead, Neolution offers the dual processes of cloning and gene editing to create new persons who are both biological clones and uniquely identifiable people. In a final blow to the heterosexual order, *Orphan Black* inserts a sterility sequence into the clones' DNA.

The same synthetic DNA sequences that give life to the clones also ensure they cannot reproduce exponentially. Neolution controls their mechanism of generation and, with it, the ability to create or restrict surplus life. Extrapolating on Marx's reflections on the counterproductive tensions of capital, Cooper argues that "as long as life science production is subject to the imperative of capitalist accumulation, the promise of a surplus of life will be predicated on a corresponding move to devaluate life. The two sides of the capitalist delirium—the drive to push beyond limits and the need to reimpose them, in the form of scarcity—must be understood as mutually constitutive" (49). In *Orphan Black*, scarcity is re-imposed through the sterility sequence. But, due to a design flaw, it not only prevents the clones from reproducing *for free* but also manifests during adulthood as a sex-linked virus. The fact that it presents as a reproductive condition with autoimmune effects in the women and a neurological STD in the men means it carries different biological, social, and economic consequences for the sexes. As indicated above, the women are a biomedical experiment; the men, a military weapon.

By disclosing Leda's disorder through the female body itself but representing Castor's through a networked web of information at the moment of revelation, *Orphan Black* links biological sex to social function. Despite the series' many compelling feminist reversals, here, it engages in an act of regression: it reduces the Ledas to their reproductive functions while allowing the Castors to serve as the brains, the conduits of information, and the social actors. In the companion scenes which reveal their respective disorders, the virus is naturalized as an integral part of the female body while the men, instead, become contagion vectors in a bioinformatic network in which the disease they carry ravages not their own sexual organs but those of their female partners. This contrast is reinforced by the scenes' divergences in *mise-en-scène* as well as the title of the episodes in which they appear: "Mingling Its Own Nature with It" (2.3) and "Certain Agony of the Battlefield" (3.6). As these titles suggest, the women's bodies have been "mingled" with an auto-immune disorder that "naturally" degrades their endometrium, while the men's neurological virus transforms the civilian landscape into a "battlefield" by inflicting "certain agony" on the women they infect by making them sterile. So even though the men's disease will eventually wreak havoc on their brains, the fact that it has no effect on their sexual organs indicates a dimorphic, gendered distinction.

In the former episode, the Dyad Institute and the female body serve as dual sites of medical discovery as Cosima learns the nature of the Leda's disorder by conducting an autopsy on her deceased sister Jennifer. In the latter, these two established sites are complemented with a third: the digital graphic, or the visual manifestation of bioinformatics. Cross-cutting between two scenes, the Castors' disorder is revealed simultaneously through Cosima performing a pelvic ultrasound at Dyad on Gracie (Zoé de Grand'Maison) (Castor clone Mark's wife) and Paul Dierden (Dylan Bruce) reading Dr. Coady's classified medical files on the Castor compound while Mark stands guard. Cosima and Paul take on the role of scientific investigators, each working with half of the wife-husband pair. The investigation begins when Gracie mysteriously collapses and is rushed to Cosima's lab. Pressing on Gracie's belly with her ultrasound wand, Cosima triggers a 3D, digital rendering of Gracie's uterus on the monitor. Her ovary shows the characteristic polyps, highlighted with flashing red arrows. The polyps, Cosima explains, are caused by a "protein in the blood. It's similar to something we found in one of your husband's brothers" (3.6). With the word "brothers," we are transported back to Dr. Coady's rustic office, drenched in military green, where Paul is arranging six or seven stacks of paper, each containing a woman's driver's license, ultrasound photo, and medical reports. Cutting in to a close-up of one of the reports, the phrase "ovaries atrophied" is circled (3.6). The hand-written commentary and thick, Manila folders contrast sharply with Dyad's high-tech *mise-en-scène*. Still, Dr. Coady's rudimentary files confirm what Cosima is looking at. Revealing Castor's disorder through the immaterial representation of information is indicative of the extent to which biology and information have become intertwined, and computerized models now stand in for the thing itself. Moreover, the visual merging of information with biology (of Gracie's fleshy stomach with the digital image of her uterus) and the frequent substitution of the former for the latter highlight the viral, contagious nature of both biological and informational networks.

In the age of biotechnology, where reproduction can take place in vitro, *Orphan Black* re-centers the female body as the locus of (in)fertility, reproduction, and venereal disease. Men transmit the virus, but it is women who must suffer its sterilizing effects. Moreover, in these two specific episodes, it is only female bodies that are examined: Jennifer's corpse, Gracie's ovaries, and medical records of Castors' female partners.[11] Cosima never even suggests Mark come in for an examination—a rather strange lack of curiosity for any geneticist, let alone one who shares his mysterious biology. This gendered division is reinforced as the cross-cutting between scenes continues. No sooner do the words "ovaries atrophied" fill the screen than Dr. Coady's office door swings open and in walks Mark—the source of Gracie's ovarian atrophy. Paul hands him a manila folder and, as he opens it, he sees a headshot of Gracie with the word "PENDING" stamped at the bottom (3.6). Even though Mark is the genetically engineered clone, it is Gracie who becomes Neolution's pending experiment.

Leda's and Castor's differences carry political and economic consequences. Unlike the Ledas, the Castors' sex organs are not affected. The side-effect they experience is neurological damage, referred to as "glitching."

Through this divergence in symptomatology, the boys are reduced to their brains; the women, their wombs. One could argue that, by causing the Castors' brains to glitch, *Orphan Black* is critiquing these reductive positions. Either way, these sex-linked variances highlight the Leda's and Castor's differing relationships with capital as it intersects with the life sciences. The Ledas follow the logic of capital accumulation in that the company holds the patent over their mechanism of reproduction and can control supply to draw higher profits. The Castors operate via a different logic: their virus is a biological weapon.

Under neoliberalism, public health, the biotech industry, and the military have become strategically indifferent. This is nowhere more true than in the bodies of the Castors. With the sterilization sequence embedded in their DNA, the line of men with piercing hazel eyes and strong jaw lines are living, breathing, human specimens of biowar. Defining the term, Thacker asserts that "in biowar, biology is both the weapon and the target, a form of 'life itself' that targets 'death itself'" (227). The Castors' bodies constitute the "weapon" and the bodies of the women they sleep with the "target." By exclusively targeting women, often using coercive strategies ranging from gaslighting to sexual assault, the Castor men become specifically patriarchal weapons. Yet, the "death itself" they target is not the women's death—or the death of current life—but, rather, future life. It is in this way they constitute a new and more virulent assemblage of earlier threats: the suicide bomber, the homosexual with HIV, and the chemical weapon.

Picking up where we left off on the Castor military compound, tucked away in an isolated pocket of the arid North American desert, walled off by miles of red sand, Paul and Sarah storm into Dr. Coady's office. Waving the Castor boys' medical files in the air, Paul confronts her. "It's a weapon. You're field testing it. You want to isolate it. Develop it in other forms" (3.6). Dr. Coady's sunken eyes enlarge: "It could end wars in a single generation without spilling a drop of blood!" (3.6). Paul turns his back in anger, but Sarah inches closer. "Who wants *it*? Who is *it* for?" (3.6) Before Dr. Coady can answer, we are transported back outside the compound's thick, iron gate. *It*. Sarah, Paul, and Dr. Coady each refer to the weapon as "it," conflating the sterilization sequence with the Castor men themselves. They are not free agents, but biological weapons being controlled by an unknown force—presumably, the same force that engineered them three decades earlier.

The wars Dr. Coady refers to here are a science fiction realization of the race wars at the center of Foucault's discussion of biopolitics in his 1975-6 Lectures, and the Castor clones are the eugenic weapons capable of performing a genetically informed racial cleansing. Biopower, Foucault argues, "takes life as both its object and its objective" which presents a conundrum. "How can a power such as this kill, if it is true that its basic function is to improve life?" (254). In answer to his own question, Foucault asserts "that racism is inscribed as the basic mechanism of power" because "racism makes it possible to establish a relationship between my life and the death of the other" in which the so-called inferior must die so that "I—as species rather than individual—can live" and "make life in general healthier" (254–5). Foucault locates racism as endemic to the dialectic of life and death, much like Cooper argues the dialectic of life and death is intrinsic to the life sciences as they ascribe to the capitalist delirium in the age of neoliberalism.

In the early 20th century, eugenic warfare was limited to the tactics of selective breeding, surgical sterilization, and euthanasia, which had to be carried out on an individual basis and were imperfect in their selection of so-called "inferior" targets. Today, the introduction of CRISPR/Cas9 technology makes it possible to engineer biological weapons that can target specific genes, cells, or chromosomes. This is one potential use for the Castor clones. If Dr. Coady identifies a specific group as the enemy, the Castors can be deployed to sterilize its female members, effectively wiping out the next generation. At present, though, Castor's victims do not appear to belong to any particular group, class, or ethnicity. The women whose files we see share no discernable physical or genetic characteristics. Whether Castor's victims are intentionally chosen or simply random targets (women they meet at bars or social gatherings, prostitutes, vulnerable women who appear more coerced than consenting), it is clear Project Castor both deviates from and extends beyond early 20th century eugenic attempts to sterilize women who were perceived to be socially undesirable. If Castor's virus can be isolated, as Dr. Coady suggests, it can be altered and mobilized. Surely her statement that the virus "can end all wars in a single generation" is an exaggeration, but its potential should not be underestimated. For instance, the virus itself could be modified so that, regardless of who is exposed, it will only affect those with genetic markers deemed inferior. While *Orphan Black* remains silent on who Project Castor's target might be, history has taught us it is likely a segment of the population that deviates from white, middle-class, heterosexual normativity. In fact, the series' attempt to capitalize on liberal "postraciality" through its emphasis on genes rather than race only reifies hegemonic whiteness, embodied onscreen through the pale, idealized bodies of Projects Leda, Castor, and Brightborn.

Unlike either traditional military combat or contemporary modes of biowarfare, the violence the Castor virus enacts is un-bloody, invisible, and silent. Examining the Castors against their real-world antecedents, listed earlier—the suicide bomber, the homosexual with HIV, and the chemical weapon—the striking differences in their appearance and strategy make them more elusive. Today, the suicide bomber is the most visible personification of terrorism and the most salient, perceived threat to a Western way of life.

The paradox the Castor clones raise is: What happens when the terrorist is us? Or, at least, he appears to be. Project Castor's bioweapons look strikingly different from those we are accustomed to seeing on CNN and Al Jazeera: they are white, Western, clean-cut, and dressed in uniforms that resemble a cross between Canadian and U.S. army fatigues. And, even more frightening, what happens when the terrorist is inside us, in our DNA, waiting to be activated?

The Castor clones are very much "body-weapons," to use Jasbir Puar's term ("Queer Times" 129), in a fashion analogous to that of the suicide bomber, but there are three salient differences which alter their mode of warfare: their weapon is incorporated into their body involuntarily, it does not fully annihilate their body or that of their victims, and its effects are invisible at the moment of detonation. The women they sleep with are unaware at the time of infection and, when symptoms surface days later in the form of red eyes and a high fever, they are unlikely to deduce the source. They will probably not know they are sterile until they undergo medical testing or try unsuccessfully to conceive. Unlike the suicide bomber whose greatest achievement is the drama of his spectacle and the fear he instills in his enemy, Project Castor's objective is to remain concealed. Its victims also do not die as a result of transmission. The death the Castor men bring about is not the death of current life but, rather, future life, which is not a *death* at all.[12] Unlike the praying-mantis who kills her partner after sex or the human martyr who annihilates himself and his victims simultaneously, the Castors do not kill their partners so that new life can be born; the living continue on and new life is never created. Neolution takes Achille Mbembe's thesis in *Necropolitics*—that "the ultimate expression of sovereignty resides [...] in the power and capacity to dictate who may live and who must die" (11)—and revises the last seven words to read: *whose life may be created, and whose life may be engineered out of existence.* Neolution's target is an entire generation who has yet to be conceived. Finally, in the act of transmission, the Castor clones' white, heterosexual, male normativity becomes dangerous and exoticized. Through the danger his body poses, the Castor terrorist, like his non–Western and homosexual counterparts, becomes improperly sexual and thus inescapably queer.

While Castor's sexually transmitted virus functions in many ways like HIV did in the late 20th century Western imaginary, by introducing it through the body of the faithfully married Gracie, *Orphan Black* positions the virus *alongside* heterosexual normativity rather than against it. Via its effect on Gracie, the Castor virus offers a feminist critique of normative domesticity and reproductive futurism. Like HIV, Castor's sterility concept is a sexually transmitted immunodeficiency virus passed through blood and other bodily fluids. It can be identified by detecting a "protein in the blood" (3.6), just as

HIV infects white blood cells which have a CD4 receptor protein on their surface. The sterility virus is first identified not through the Castors' escapades with prostitutes, but through Gracie, the Prolethean girl who had sex for the first time on her wedding night. Identified with an act of loving, married heteronormativity, the threat posed by the Castor virus figures differently than that posed by the homosexual with HIV in 1980s and 90s social discourse. In *The Spectacle of AIDS*, Simon Watney argues that, in the cultural imaginary, "the spectacle of AIDS operates as a public masque in which we witness the corporal punishment of the 'homosexual body'" that resists "marriage [and] parenthood" (209). The body with HIV—weak, pale, disease-ridden— becomes the locus of punishment for sexual deviance. Defined through opposition to one another, the homosexual with HIV and the family are prescribed as cultural antagonists: the former is reprimanded for his transgressions against marriage and parenthood while the latter, the "family unit—understood as the locus of the 'the social'—is cleansed and restored" (208). In contrast, the ravages of the Castor virus are depicted through the body of Gracie, the virtuous Prolethean girl. Already impregnated through IVF (with embryos created from her father's sperm and Helena's eggs), Gracie is an unwitting Prolethean Virgin Mary. The sterility virus thus has two effects: it aborts the artificially engineered (and, arguably, incestuous) child she is carrying (the Prolethean baby Jesus) *and* it prevents her from conceiving any future children with her husband, who would be the natural product of a heterosexual family. By disrupting both, *Orphan Black* circumvents the attribution of social value to either one child, or method of reproduction, over another.

What remains unclear in *Orphan Black* is whether the Castor sterility concept can be passed among men. While the Leda clones are shown to be diverse in regards to their gender identities and sexual orientations, all of the Castor clones we encounter are male-identified and heterosexual.[13] Neither Cosima's nor Paul's medical investigations examine whether the Castor virus can be passed among men, or through oral or anal sex with partners of any sex. Though, if it can be passed through blood and bodily fluids like HIV, one would surmise it could be transmitted among men. If so, it begs the question: would it make their male partners sterile (like their female counterparts) or would it transform them into contagion vectors who could then pass the disease on to other partners? In either case, it seems an army of Castors who have sex with men would constitute a desired arsenal of bioweapons for Neolution.

Unlike traditional chemical warfare's objective of instilling fear in the many by engendering what Agamben refers to as an ongoing "state of exception" (1), the Castors' mode of biowarfare operates by avoiding detection in the "battlefield" of mainstream society. The threat of chemical warfare garnered widespread attention following the 2001 anthrax attacks carried out via U.S. mail and has since been dramatized in numerous films and television shows including *The Crazies* and *CSI*. What these real-life and fictional examples have in common is the ability to create a pervasive sense of fear disproportionate to the number of victims, which persists even after a threat has been extinguished. As Thacker argues, this kind of biowarfare "*affects many by infecting a few*. In this sense, it would be more appropriate to refer to biowar as utilizing not a grandiose, genetic bomb but, rather, deploying a number of genome 'messages.' [...] *It is the message, not the bomb, that is the guarantee of the continuing effectiveness of the threat of biowar*" (241; original emphasis). What allows biowarfare to terrify us, even if its actual threat is minimal, is its relation "to a certain horror of the body, or, more specifically, to a horror of what biological warfare" can "do to [our] body" (239). Yet, Project Castor depends on acquiring cooperation rather than eliciting fear. Of course, while these women are (in most cases) choosing to sleep with the Castor men, they are not choosing to be infected.[14] Much like the early 20th century victims of eugenic sterilization, even when they are giving consent, it is not informed consent.

Unfortunately for Neolution, Paul's fury over the genetic implications of Project Castor leads him to burn down the military compound in the penultimate episode of Season 3, and the majority of the Castors expire as the flames engulf the base. Not even bioweapons can survive the fury of Nature's deadliest instrument. By the series finale, Neolution's principle actors are dead, and the Ledas have secured the rights to their own bodies and lives... or so we are led to believe. But, as series creators Graeme Manson and John Fawcett tease the possibility of a movie spin-off (Patterson), we cannot help but think Neolution's corporate subsidiaries would not abandon their objective of acquiring, harnessing, and selling the capacity for surplus life and biowar embedded in the clones' DNA.

Conclusion

As implausible as *Orphan Black*'s clones might seem, the idea of re-engineering our DNA is not. Through the cross-pollination of ideas between science and science fiction, those in lab coats and those in director's chairs are collaboratively rethinking the biological, social, and political boundaries of our DNA. On November 21, 2012, *Nature* introduced the world to "DNA's new alphabet." Teams of scientists, headed by Floyd Romesberg and Erik Kool, have been "tinker[ing] with DNA's basic building blocks" to engineer "unnatural base pairs": DNA bases beyond nature's A, T, C, and G (Kwok 516). With the merging of capitalism and the life sciences, these new DNA bases carry the ability to maximize both life and profit. Given the Supreme Court's ruling in *Myriad*, these new DNA bases—and the surplus life they promise—will be the intellectual property of their engineers. This reality is being overlooked as both scientists and reporters emphasize a progress narrative. As Kool tells *Nature*: "Why is the chemistry of living things the way it is? Is it because it's the only possible answer? [...] I believe the answer to that question is no. And the only way to prove it conclusively is to do it" (518). Like *Orphan Black's* Neolutionists, our 21st century scientists have no roadmap for implementing a humanitarian future or "Neotopia." Perhaps Cosima says it best: "Nobody's got any idea. We're just poking at things with sticks." We're not sure what we're going to find, we're not sure what we're going to build, and we're not sure what effect it's going to have. It is simply in our nature—in our DNA—to keep building, both in the lab and on the science fiction screen. Meanwhile, we should remember genetic engineering's eugenical roots and allow these historical lessons to inform us as we, inevitably, continue to build.

NOTES

1. Formed in 1987, the Critical Art Ensemble is a collective of five tactical media practitioners of various specializations: computer graphics and web design, book art, performance, photography, and film/video. Focusing on the intersections among art, critical theory, and political activism, the CAE works to create fissures and disruptions in authoritarian culture. The primary objects of the CAE's critique include cyberculture, biotechnology, and U.S. defense policy.

2. A genetic chimera is a single, living organism composed of cells from more than one zygote. In humans, genetic chimerism is the result of a merger, in utero, between two (or more) different fertilized eggs. Human chimeras can have two blood types, two different colored eyes, male and female organs, and numerous other variations in form. See: Norton and Zehner.

3. In this essay, I use the term "synthetic DNA" in the way that the U.S. Supreme Court uses it in Clarence Thomas's majority opinion in *Association for Molecular Pathology v. Myriad Genetics, Inc*. In other words, I use it to refer to any DNA segment that is not native, meaning it has been altered, in the lab, by humans. Under this definition, cDNA is considered "synthetic DNA" because it has undergone the removal of its introns. In the scientific community, however, the term "synthetic DNA" is sometimes reserved exclusively for DNA that has been created by artificial gene synthesis.

4. Lobbying expenditures reported by the Senate Office of Public Records. An analysis of Myriad's lobbying expenditures is available from The Center for Responsive Politics.

5. In 2015, Myriad was the respondent in a gene patenting case, *D'Arcy v. Myriad Genetics, Inc,* heard before the High Court of Australia. The Australian court held that claims to isolated genes, cells, and proteins "are 'excluded where they merely replicate the genetic information of a naturally occurring organism.' However, where the utility of the invention lies in genetic information that has been 'made' (e.g. created or modified by human action), these types of claims may be patentable" (Szweras and MacLean 1). The biological patent landscape in Europe, regulated by the European Patent Organisation, is more permissive. While discoveries such as the sequence of a gene are not patentable in and of themselves, "[b]iological material, whether isolated or produced by means of a technical process, is patent eligible even if it previously occurred in nature provided its industrial application is disclosed in its patent application" (1). The *Directive of the European Parliament and of the Council of 6 July 1998 on the legal protection of biotechnological inventions* states that it is legal to patent

inventions "including industrially applicable parts obtained in a technical manner from the human body in such a way that they can no longer be ascribed to a particular individual" (quoted in Strathern 26).

    6. During the American Revolution, Benedict Arnold and John André developed a book cipher using William Blackstone's *Commentaries on the Laws of England* to communicate, including planning Arnold's unsuccessful attempt to surrender West Point to the British Army. See "Secret Methods and Techniques." Other common books used to develop book ciphers include the Bible, the dictionary, and the Declaration of Independence.

    7. In 2007, Craig Venter filed patent applications US2007 0264688 and US2007 0269862 to cover *Mycoplasma laboratorium*, the first synthetic species ("Patenting the Parts").

    8. Each Leda clone carries the last name of the family who adopted her. Rachel, who was adopted by Susan and Ethan Duncan, carries their last name—but she is the only one. Every other clone has a different surname.

    9. As of 2007, 5,002 secrecy orders were in effect in the United States. Though the types of inventions classified under the Invention Secrecy Act are not disclosed, the majority of inventions that were previously classified (but have since been published) are in the areas of military defense and weapons development. As I will discuss in the following section, the Castor clones, even more so than the Ledas, fall into this area.

    10. The bifurcation of body parts visually resembles the early stages of clonal fragmentation, a type of asexual reproduction in which a multi-cellular organism splits into fragments, each of which eventually develops into an adult organism that is a clone of the original.

    11. In other episodes, however, we do see the Castor clones serve as the human experiments of Dr. Coady's military faction, such as when Parsons is tied to a chair, his brain exposed, and connected to electrodes (3.4).

    12. In the case of Gracie, the Castor virus also aborts the recently implanted embryo she is carrying. In so doing, the Castor virus not only prevents new life from being conceived but also life-in-gestation from being born.

    13. While, as far as we can tell, each of the Castor clones identify as heterosexual and/or participate in heterosexual activity, there is speculation among fans that Ira—despite his romantic relationship with Susan Duncan—is coded as homosexual through his mannerisms, dress, and speech. Mark also makes a comment to Gracie about life on the Castor compound that is open to interpretation. On their wedding night, he tells her: "At the military academy, the other boys did sex things and chased girls, but not me. I was waiting" (3.3). It is unclear whether Mark is referring to "sex things" *among* the Castor boys, or between the Castor boys and local girls.

    14. Throughout Season 3, we see the Castor clones court various women. In most cases, the women appear to be consenting. However, in "Transitory Sacrifices of Crisis," a consensual encounter between Rudy and a young woman, Patty, becomes non-consensual when his brother, Seth, joins them in bed. Presumably, the brothers have a pattern of this kind of tag-teaming. Several episodes later, in Rudy's death scene, Helena accuses him of having "poisoned women" and calls him a rapist (3.10). Krystal is also attacked by them.

Works Cited

Adorno, Theodor, and Max Horkheimer. *Dialectic of Enlightenment*. Stanford UP, 2007.
Agamben, Giorgio. *State of Exception*. Trans. Kevin Attell. U Chicago P, 2005.
Baudrillard, Jean. *Simulacra and Simulation*. University of Michigan Press, 1994.
The Center for Responsive Politics. "Myriad Genetics." 9 August 2016. https:/opensecrets.org/lobby/clientsum.php?id=D000064923.
"Certain Agony of the Battlefield." Writ. Aubrey Nealon. Dir. Helen Shaver. *Orphan Black*. Season 3, episode 6. First aired 23 May 2015.
Cooper, Melinda. *Life as Surplus: Biotechnology and Capitalism in the Neoliberal Era*. U Washington P, 2008.
Critical Art Ensemble. *Flesh Machine: Cyborgs, Designer Babies, and New Eugenic Consciousness*. Autonomedia, 1998. http://critical-art.net/?p=272.

Deleuze, Giles. "Postscript on the Societies of Control." *October* vol. 59 (Winter), 1992, pp. 3–7.
Ellis, Edith Lees. *The New Horizon in Love and Life.* A. & C. Black Ltd., 1921.
"Endless Forms Most Beautiful." Writ. Graeme Manson. Dir. John Fawcett. *Orphan Black.* Season 1, episode 10. First aired 1 June 2013.
Fisher, Irving. "Impending Problems of Eugenics." *Scientific Monthly* Vol. 13 no. 3, 1921, pp. 214–231.
Foucault, Michel. *The History of Sexuality Volume 1.* Vintage Books, 1990.
_____. *The Order of Things: An Archaeology of the Human Sciences.* Routledge, 1989.
_____. *Society Must Be Defended: Lectures at the Collège de France, 1975–1976.* Picador, 2004.
Kwok, Roberta. "Chemical Biology: DNA's New Alphabet." *Nature* vol. 491, 2012, pp. 516–518.
Liptak, Adam. "Justices, 9–0, Bar Patenting Human Genes." *The New York Times.* 13 June 2013. nytimes.com/2013/06/14/us/supreme-court-rules-human-genes-may-not-tobe patented. html?r=0.
Marx, Karl. *Capital: Volume 1: A Critique of Political Economy.* Penguin Classics, 1992.
Mbembe, Achille. "Necropolitics." *Public Culture* vol. 15 no. 1, 2003, pp. 11–40.
Mililo, Diana. "Rape as a Tactic of War: Social and Psychological Perspectives." *Affilia Journal of Women and Social Work* vol. 21 no. 2, 2006, pp. 196–206.
"Mingling Its Own Nature with It." Writ. Alex Levine. Dir. TJ Scott. *Orphan Black.* Season 2, episode 3. First aired 3 May 2014.
"Myriad Genetics," *The Center for Reproductive Politics*, 2016, opensecrets.org/lobby/client sum.php?id=D000064923.
"Nature Under Constraint and Vexed." Writ. Graeme Manson. Dir. John Fawcett. *Orphan Black.* Season 2, episode 1. First aired 19 April 2014.
Norton, Aaron, and Ozzie Zehner. "Which Half Is Mommy?: Tetragametic Chimerism and Trans-Subjectivity." *Women's Studies Quarterly.* Fall/Winter (2008): 106–127. "Patenting the Parts." *Nature Biology*, 2007, www.nature.com/articles/nbt0807–822.
Patterson, Dominic. "*Orphan Black* Co-Creator Talks Series Finale, Movie Reunion & #Clone Club." *Deadline.* 12 August 2017. deadline.com/2017/08/orphan-black-series-finale-spoilers-clone-club-tatiana-maslany-john-fawcett-bbc-america-1202147260/.
Puar, Jasbir. "Queer Times, Queer Assemblages." *Social Text* vol. 23 no. 3–4, 2005, pp. 121–139.
_____. *Terrorist Assemblages: Homonationalism in Queer Times.* Duke University Press, 2007.
Rice, Waubgeshig. "CHEO Reaches 'historic' Settlement with Gene Patent Owner." *CBC News*, 2016, cbc.ca/news/canada/ottawa/cheo-gene-patent-lawsuit-settlement-1.3483433.
"Secret Methods and Techniques." Clements Library, University of Michigan. Archived from the original on 11 June 2010. web.archive.org/web/20100611042144/http://www.clements.umich.edu/Spies/methods-code.html.
Smith-Spark, Laura. "How Did Rape Become a Weapon of War?" *BBC News*, 2017, news.bbc.co.uk/2/hi/4078677.stm.
"So Now What? Implications of the Supreme Court's Myriad Ruling." *Foley Hoag*, 2013, foley-hoag.com/publications/alerts-and-updates/2013/june/implications-of-the-supreme-court-myriad-ruling.
Stacey, Jackie. *The Cinematic Life of the Gene.* Duke UP, 2010.
Strathern, Marilyn. "Potential Property: Intellectual Right and Property in Persons." *Social Anthropology*, vol. 4, no.1, 1996, pp. 17–32.
Szweras, Melanie, and Teresa MacLean. "Canada to Consider Gene Patent Eligibility: Looking Abroad for Insight." *Biology Focus*, 2016, biotechnologyfocus.ca/canada-consider-gene-patent-eligibility-looking-abroad-insight.
Thacker, Eugene. *The Global Genome: Biotechnology, Politics, and Culture.* the MIT Press, 2006.
"35 U.S. Code § 181: Secrecy of Certain Inventions and Withholding of Patent." *Cornell University Law School: Legal Information Institute*, 2007, law.cornell.edu/uscode/text/35/181.
Thomas, Clarence. "Association for Molecular Pathology V. Myriad Genetics, Inc.," 2003, *Supreme Court of the United States*. supremecourt.gov/opinions/12pdf/12-3981b7d.pdf.

"United States Patent 6,200,806." *USPTO Patent Full Text and Image Database*, 2001, patft. uspto.gov/netacgi/nphParser?Sect2=PTO1&Sect2=HITOFF&p=1&u=/netahtml/PTO/searchbool.html&r=1&f=G&l=50&d=PALL&RefSrch=yes&Query=PN/6200806.

Watney, Simon. "The Spectacle of AIDS." *The Lesbian and Gay Studies Reader*, edited by Henry Abelove, Michele Aina Barale, and David M. Halperin, Routledge, 1993, pp. 202–211.

Williams, Robert W. "Politics and Self in the Age of Digital Re(pro)ducability." *Fast Capitalism*, 2005, uta.edu/huma/agger/fastcapitalism/1_1/williams.html.

About the Contributors

Erin **Bell** is an assistant professor of English at Baker College in Allen Park, Michigan. Her areas of research include women's writing, gender and sexuality studies and popular culture and her work has appeared in *The Explicator, Lilith*, and *The Journal of American Culture*. She is coediting a collection of essays about *Breaking Bad* and finalizing her dissertation project at Wayne State University.

Jenny **Bonnevier** is a senior lecturer in English at Örebro University, Sweden, where she teaches courses in contemporary literature, literary theory, and American studies as well as second language acquisition and the teaching of literature. She is also the Vice Head of Teacher Education. Her main research focus is representations of assisted reproductive technologies in contemporary American culture. She has forthcoming publications on the role of reproductive technologies in feminist utopias as well as on IVF and single motherhood in Hollywood rom-coms.

Brandi **Bradley** is a fiction writer and the creator of the website *Books and Boots*. Her work has appeared in *Juked, Louisiana Literature,* and the *Lincoln Humanities Journal*, among other publications. She was a finalist for *New Letters*' Alexander Cannon Prize for Fiction and for the William Faulkner–William Wisdom Creative Writing Competition. She is pursuing a Ph.D. in creative writing at Florida State University. For more information visit brandibradley.com.

Alyson R. **Buckman** is the chair of and a professor in the Humanities and Religious Studies Department at California State University, Sacramento, where she teaches courses in film, popular culture, American Studies, and multiculturalism. She is the secretary of the Whedon Studies Association and a winner of the coveted Mr. Pointy from the WSA. She has published multiple essays on science fiction and fantasy, especially the work of Joss Whedon. Her next project is a coedited volume on the representation of trauma, memory, and disability in the works of Joss Whedon.

Bronwen **Calvert** is an associate lecturer at the Open University in the North of England. She has been a senior lecturer at Sunderland University and is the author of *Being Bionic: The World of TV Cyborgs* (2017) and of a range of essays on television series including *Buffy the Vampire Slayer, Angel, Heroes, The X-Files, Fringe,* and *Dollhouse*. Her research examines embodiment in fantasy and science fiction narratives, with particular focus on cyberpunk fiction, horror, and versions of the television action hero.

About the Contributors

Janet Brennan **Croft** is the Liaison to the School of Communication and Information and Librarian for Disability Services and Copyright at Rutgers University libraries. She earned her MLS at Indiana University in 1983. She is the author of *War in the Works of J.R.R. Tolkien* (Praeger, 2004) and several book chapters on the Peter Jackson films; she has published articles on J.R.R. Tolkien, J.K. Rowling, Terry Pratchett, Lois McMaster Bujold, and other authors, and is editor or coeditor of many collections of literary essays. She has also written widely on library issues, and is the author of *Legal Solutions in Electronic Reserves and the Electronic Delivery of Interlibrary Loan* (Haworth, 2004). She edits the refereed scholarly journal *Mythlore* and serves on the board of the Mythopoeic Press.

Jennifer **DeRoss** earned her master's degree at the University of Oregon, where she studied comics with a main focus on the modern American superhero. Her other fields of focus include queer studies, television studies, and biographical studies. She is working as an instructional specialist at Lane Community College. She has written on *Swamp Thing*, *Buffy the Vampire Slayer*, *Wonder Woman*, and *Bitch Planet*. She is writing a biography of Gardner Fox and contributing to the female-led fandom website *Sirens of Sequentials*.

Dani **Howell** has a master's degree in literary and textual studies from Bowling Green State University. Her work analyzes popular culture's role in supporting hegemonic views of sexuality and gender, and it explores the ways radical portrayals of marginalized identities can potentially validate stigmatized groups. She previously worked as an assistant editor for the *Mid-American Review* and is a writer and managing editor for the popular culture website *Cultural Dérives*.

Jessica Lee **Mathiason** is a faculty member in the Department of Women's Studies at the University of Maryland, where she co-leads a working group in medical humanities & bioethics and teaches courses in feminist science studies, feminist and queer theory, and LGBTQ media studies. She also serves as a member of the University's Consortium for Race, Gender, and Ethnicity. Her work has been published in *Cultural Critique* and *Transgender Studies Quarterly* and is forthcoming in the edited collection *Ethical Fashion and Empowerment* (ed. Katrina Sark).

Graeme J. **Wilson** is pursuing a Ph.D. in media and communication at Bowling Green State University, where he works as a teaching associate. In December 2017, he received a graduate certificate in women's studies from the university. His research interests lie in the visual representation of gender and racial identities in popular narrative media. He has presented at the Broadcast Education Association (BEA), National Communication Association (NCA), and Popular Culture Association (PCA) annual conventions, among others.

Laine **Zisman Newman** received her Ph.D. from the University of Toronto's Centre for Drama, Theatre and Performance Studies and the collaborative programs in sexual diversity studies and women and gender studies. Her research focuses on the influence of space on queer women's performance practices. She was the founder and chair of Toronto's Queer Theory Working Group at the Jackman Humanities Institute and co-founder of Equity in Theatre. She teaches theatre and sexual diversity studies at the University of Toronto.

Index

the abject 137
abortion 9–10, 50, 128
abusive relationships 66–67, 69, 80, 107, 117, 120–129 *passim*, 135, 137
accents 155–156
action-adventure film (genre) 152
Adele (character) 75n1
adoption 8, 11, 27, 41–42, 72, 86, 153, 162
adrenaline 186
AIDS/HIV 196–199
alcohol consumption, alcoholism 49, 51, 53, 124, 140
Alexandre, Kathryn 4, 155–156, 159–161, 163n8; other acting doubles 160
Alexis (character) 66–67
Aliens 80
Amelia (character) 28, 42, 65, 71, 80, 83, 93n1, 100–103, 109, 121–122, 135
Ancestry.com 146n18
androgyny 36
animus (Jungian psychology) 96
anthrax 200
Aphrodite (Greek goddess) 98–99, 108; *see also* Venus
Apuleius: *The Golden Ass* 98, 110n2
artificial wombs 44
Association for Molecular Pathology vs. Myriad Genetics, Inc. see Myriad case
Athena (Greek goddess) 116, 130, 161
autonomy (freedom of choice, agency, self-determination, bodily autonomy) 22, 38, 49–51, 78, 84–85, 93, 132, 142, 166–167, 173, 177

bad girl archetype 77–78, 80
Bailey Downs (location on show) 50, 119
Battlestar Galactica 152
Baudrillard, Jean: *Simulacra and Simulation* 193
BBC America 1, 5, 45, 78, 160–162, 177
Beckwith, Janis (character) 27
Bell, Art (character) 27–28, 30, 37, 39n4, 42, 115, 131, 135, 140, 144, 145n8, 146n20, 160, 174
The Belle Game: "Blame Fiction" 189
bioinformatics 188, 190, 194
biology and sexuality/gender 34, 70
bio-technology 41–43, 56, 134, 185, 195
bioweapons, biowarfare 182, 196–200
bisexuality 15, 34
Blair, Ira (character) 71, 75n4, 84, 202n13
blood symbolism and imagery 92, 108
body modification 193, 202n10
"bots" (nano-robotic implants on show) 48, 129, 137, 163n3
Bowles, Charlotte 85, 91, 163n11; as clone of Rachel 64–65, 71, 85, 91, 124; disability 91, 171
The Brady Bunch 51
Breaking Bad 5
Brightborn Industries/Clinic (location/business on show) 28, 69, 133, 158, 162, 197
Brown, Louise 70
Bubbles (location/business on show) 25, 52, 54, 142
Buffy the Vampire Slayer 92, 99; Buffy Summers 92, 100, 106–107, 110n10
Burke, Tarana 126
Butler, Judith 35, 37

Campbell, Joseph 95–95, 99; *The Hero with a Thousand Faces* 130
cancer 63
Candolle, Augustin Pyramus de 181
capitalism 183–185, 194, 196–197, 200
carnival 103
Castor and Pollux (Greek mythological figures) 110n3, 130
Castor clones, Project Castor (characters, male clones as a group) 10–14, 17, 42, 44, 61–62, 71–72, 88, 100, 102, 104, 106, 114, 128, 132, 137, 140, 159, 181–183, 191, 193, 202n11; gender and sexuality 145–146n12, 199, 202n13, 202n14; "glitching" 195–196;

207

208　Index

as vectors of sterility 188, 192–200, 202n12
Castor compound (location on show) 69, 96, 110n7, 141, 195–196
CGI (computer-generated effects) 152, 159, 162
chemical weapons 196–200 passim
Chen, Maggie (character) 28, 100–101, 122, 135
Chevalier, Ferdinand (character) 47, 125, 134, 138–141, 157, 167–169, 174–177, 179n1
child archetype 79–81, 89–91
childbirth 69, 74, 91–92, 109, 132; death and trauma in childbirth 145n10, 145n11, 146n13
Children's Hospital of Eastern Ontario case 188
Childs, Beth (character) 22, 28, 46–47, 49, 59, 101, 110n4, 114–117, 122, 128, 135–137, 139, 141, 146n20, 152, 169, 171
chimera, human (biology) 42–43, 62, 65, 188, 193, 201n2
Cho, Evie (character) 28–29, 122, 137
choreography 155
Christianity 174, 183
cisgender individuals 13–14, 16, 37
Citizens United case 143
Clinton, Hillary 145n9
Clone Club (characters on the show: female self-aware clones and their allies as a group working together) 6, 8–9, 12–13, 15, 17, 33, 117–118, 135, 140, 145n8, 166, 172, 174, 177, 184, 189–190, 192
"clone dance party" (multi-clone scene) 103, 125, 140–142, 155, 158, 160–161
"clone swaps" (one clone playing another) 154, 156–158, 162
cloning (in general) 6, 42–43, 58–59, 66, 133, 170, 182, 185, 191, 193
Coady, Virginia (character) 11, 42, 61, 70–72, 75n3, 79, 86–87, 104–105, 108–109, 137, 141, 144, 183, 195–197, 202n11
Coates, Marci (character) 27–28
Colin (character) 179n3
communication as a value 138, 140, 142
community as a value 24, 33, 129, 140–143
concentration camps 190
copyright of genetic modifications *see* intellectual property
Cormier, Delphine (character) 17, 30, 32–37, 44, 54, 84, 117–118, 141–142, 157, 159, 180, 189–190; sexuality 179n3, 180
corporations as antagonists, corporate control 22, 84, 89, 93, 114, 128, 130, 142, 144, 181, 185
cosmetics industry 130, 145n5
The Crazies 200
Critical Art Ensemble 181, 201n1
CSI 200
cyborg (technology) 44, 151–152

cyborg (theory) 43, 51; *see also* Haraway, Donna

Darwin, Charles 143
Davydov, Shay (character) 35–36, 179n3
Dawkins, Felix (character) 16, 37, 45–46, 48, 68, 72–73, 75n1, 86–87, 103, 113, 115–116, 120, 122, 125, 131, 135, 137, 139–141, 146n20, 153, 156–157, 160–161, 176; art show 116, 130, 145n9, 161–162; artwork 55, 130, 162, 189; sexuality 12–13, 18, 31–32, 35–36, 73, 179n3
death: fear of 17
death/life binary 60, 133
Deleuze, Gilles: *Postscript on the Societies of Control* 184
Demeter (Greek goddess) 97–98
Desperate Housewives 14
detective story (genre) 130, 142–143
Dick, Philip K.: *Do Androids Dream of Electric Sheep?* 172
diegetic and non-diegetic elements 155–156, 159, 162
Dierden, Paul (character) 32, 35, 47, 68, 105, 115, 117–118, 131, 135, 141, 159, 195–196, 199–200
disability studies/theory 79, 89; ableism 88–89, 91
Dizzy (character) 48
DNA (science of) 131, 144, 183–187, 190–191, 200–201; cDNA (DNA with introns removed) 181–183, 187, 189, 201n3; mRNA 189; RNA 187; synthetic DNA 182, 185, 187, 189, 194, 201n3; testing 62, 146n18
Dolly the sheep 146n23, 170–171, 174
The Donna Reed Show 51
donor insemination 75n2
dreams 146n22, 172
drug dealing, use, and addiction 25, 32, 45, 48–49, 51, 53–54, 67, 79, 105, 117, 140
Duko, Martin (character) 137
Duncan, Ethan (character) 9, 41, 44, 58, 64–64, 83, 88, 100, 114, 125, 132, 134, 138, 141, 144, 146n14, 188–190, 192, 202n8
Duncan, Rachel (character) 6, 8–9, 13, 15, 42, 44, 49–50, 63–65, 70–71, 81, 83–86, 88–91, 102, 107, 123–125, 131, 134, 137–138, 140–142, 146n16, 146n22, 155, 157–159, 162, 163n11, 166, 168, 172, 175–176, 185, 202n8; bionic eye 134, 136, 163n3; father figure fixation 134; infertility 42, 44, 63–64, 81, 85, 124, 132–133; meaning of name 172; self-awareness 64, 100, 123–124, 171, 173; sexuality 35, 47, 125, 134, 140
Duncan, Susan (character) 36, 42, 63–65, 70–71, 75n3, 75n4, 79, 83–86, 100, 114, 124–125, 133, 136, 138, 141, 144, 146n14, 188–190, 192, 202n8, 202n13
Duval, Olivier (character) 193
Dyad Institute 6, 9–10, 15, 17, 30, 32, 44–52

passim, 56, 68, 70, 92, 99–100, 103, 108–109, 114, 117–118, 120–121, 123–125, 128, 137, 139, 141, 153, 157, 162, 167, 171, 174, 176, 180–181, 184–185, 188–189, 191–192, 194–195

Edwards, Robert 70
Eleusinian mysteries (Greek religion) 97–98, 110n1
Elle (character) 48
encryption (codes, keys, passwords) 184, 188–189, 191–192; in American Revolution 189, 202n6
Ereshkigal (Sumerian goddess) 97, 101
Eros (Greek god) 98
ethics of care 33
eugenics 143–144, 180–183, 191, 193, 196–197, 200–201
Eurydice (Classical mythological figure) 95, 99
euthanasia 197
evolution 143, 152, 184–185
extramarital sex 35, 47, 53; fidelity as a value 33
eye imagery and symbolism 146n21

family: alternative structures 78, 83, 93; bond as tool of resistance 114–115, 125–126; chosen 56, 85; foster 86, 122; nuclear 73, 75, 85; restoration of 96, 101–103, 105, 107, 109–110, 121; subversion of normative family values 33; as theme 41, 65; as a value 33, 199
fans, fan response 161, 177; Clone Club (fandom) 18, 177; Clonesbians (fandom) 18
fascism 144
fathers 58; father figures 41–42, 82–83, 134; fatherhood 58, 70
Fawcett, John (producer) 5, 7, 16, 114, 146n23, 171, 200
Fay and Femke (characters) 146n19
female bodies 24–25, 38, 44, 46, 61, 91–92, 116–117; *see also* Western ideal female body
feminine archetype 60
femininity 5, 32, 36, 38, 39n1
feminism 8, 14, 17–18, 22–24, 33, 38, 56n3, 69, 74, 78, 93, 143, 194; criticism and theory 7, 30, 39n2, 42–43, 49, 198; intersectional 12, 24, 30, 38; media 22, 24; second wave 51; themes 6–7
fetish objects 131
film noir (genre) 130–131, 142
Final Fantasy 153
Fitzsimmons, Jennifer (character) 194–195
food symbolism and imagery 102, 105
Foucault, Michel: *Discipline and Punish: The Birth of the Prison* 113–126, 184; failure to account for family bond 114, 118, 125–126; *The Order of Things* 181; *Society Must Be Defended* and biopolitics 183–184, 196–197
fraternities 11–12

Freud, Sigmund 136; *see also* the uncanny
Friedan, Betty: *The Feminine Mystique* 51

Galant, Cynthia 163n11
gaslighting 196
Gavaris, Jordan 160, 163n10
gender 23–24, 26, 36, 38, 43, 56, 129, 132, 183; equality 24; performativity 35–37, 78; roles and stereotypes 14, 18n5, 23, 31, 37, 78, 82, 88; subversion 7, 13–18, 24–26, 30–31, 36–37
genetic engineering 41–42, 44, 60, 135, 143, 183–184, 187, 193; CRIPR/Ca9 technology 197
genocide 184
genome, human 62; Human Genome Project 189
genre 56, 129–130, 142; *see also individual genres*
germ cells (totipotent cells) 182, 186–187
GLAAD 16
Glee 39n8
goddesses 95–99, 130; gods 95
Goderitch, Krystal (character) 14–15, 28, 145n5, 146n20, 158, 202n14
Golden Globe Awards 126
gothic (genre) 129–130, 137, 142, 145n4
government as antagonists 22, 131, 142, 144, 181, 184
Gramsci, Antonio 23
Greek mythology 97–98
Grossman, Portia (character) 133

Hades (Greek god) 97–99
Haraway, Donna 43, 56, 70, 78; *see also* cyborg (theory)
healing, accelerated 44, 49, 107; *see also* LIN28A gene
Hecate (Greek goddess) 97
hegemony 23–24
Heidegger, Martin 135
Helena (character) 6, 8–14, 17, 42, 44, 49, 54–56, 61, 65–74, 79–92 *passim*, 93n1, 93n2, 95–110, 114, 117, 120–121, 132–142, 144n1, 146n15, 153, 159–160, 162, 171, 178, 181, 192, 202n14; angel imagery/wings/self-mutilation 96, 101, 106, 109, 110n7, 121–123, 136, 139–140; brought up in convent 65, 83, 100–101, 107, 123, 135; children 54, 72, 87, 92, 103, 105–110, 110n3, 122, 124–125, 162, 166, 192; musical cue 163n7; self-awareness 120; *situs inversus* (mirror physiology) 100, 136
hell/underworld/Hades 95–100, 103–105, 107–108, 110
Hellwizard (character) 145n9
Helsinki (event on show) 101, 138–139, 146n22, 168, 171, 174–176
Hendrix home (location on show) 74, 105–107, 109; garden 104, 106, 109, 125, 162

Index

Hendrix, Alison (character) 6, 8, 14–15, 17, 22, 25–28, 35–36, 41–43, 45, 48, 50–56, 63, 67, 72–74, 83–84, 86, 92, 103, 105–107, 110–111n11, 115–120, 122–123, 136, 138–141, 146n20, 153, 155–162; acting experience 27, 156, 163n9; infertility 8, 27, 54, 106, 133, 146n15; intervention 53; sexuality and gender expression 25–26, 35, 47, 54–55, 109, 174; in treatment center 54
Hendrix, Connie (character) 25–26, 52, 63, 83
Hendrix, Donnie (né Donnie Chubbs) (character) 8, 14, 25–27, 32, 35, 41, 50, 52–53, 67, 72–73, 83, 105–107, 109, 117, 119–120, 122, 133, 138, 140, 160
Hendrix, Gemma and Oscar (characters) 8, 27–28, 42, 48, 50, 52, 55–56, 72, 86, 91, 105, 122
Hermes (Greek god) 97
hero's journey 95–96, 130; female 107, 109
Herter, Cosima (science consultant) 6–7
Hestia (Greek goddess) 130, 161
heteronormativity 7, 11–12, 23, 31–33, 44, 90, 146n12, 173, 199
Hidden Figures 143
hierarchies 23–24, 30, 37, 113, 121, 178
Hitchcock, Alfred 131; *see also* names of films
Homeland 18n1
homophobia 12
homosexual men 12–13
hooks, bell 145n7
horror (genre) 137
Hurston, Zora Neale 143
Husserl, Edmund 171–172
Huxley, Aldous: *Brave New World* 180
hybridity 62

Iceland (location on show) 73, 82
icon theory 166, 169–170, 178
identity 62, 78, 130, 161, 167
immortality 100, 114
in vitro fertilization (IVF) 41, 59, 63, 67, 69, 100, 133, 181, 195, 199
Inanna (Sumerian goddess) 95–97, 99, 105, 107
infertility 8–10, 15, 42, 44, 54, 61, 79, 84–89 *passim*, 132–133, 145n11, 146n12; infertility/fertility binary 60, 89; male 61, 132; treatments 69
intellectual property, artificial genes as (copyright, patent, trademark) 17, 44, 60, 68, 163, 175, 181–201; European Patent Organization 201n5; Invention Secrecy Act 191, 202n9; US Patents and Trademarks Office 186, 191; *see also* legal and legislative issues
Intelligent Creatures 153–154
Irina, Sister (character) 107
island (location on show) 36, 70, 124

isolation (as technique of abuse or punishment, or cause of trauma) 122–123, 125, 130, 141–142

Jesse (character) 73, 103, 106, 109
Johanssen, Bonnie (character) 102
Johanssen, Gracie (character) 67, 70, 102–103, 108, 137, 195, 198–199, 202n12, 202n13; as Virgin Mary figure 199
Johanssen, Henrik (character) 9, 66–67, 70, 102–103, 106, 110n3, 139, 144
Jung, Carl 95; *see also* animus, shadow

Kahlo, Frida: "The Two Fridas" 108, 111n12
Kali (Hindu goddess) 60
King Kong 154
kinship terminology and structures (as complicated by reproductive technologies) 59, 65, 74, 84, 89, 93
Kumar, Meera (character) 27
kyriarcy 24, 31

Lacan, Jacques 135, 146n17
Lamarck, Jean-Baptiste 181
Leakey, Louis 180
Leave It to Beaver 51
Leda and the Swan (myth) 9–10, 130
Leda clones, Project Leda (characters as a group, including non-self-aware clones) 6, 8–10, 14, 17, 22, 28–35 *passim*, 42, 58, 64–65, 68, 70–71, 73, 78, 83, 85, 88, 90, 92, 93n1, 99–100, 106, 109–110, 115–118, 121, 124, 128, 131–132, 136–137, 141, 151, 162–163, 170, 177, 181–183, 188–189, 191–193, 197, 200, 202n8; gender and sexuality variations 145n12, 199; infertility/auto-immune disorder 44, 60–62, 64, 88, 171, 174, 188–189, 191–195
Leekie, Aldous (character) 26, 42, 100, 120–121, 134, 140, 146n14, 180, 184–185, 189
legal and legislative issues (around cloning, genetic engineering, and eugenics) 170, 181–202; *see also* intellectual property
lesbians 13, 34; butch stereotype 15; femme stereotype 36
Lewis, C.S.: *Till We Have Faces* 110n2
LGBTQIA+ community 13; fandom for *Orphan Black* 18
lighting (of scenes) 119, 152, 155
Lintula, Niki (character) 139, 168–169, 175–178, 179n1; sexuality 168, 179n3
LIN28A (gene) 49
The Lord of the Rings 154
Lovelace, Ada 143

Mad Men 5
male bodies 29–30
male gaze 32, 44, 48, 130–131, 134, 136, 145n7
Malone, Kendall (character) 28, 42, 48, 62–

63, 65, 73–74, 137, 139–140, 181, 188, 190, 193
Manning, Kira (character) 8–10, 15, 45–52 passim, 55, 59–61, 63–64, 66, 68, 72–74, 77, 79–82, 86, 89–92, 93n2, 96, 101–104, 107–109, 114–115, 122–123, 133–134, 136, 139, 142, 153, 156–157, 161, 167, 176–177, 191–192; self-mutilation 139; telepathy/empathy 89–90
Manning, Sarah (character) 5–6, 8–11, 13–17, 22, 28, 32–33, 35–37, 41–46, 49–56 passim, 59–68 passim, 72–74, 77–80, 82, 85–86, 88–92, 93n1, 100–110, 110n7, 113–119, 121–124, 128, 131–144 passim, 145n5, 145n8, 146n20, 152, 155–162, 163n9, 166, 169, 171–178 passim, 190–192, 196; sexuality 15, 47–48, 140, 145n12, 174, 179n3
Manson, Graeme (producer) 5, 7, 16, 109, 114, 154, 171, 200
Marnie 131
martial arts films (genre) 152, 163n2
Marx, Karl: *Capital* 188, 194; theory and criticism 24, 187–188
masculinity 5, 10, 12–13, 26, 32, 49; hegemonic 12, 49; military 12; and science 70; *see also* patriarchy; toxic masculinity
Maslany, Tatiana 4, 6, 15, 22, 29, 41, 93n1, 105, 141, 145n3, 145n9, 146n16, 146n23, 151–165, 168; Emmy award 6, 41, 151; use of music playlists 155
maternity *see* motherhood
Mathiason, John *see* Westmorland, P.T.
McCloud, Scott: *Understanding Comics* 169–170
melodrama (genre) 129, 142, 152
mental health 142; *see also* trauma, PTSD
Metis (Greek goddess) 130, 161
#metoo movement 126
Mettray prison 113–123 passim; *see also* Foucault, Michel
Milano, Alyssa 126
Millen, Ari 145n3
mirror imagery and symbolism 136, 146n20; *see also* Lacan
miscarriage 108
mise-en-scène 162, 168, 188, 194–195
misogyny 12, 138, 145n9
M.K. (Mika) (character) *see* Suonimen, Veera
Modern Family 39n8
monitors 46, 52–54, 72, 78, 88, 91, 102, 116–119, 124, 138, 171; as lovers 117
monogamy 33
Morrison, Cal (character) 41, 72–73, 82, 131
motherhood 7–10, 18, 41–46, 51, 54–93 passim, 107, 109, 123; biological 59–60, 66, 78–79, 82, 84–88, 92; global North/global South 83; as redemptive 78–80, 92, 107; subversion of societal expectations 45, 47–48, 51, 55, 109, 115, 131; on television 51, 55

mothers 58; absent 78, 81–83, 130; archetype 79, 91, 109; bad mother archetype 8, 11, 59–60, 63, 85–86, 92, 105; good mother archetype 82, 86; mother figures 42; violent 79–80, 92
motion capture technology 153–154
Mrs. S *see* Sadler, Siobhan
multi-clone scenes 155–156, 158–162; *see also* "clone dance party"
multi-platform storytelling 166–169, 178
Mulvey, Laura 131, 145n7; *see also* male gaze
murder 54, 128, 138, 140
Myriad case 183, 185 187, 201, 201n3, 201n4, 201n5
mystery (genre) 131
mythology 95–99

names and naming 54, 172, 190; derogatory 173–174, 177
Nazism, Nazi Gemany 144, 190
neoliberalism 181–184, 191, 196–197
Neolution, Neolutionists 6, 10, 15, 17, 26, 29, 46, 49, 68, 71, 85–86, 100, 106–108, 110, 128, 131, 134, 136–138, 143–144, 145n5, 152–153, 162, 163n4, 176, 181–182, 184, 192–195, 198–201
Neumann, Erich: *The Great Mother* 60
New Order Prolethean compound (location on show) 66–67, 96, 101–103, 105, 108, 110n5, 122, 138
Niehaus, Cosima (character) 6, 8, 13–15, 17, 22, 28, 32–37, 44, 54, 56, 74, 83–84, 87–90, 92, 103, 115–118, 121, 125, 133, 136–137, 139–142, 144, 146n20, 153, 155, 158–162, 163n9, 166–167, 174, 180, 189–191, 194–195, 199, 201; parents 84, 141; sexuality 13, 18, 32–36, 88, 118, 145n12, 174, 179n3
non-binary individuals 35
Norris, Aynsley (character) 53–54, 119–120, 122, 138
Norris, Chad (character) 35, 47, 53, 120
Nurse Jackie 18n1

Obinger, Katya (character) 27, 139, 141, 146n20
obstetrics 56n2
Olympus (Greek mythological location) 98
omphalos 105
Once Upon a Time 82
The 100s 82
Orange Is the New Black 18n1
Orphan Black Classified Clone Reports (tie-in volume) 138, 144, 146n22, 163n9, 168, 179n1
Orphan Black games 167
Orphan Black graphic novels 99, 101, 104, 110n4, 135–136, 138, 146n19, 146n22, 166–169, 172

212 Index

orphans 58, 80, 83, 91–92, 113, 116, 123
Orpheus (Greek mythological figure) 99; imagery 99, 103, 106–107, 110*n*10
Orwell, George: *1984* 181
the Other 77
Ovid 99

pacifism 80
panopticon 113, 119, 123,126, 184; *see also* Deleuze, Gilles; Foucault, Michel
pansexuality 15–16
paranoia 118–120
paratexts (DVD extras, publicity releases, etc.) 160–162, 163*n*10, 163*n*11; *see also Orphan Black Classified Clone Reports*
parental figures (in general) 41–42
Parsons (character) 104–106, 202*n*11
patents *see* intellectual property
patriarchal culture, society, and institutions 7–8, 12, 19, 23–24, 29–30, 38, 49, 75*n*3, 78, 89, 110*n*3, 131, 133–134, 145*n*9, 146*n*12, 177, 196; phallagocentric symbolism 131; systems 190
Patty (character) 11, 202*n*14
Peaches (performer) 48
people of color 27, 29, 39*n*4; trope of killing characters on television 28–29, 39*n*5; *see also* women of color
Persephone (Greek goddess) 95, 97–99, 102, 104–105, 107–108, 110*n*1, 110*n*3
"phallic girl" 49
Plato 99, 129
Pleasure (Classical mythological figure) 98, 110*n*3
plus-sized women 27, 30
point of view characters 131
popular culture 24, 30, 78
pornography 53
postfeminism 42–45, 47–49, 51–52, 55, 56*n*3
posthumanism 42–44, 49, 56
Pouchy (character) 67, 105–106, 122
power and control dynamics, structures, and relationships 31, 38, 47–50, 64, 97, 114–115; *see also* Foucault, Michel; surveillance
pregnancy 41, 50; trauma in pregnancy 145*n*11
prisons and prisoners *see* Foucault, Michel; Mettray prison; surveillance
privatization, private property 181–183, 185
Proletheans, New Order (characters) 9, 66–67, 101–102, 139–140, 199; *see also* New Order Prolethean compound
Proletheans, Old Order (characters) 6, 9, 88, 100–101, 110, 114, 120–122, 135, 137
Promethea 105
Prometheus (Greek mythological figure) 110
Prychidny, Jay (editor) 160

Psyche (Roman mythological figure) 95, 98–99, 103–105, 107–108, 110, 110*n*3
PTSD 137
public schools 27–28, 52
Pupok (character) 96, 104–105
Pygmalion 156

queer studies/theory 7, 16, 24, 33, 78–79, 193, 198; bodies 31; characters (in general) on television 35, 39*n*8, 88; kinship *see* family, chosen; reappropriation of term 167, 173; sexuality 24, 31–34, 36; values 39*n*2; women 31, 87
Quigg, Donald 186

race and race theory 24, 93*n*1, 196–198; intersectional antiracism 30; *see also* people of color; women of color
rape 9, 61, 102, 108, 126, 196; culture 11–12, 18*n*5, 126, 134
Rear Window 131
religious institutions as antagonists 22, 114, 128, 130, 142, 144, 181
reproduction (in general) 41, 58, 78, 85, 89, 92, 132–133, 182, 193, 195; rights 11, 44, 60; technologies 58–59
Resurrection 82
Rollins, Mark (character) 86–87, 102–103, 108, 195, 202*n*13
Rosen, Daniel (character) 102–103, 122
Rowling, J.K.: *Harry Potter* series 79–80, 92
Roxie (character) 28
Rudy (character) 11–12, 106, 109, 202*n*14

Sadler, Siobhan (Mrs. S) (character) 8, 10, 13–14, 42, 46, 50, 55, 63, 65, 68, 73–74, 79, 81, 86–87, 91–92, 101–105, 113–115, 122, 137, 139–140, 153, 157, 159–160, 176
sadomasochism, sadomasochistic sex 35, 47, 125
Sawicki, Tony (né Antoinette Sawicki) (character) 16, 37–38, 145*n*12, 179*n*3
scapegoating 130
Schmidt, Victor (character) 8, 12, 39*n*4, 135, 139
science fiction (genre) 6, 41, 82, 92, 143, 151–153, 162, 178, 182, 196, 200
scorpion imagery 104–105, 109
Sedgwick, Eve Kososky 33, 130
Serkis, Andy 154
sestra (term used on show for chosen family of self-aware Leda clones) 74–75, 78, 85, 96, 107–108, 114–116, 120–126 *passim*, 136, 142, 178; *see also* Clone Club; Leda clones; sisterhood
Seth (character) 11, 202*n*14
sexual acts, depiction on television 31, 34–35, 38*n*1, 47
sexual harassment 126

Index 213

sexuality 23–24, 31, 47–49, 56; sexual identity 33–34; sexual objectification 11; subversion of sex roles and stereotypes 24; *see also* individual sexual identities
shadow (Jungian psychology) 96, 99–101, 108, 110
shamans, shamanic imagery 96, 105–110
sheep imagery 121, 146*n*23, 171–178 *passim*; *see also* sheep mask *under* Suonimen, Veera
Shelley, Mary: *Frankenstein* 39*n*1, 64, 138
single mothers 78
sisterhood 65–66, 74–75, 89, 96, 101–103, 108, 114, 142, 144
slavery 191
Smith, Adam 181
Smith, Scott (character) 160
social contract 121
social media 151
somatic cell nuclear transfer 181
The Sopranos 5
special effects 151–165; *see also* CGI; Intelligent Creatures; motion-capture technology; TechnoDolly
Spin City 16
sports 52
Steel Magnolias 156
stem cells (pluripotent cells) 182, 184, 186–187
Steptoe, Patrick 63, 70
sterility 104, 133, 182, 197; *see also* Castors; infertility; infertility *under individual characters*,
storytelling 108–110, 129, 142–144
straight men 25–26
Stubbs, Sarah (character) 27
suburbia 25, 27, 50, 67–69, 118–119, 126
suicide 46, 59, 101, 108, 116, 128–129, 137–138, 141, 152
suicide bombers 196–198
Sumerian mythology 96–97
Suonimen, Veera (character) 29, 136, 138–139, 141, 146*n*20, 146*n*22, 146*n*23, 166–179; burn scars 139, 172, 176; death 167, 176–178; self-awareness 171, 173; sheep mask 29, 139, 166–179 *passim*
Supreme Court, US 185–187, 201; High Court of Australia 201*n*5; Supreme Court, Canada 188; *see also* Thomas, Clarence
surplus life 182, 186, 191–192, 194, 200–201
surrogate mothers, surrogacy 44, 59, 65–66, 69, 100
surveillance 46, 52–54, 78, 113–126, 128–129, 131, 136, 184
swan imagery 133, 136; *see also* Leda and the Swan

TechnoDolly 154, 159
television series (in general) 5, 18*n*1, 42, 142, 168

testosterone 16, 37
theatre, amateur/community 27, 52
Thomas, Clarence 187, 201*n*3
Thomson, James A. 186
thriller (genre) 152
Time's Up Legal Defense Fund 126
Tito (character) 48
Tomas (character) 66, 100–102, 120–121, 123, 133, 135–139
Topside 104, 125, 128, 139, 174
Toronto (location on show) 1, 59, 163*n*5
toxic masculinity 7, 10–13, 17; *see also* masculinity
transgender individuals 16, 37; trope of killing on television 37
Transgenomic (company) 188
trauma 128–150
Trevor (character) 93*n*2
trickster imagery 166
Trump, Donald 145*n*9
Twilight series 80

the uncanny 136, 154–155

Van Lier, Ian (character) 158
venereal disease 195
Venter, Craig 189, 202*n*7
Venus (planet) 97; Venus (Roman goddess) 98; *see also* Aphrodite
Vertigo 131
violence 10, 13, 73, 79–80, 83, 92, 105–106, 128–130, 138, 142; against women 18*n*5; *see also* rape
Virgil 99

Walker, Alice: "In Search of Our Mothers' Gardens" 143
war, warfare, military 61; *see also* bioweapons
Webster, Peter (costumer) 50
Weeds 18*n*1
welfare state 182
Wells, H.G.: *The Island of Doctor Moreau* 144, 189–190
Western ideal female body (thin, white, feminine) 23, 25–31, 37, 39*n*6; *see also* female bodies; plus-sized women
Westmorland, P.T. (alias of John Mathiason) (character) 17, 36, 42, 72, 75*n*3, 84, 92, 108, 114, 118, 124, 131, 133–134, 136–138, 144, 145*n*8
Wexler, Skyler 160
Whatever Happened to Monday (alternate title: *Seven Sisters*) 80
whiteness 23, 93*n*1, 197; bodies 28, 30; maleness 23, 144; nationalism/supremacism 18, 144; privilege 28
Will & Grace 16
Williams, Serena 145*n*10
women of color 24, 27–30, 132, 145*n*10

women scientists 70–72, 75n3, 86, 143–144
women's rights 7
women's roles on television 5–6, 17, 18n1
working class 15
World War II 190–191; World War I 191

Yanis (character) 137
yin-yang symbol 102
Yvonne (character) 27

Zeus (Greek god) 9, 97

www.ingramcontent.com/pod-product-compliance
Lightning Source LLC
Chambersburg PA
CBHW032043300426
44117CB00009B/1170